Verónica Galindo de Otazo

D0560717

My Lover, Myself

Self-Discovery Through Relationship

My Lover, Myself

David Kantor, Ph.D.

Riverhead Books
a member of
Penguin Putnam Inc.
New York
1999

Certain names and identifying characteristics of
individuals portrayed in this book have been changed
to protect their privacy.

Riverhead Books
a member of
Penguin Putnam Inc.
375 Hudson Street
New York, NY 10014

From "Home Burial," from *The Poetry of Robert Frost*, edited by Edward
Connery Lathem, © 1958 by Robert Frost. © 1967 by Lesley Frost
Ballantine. Copyright 1930, Copyright 1939, © 1969 by Henry Holt and
Company, Inc. Reprinted by permission of Henry Holt and Company, Inc.

Library of Congress Cataloging-in-Publication Data

Kantor, David
My lover, myself : self-discovery through relationship / by David Kantor.
p.   cm.
ISBN 1-57322-140-6
1. Marital psychotherapy.   2. Man-woman relationships.   I. Title.
RC488.5.K36   1999   98-51090   CIP
616.89'156—dc21

Printed in the United States of America

1   3   5   7   9   10   8   6   4   2

This book is printed on acid-free paper. ∞

BOOK DESIGN BY
JUDITH STAGNITTO ABBATE/ABBATE DESIGN

Acknowledgments

To Jules Chametzky, for taking me and my ideas seriously over more than fifty years of friendship, respect, and love.

To Meredith (my revered "teacher," who keeps pushing my capacity for love beyond its limits), for never letting up on being gentle wife, honest critic, fearless protector, and uncompromising monitor of my given tendencies to make trouble for myself.

To my seven children—Marcia, Mathew, Richard, Jessica, Pamela, Melissa, and Sam—for their forty-five years of trying to figure out my ways of loving them, and then, when I least expect, courageously challenging my most cherished assumptions about how a father should love his children.

To our "Family Farm," for its thousands of hours of play, exploration, meditative space, and contemplative time.

To Sally Jackson, for being friend, reader, tireless supporter, and gracious guide to everything I've written in the past twenty-five years.

To Michael Miller, for those spirited and spirits-fed

"monthlies" at The Harvest, during which ideas took wing and I tried to discover what real writing is about.

To Diana Smith, for pretending that she needs my intellectual companionship when more than half the time it is the other way around.

To Charlie Keifer, Bill Isaaks, Thomas Rice, Steve Ober, and Joel Yanowitz, for finding ways to pay me for thinking with them while I was writing this book.

To Our Book Club (Molly Power and John Ordway, Mary Weisblum, and David and Meredith Kantor), for about ninety books of mostly great reading, bountiful conversation, and gourmet meals over a nine-year span, the last three of which were an exercise in restraint while waiting to see whether this book met the club's high standards for selection.

To Sib and Judy Wright, for never failing to ask the "wright questions" about the book's content and politics, from the beginning to the very end of its sometimes circuitous journey; and for those artful meals and drinks at sunset after sunset on their porch overlooking Ipswich Bay.

To Molly Sherden, intellectual property lawyer, for protecting my interests with a grace unbecoming a lawyer.

To Marietta Whittlesey, for her calm competence in helping me transform what must be close to two thousand pages of rambling prose into a readable manuscript.

To Ulrike Dettling, for those years of overseeing my office and all of its projects with poise, skill, caring, and an unflappable ability to make order out of chaos.

And to Amy Hertz, who, when the book stumbled and then tumbled headlong into the darkness of an endangered mineshaft, used the same clear vision she is valued for as a premier editor to guide it and me back into the light.

Contents

My Lover, Myself

But we are so foolish and fixed by our limited ideas. A man says: "I don't love my wife anymore. I don't want to sleep with her." But why should he always want to sleep with her? How does he know what other subtle and vital interchange is going on between him and her, making them both whole in this period when he doesn't want to sleep with her?

—D. H. LAWRENCE, *We Need One Another*

Introduction

We enter the infatuation phase of love glutted on hope, wild fantasies, and dreams of a perfect future. Why, then, do the promise of safety, the allure of charisma, and the joy of uncensored sex seem to fade? I would estimate that ninety-five percent of all long-standing (one year and beyond) sexual partners stop "making love"—though many continue to "have sex." Everyone accepts that these things happen, that they are inevitable "after the honeymoon." I do not believe this fate need befall you and your partner.

We have come to expect that love with good sex is an inalienable right. It isn't. It must be earned, through a kind of discipline that has been shrouded in mystery. As a practicing psychotherapist, I have been aware for some time that people are confused about sex—as well they might be, for it is truly a riddle. I hope to help solve the riddle of what happens to sexual desire in marriage and other long-term committed relationships.

I have written *My Lover, Myself* to provide real answers to these and other questions about relationships. One of the important messages of this book is that the disappointment that seeps into relationships need not inevitably lead to the loss of intimacy, caring, and desire. Couples can stay connected after infatuation. My purpose is to guide lovers who are interested in doing "the work of love" toward a renewal of desire. This book is intended as a map to help couples find their own way through the changes and conflicts that are inevitable in serious relationships. If these forces are harnessed in the service of love, they will take you and your lover on a wondrous journey. But if they are misunderstood, or an attempt is made to ignore them, couples start down another pathway, one that all too often leads to withdrawal and, eventually, loss of desire. This need not happen to you. Have the courage to embark on this journey together. Use this map as your guide to help you negotiate your way through the conflicts and redefinitions that, threatening though they may seem, are the necessary impetus for the exploration and deep knowing of self and other.

This map offers a way to take apart and reconstruct with renewed hope and insight three of the most disheartening and debilitating declarations many couples are heard to make:

- We are so different.
- We can't communicate.
- We don't make real love anymore.

These statements are symptoms arising from our childhood mythologies, which influence our choice of partner, our expectations from our adult relationships, and our sexuality in ways that are both conscious and unconscious. Parts of our mythologies are known to us, while others can become known only through the mirror of a long-term committed relationship. Over many years as a practicing couple and family therapist, I have developed a way for people to learn about their guiding mythologies. Delving into our own and our partner's myths and childhood stories, telling our partners in a compassionate way things we see about them of which they may be unaware, and allowing our partners to mirror back to us the parts of ourselves that are hidden to our view can restore intimacy and desire even when they have been absent for years. This clarification of each other through relationship is one of love's greatest gifts.

My Lover, Myself offers hope that is founded not on the false promises of pop psychology, but on my work as a scholar, teacher, and clinician. I have tested and refined the approach to relationships described in this book on both the playing fields of happy lovers and the battlegrounds of unhappy ones. It tells the truth about what is and is not possible. If there is one primary cause of love's demise, it is our failure to understand the complex nature of communication in close relationships. Many authors have tried. Some recent efforts shed some light, but none is able to provide much help when the emotional stakes are high. At these crucial times, lovers speak different languages—languages that are in no way based on male–female differences. If that were all there was to it, there would be much less despair and fewer divorces by far. My Lover, Myself sets out to break the communication code. I hope hereby to clarify the relationships among the perception of difference, failure in communication, and loss of desire, a territory that has not been explored until now.

DAVID KANTOR
Cambridge, Massachusetts
December 1998

Chapter One

Portrait of a Marriage:
The Birth, Death, and Rebirth of Desire

Love Engulfs You

It begins in innocence. Someone enters your life and unexpectedly awakens you. Suddenly, your life force is galvanized and it burns a little brighter. Love engulfs you, overwhelms every waking moment. *He* has changed your world. *She* has restored you to your best self—not only in her eyes but in your own. Miraculously, all your dreams seem possible again. Your very soul alerts you to the fact that he or she, who stands before you, is the source of this new life. So much pessimism dissolves. All those grim statistics about marriage and divorce are forgotten. The rational faculties themselves are put to sleep amidst the vapors of love's intoxication.

Hope in Love Everlasting

It doesn't take long before you are wanting all of him. Soon you are fantasizing about what it would be like to make love to her, to take her into your arms and devour her beauty. Sexual hunger becomes overwhelming and unbearable. There is no middle ground now. You must have this person.

"She's the one I've been looking for," you tell a friend. "She's completely different from the others."

"He's the only man who's ever really understood me," she tells herself. "This time it's going to work."

In fact, you are seeing less the person who is than the partner you long for, the *other* you need to feel whole. Having him will bring love everlasting. The ancient Greeks recognized this state of intoxication as the blessing of Eros, the god of Love and Desire. The two of you do not know it yet, but you have embarked on a quest that contains the very essence of life. At last comes that magic day when you first make love. Sex is so effortless and exciting for many couples at this stage that they never dream it could be otherwise. Thus, driven by erotic passion, you find yourself racing toward those exciting yet dangerous reefs called commitment and marriage, beyond which lies an uncharted sea where lives are transformed, sometimes for the better, sometimes for the worse.

All couples just starting out expect that this time it will be for the better and that they will be able to sustain this level of communication, both intellectual and sexual, for the rest of their lives. No matter how many other relationships have failed in the past, this time both believe they have found the perfect other. And certainly some couples, though in my experience they are the minority, are intuitively equipped to do the work necessary to sustain their desire and appreciation for each other.

The Shock of Leavened Bliss

Early on in the journey you discovered that you could "talk about anything." This was part of the attraction. She understood and appreciated what was important to you. He appreciated how

you spoke about and defined your needs, and would be there to
fulfill them. This was part of the magic of the relationship. The
ability to discuss significant themes in world affairs, in raising a
family, in relationships. Early on in the partnership, lovemaking
was automatic, rhythmic, and rhapsodic. Little was denied to curiosity and experimentation in the ways of making love. It just
happened, and it was blissful. But then something began to
change.

The Ritualization of Difference

At first it's the little things you disagree on. Who takes the garbage
out? Do you share the cooking? What is a safe speed to drive at?
Did you or did you not dominate the other guests at the dinner
party? The small doubts which you had smothered during the ecstatic days of courtship and early marriage, the little differences of
opinion that were so easy to dismiss then, now loom large.

Suddenly the battle lines are drawn. Now your arguments are
about who you are, who your partner is, where you are going together. It is this fundamental disagreement over identity that
threatens to transform your original love and passion into doubt.
If you are the average couple in this portrait, sex comes to the rescue. "Let's drop this nonsense and make love," one of you says, and
if this part of your relationship is relatively secure, you do. This allows you to treat your differences as those "little 'scraps' that all
couples have, it's the 'universal lover's quarrel,' " you say. Still, the
fights begin to follow a pattern, with a small number of recognizable themes. This repetition of themes puzzles you, but you ignore
or dismiss this. Each time a button-pushing theme comes up you
try to warn yourself, but you get drawn in anyway. You even know
in advance the position your partner is going to take, what **he** will
say and how **she** will say it. Even while you are escalating the conversation, you are aware of the position **you** will take, what **you**

will say, and how **you** will say it. You end up either in silence, anger, or, in some cases, absolute rage.

At These Times Your Shadows Enter the Room

Our shadows are the dark side of love. Were it not for the shadow we could love purely, as we intend, and do, most of the time. We wouldn't have so much trouble with love, with expressing it, with taking it in. Were it not for the shadow we could feel *the tender touch of love*, whenever it was being offered. But alas! When the shadow is present, our skin hardens to the touch, repelling it along with the one who offers love. Were it not for the shadow, we would be able to talk straight, say what we really mean, whether what we mean comes from the mind, or the heart, or the genitals. And we would be able to do this most of the time, not only in those too infrequent moments when we run so scared of losing love entirely that we appeal to our lover to ignore our shadow, to love us in spite of ourselves. Were it not for the shadow, we could accept the bliss which our sexual drives promise as our due, and give sexual pleasure freely and lovingly to those we love.

Paths Diverge

At this time, couples may take different routes on the journey of love, but all will run into roadblocks, detours, storms. They will get stalled, start up again, gain ground, and stall again. In most cases, those who are determined to succeed, will. For some, the journey will simply be easier than it is for the vast majority. The difficult "work" that all marriages require, these couples manage without, or with just a little professional help. But work they must. For communication breakdowns and the interruption of lovemaking are typical of any pursuit of the elusive grail we call sustained sexual intimacy. Or so I believe. I also believe that those couples who "make it" with relative ease are a smaller minority than is assumed, not only by the public but by most experts. Like the rest, these lucky couples will go through stages, from bliss, to lost innocence, to the dark side of love, which drags each partner down into the pits of their own psyches, where they encounter their own demons. But these lucky ones ascend again, more whole as individuals, more in love, and better able to deal with whatever they encounter on the rest of the journey. Sex, if it is affected by temporary detours, will prevail.

A much larger number of couples are not so fortunate. They may simply lack the fortitude to press on in the journey, they may get frightened by their own or their partner's demons, or they may have no adequate models for what is possible in love. In this quite common scenario there is a gradual diminution of sexual desire and intimacy, an acceptance of less than what could be. These couples often appear firmly committed to one another, and may indeed function very well together at family, professional, and social gatherings, but they have settled for less than what they started out with. At best, they live side by side in a cozy world, directing their attention outward toward their children, their careers, or the needs of others.

They have an "adequate" sex life and "enough" intimacy, they say. In fact, many may all but give up sex, but do not talk about it. Characteristically, they do not seek therapy until another crisis occurs later in their lives. The fact that they have not made love for months or even years is only discovered accidentally.

Two of the couples featured in this book fall into the first category, the "fortunate ones." The second group is not dealt with here. Our focus, instead, is on a third, very large group who do not settle for less than they believe they can have. They struggle on their own, speak with doctors and ministers, read self-help books ravenously, attend workshops, and come for therapy. All, in their fashion, are trying to "work" on their relationships. All want to sustain, salvage, or restore desire. This book may help them.

Disappointment, Broken Contracts, and the Threat to Desire

Most of your disagreements run off your hide without consequence—when the stakes are low, that is. Men act and fix; women emote and talk, says the common wisdom. But when the stakes are high—in matters of identity, or when buttons are pushed—this can become a matter of psychological life or death. At the end of each of these failed conversations, you feel abandoned, betrayed, not understood, and above all, disappointed in the business of love. Despair and melancholy (which can even be mistaken for clinical depression) set in. The unspoken agreements you made to one another during courtship, your mythic contracts, are being battered. Your relationship can sustain itself this way for a long time, but ultimately the difficulties will deepen. What I am about to describe may not happen to you, but if you have started down the road I have described so far, this is where many of you may end up. If you recognize even a little of your relationship in this scenario, take it as an early warning sign that trouble lies ahead—trouble that can become the greatest opportunity for growth and happiness you will ever have.

The Withdrawal or Loss of Desire

You can't identify a particular incident, a moment where it all changed. It is almost unbelievable that you two, who once seemed to complete each other, who once were each other's best friends, now live in a state of roiling daily discontent. Where once the

evenings were a time for the pleasurable sharing of the day's stories, the airing of opinions, and curiosity about each other, now
communication falters.

You learn to stick to neutral topics lest dinnertime conversation degenerate either into arguments, often with the same theme,
or into the painful silence of two people living in separate worlds.
Where once a trip together in the car was an occasion for happy
intimacy, now each of you stares straight ahead, perhaps even plot-
ting a better future in which you won't make the same mistake
again.

The two of you no longer bother to make your accustomed efforts at reconciliation. At the same time, you can't ignore the conflict. It surfaces periodically, nagging at you. Time does not restore
your relationship to its former buoyancy. Talking it over doesn't
help the way it once did. As the pressure builds intolerably inside
you, you find yourself criticizing your spouse to a friend. You realize that this is a betrayal. You're even a little shocked that you've
done such a thing, but the tension and the emptiness inside you
are too much to bear alone.

When you are no longer excited by who your partner is, you
are no longer impassioned about sex. Sex is the most delicate part
of your relationship and its most sensitive barometer. Your lovemaking becomes less frequent. You may realize that it has been
weeks or months since you've even approached one another. Or,
lovemaking is reduced to a sexual exercise from which you withdraw your soul. Eyes shut, each in your separate worlds, you go
through the movements to relieve tension, perhaps to foster the illusion that things are still all right between you.

The death of desire is the cruelest death of all, in part because
desire succumbs in a series of painful disappointments. With each
one, you expect a little less from your partner, from yourself, and
even from life. You and your spouse are diminished in each other's
eyes. You physically withdraw to your respective corners of life and
stay there. With the loss of desire and lovemaking comes the loss
of intimacy. He is a stranger now. He speaks only of unimportant

things, and is reticent about his inner life. He always seems impatient. She has withdrawn and become unreachable. She is possessed by a cold, brittle tension or seems always on the verge of tears. You assume defensive postures against each other, your arsenal of angry accusations always at the ready.

If you have reached this point, you are alone and lonely. You don't know how to reach your partner, and perhaps you aren't willing to try. At some point in your isolation, you realize that all the disappointments have piled up to form a single heartbreaking revelation: you are no longer special in your partner's eyes and neither is your partner heroic in yours. For the first time, you are shocked to realize that you are considering leaving or having an affair. Worse, you fear that your partner too may be having these once-unthinkable thoughts.

A terrible paradox traps so many relationships today. We enter into monogamy in the hope that we will experience love, intimacy, and sexual fulfillment until death parts us. Yet as time goes by, we discover that just the opposite has occurred. To add to our pain, the media bombards us with fantasies and explicit sexual images. The average couple, we are told, has sex three times per week. Love, intimacy, and ecstatic sex are available to all, we are made to believe. They just didn't happen for us.

The Rebirth of Desire

In more than thirty years as a clinical psychologist and family therapist, I have treated hundreds of couples. Over this career, I have taught undergraduates, graduates, and medical students at Harvard, Tufts, and Northeastern universities. At the Boston, Cambridge, and Kantor Family Institutes, I have trained more than a thousand professionals who specialize in couple and family therapy. I can tell you with assurance that contrary to what we read in popular surveys, a great many couples—far more than is commonly reported—have undergone exactly the journey described above and are not making love as much as they used to or have stopped altogether. In fact, one of the most consistent refrains with which couples confront me in my office is that they no longer make love.

This tragedy need not befall you. Let this book serve as a blueprint for maintaining the vitality and excitement of those early days and at the same time going deeper into each other, learning each other's mysteries, and respecting, not fearing, your differences.

If you have lost your desire for each other, there is a way back. Couples *can* experience again the joys for which they long. They can restore love, intimacy, and sex to their partnerships. The capacity for lasting love, intimacy, and fulfilling sex lives lies within all of us. But in order to retrieve it we must understand the true meaning and nature of love and relationships. Ironically, our culture leads us away from the very abilities that would return these gifts to us.

The memory of that perfect early love may lead you to ask why it all went even a little bit wrong. Was it because you made the wrong choice and now must struggle to live with your choice, to right the sinking ship and get by with a fraction of the former bliss?

Nearly every couple reaches an impasse. The high-stakes argument in which you find yourself unwilling to give an inch is your way of saying, "Here's who I am; my identity, my very being is at stake. Back off or I will fall into a black hole." When you are pushed more, your partner is saying, "There is darkness in you that you haven't a clue to, things I can help you see." These important issues lie beneath your ritualized disagreements and fuel its fires. As long as they remain subconscious, they will bring disappointment. This too is unavoidable; it may even be necessary: no adult can continue to mature without dealing with disappointment.

If you and your lover have ever had high-stakes arguments, if you have ever gone to bed withholding intimacy, if the polish has worn off a committed relationship, if you see any of yourself or your relationship in what I have described, this book can help you rediscover the promise of love, growth, and happiness you felt when you first set eyes on each other.

The only way to lasting love and desire is through a guided exploration of the stories you bring into the intimate relationship: stories about what defines love, about how to express your heroic identity in the name of love, and about how to achieve sexual ecstasy. When two people have the courage to undertake this sometimes frightening and often painful journey, each becomes exciting and fresh to the other: joint exploration and growth is the ultimate aphrodisiac. But the inner search requires courage, honesty, and commitment, for in the end it is a confrontation with all that is most frightening in each of us. Yet each of us knows in his deepest soul that this struggle to evolve is the essence of life.

As you will come to understand, it is for this very reason that you and your lover came together in the first place, the reason that you chose *this* person above all others. On an unconscious level you and your partner agreed—as a prerequisite for commitment—to play a heroic role in each other's personal story. "I will be all that you need," you and your partner unspokenly said to each other. "You will be all that I need," each of you replied. That promise made to each other during courtship inspired great excitement and deep feelings of safety and security, and was the basis for your courageous leap into the unknowns of long-term commitment and marriage. It is when this agreement breaks down—as inevitably it must between two separate beings—that intimacy and sexual desire is threatened. The original agreement inevitably breaks down because neither partner has fully seen the other. Instead, they have unconsciously empowered each other, indeed demanded of each other, to play a starring role in a drama with an incomplete script.

Inside each of us is a tangle of long-repressed secrets, dark desires, inner wounds, and heroic aspirations. These hidden parts of you shape your personality and your needs, including your sexual desires. It is for this reason that you must dare to become an adventurer who enters the world of the psyche, the world of the un- known, and brings back discoveries to share with your lover.

Three Stories That Must Be Told

We are all storytellers. You make sense out of your life by organizing the raw facts into stories that give shape to your experience. By telling and retelling your stories, you define yourself to yourself and to others. It follows that the best way to gain insight is to understand your inner stories. In short, you must elucidate your own mythology.

Among the many stories that are inside all of us, three are cru- cial to the territory I am mapping here.

The Personal Myth is our single most compelling story of love. It is "written" in childhood, at a time when we realize that the pure, unconditional love that seems to be our birthright may not be ours. Indeed, it is The Story of Imperfect Love. In the child's mind it contains villains, conspirators, betrayals, melancholic disappoint- ment, and wished-for heroes who will make the love story come out right. In this story we form the dim outlines of our future "heroic self"—the hero-lover we will be when we grow up—and the hero for whom we search.

The Gender Myth **is** the story of our adult heroic self. In this story we assert who we are or want to be as we make our mark in work and in society. In particular, it is the heroic persona we will present to the ideal lover. Our Gender Myths tell the stories of three prototypical heroic figures. These are you as *the* Survivor, *the person who is capable of enduring, adapting, showing tolerance of ex- treme hardship, and able to await the moment of victory at some future point; the* Fixer, *the person who is capable of overcoming obstacles that block the path to goals and causes worthy of support; and the* Protector, *the person who is driven to shield anything or anyone who is vulnerable to powerful external or internal forces.*

The Sexual Fantasy Myth is your sexual story. It contains the rich storehouse of all your sensual yearnings and lustful fantasies. In this myth lies your desire; it describes how you wish to express yourself sexually, the ways you prefer to make love. It also contains your secret yearnings for sexual adventure, ways of making love which you keep hidden, sometimes from yourself.

If love and sexuality are to be sustained, you must get to know your own and your partner's myths, along with their shadows.

Many people refuse to do this work. Instead they search for a secure niche and fight with all their might to stay there. By not daring to look within themselves and grow, they become stale and predictable. They become stuck in their own sameness and therefore no longer have the power to inspire excitement or even respect. A superficial understanding of oneself is, in the end, boring, and boredom is at the bottom of countless failed relationships.

No one can take up this work without a map of the inner world and some knowledge of what he or she is looking for. In my work as a family and couples therapist, I have developed an approach to the psyche that allows couples to explore and understand themselves on a deep, intimate level. The key that will unlock these secrets lies in understanding the nature of your own mythology. These myths are compelling stories that we use as models and guidelines for living and loving. What makes them different from other memories we have stored is their larger-than-life character. The myths I will introduce you to have the character of all myths, but they are more personal than cultural, because we have created them ourselves and internalized them as parts of our identities. The three myths we will explore in this book all contribute to our sexual lives and to desire. They draw us to love, sustain us in love even when all else seems to be failing, and, when violated, they lead to the loss of desire and threaten the meaning of love.

Should you take up the call to look within yourself, examine your own mythology, and grow, my approach will provide you with a safe means to communicate your discoveries to your spouse so that intimacy and sexual fulfillment can be sustained, reinspired or reborn.

This book is intended as a new psychology of committed relationships. The theory it describes has evolved from decades of learning from the hundreds of couples I have seen in therapy, the nearly one thousand therapists whom I have trained, from public workshops, and from a perhaps too closely examined study of my own two marriages. In a career devoted to research, teaching, clinical practice, organizational consulting, and writing, nothing has commanded more of my serious attention and study than the couple in an intimate relationship. No institution created by humans comes close to this one for the effort required to assure its survival.

I am attempting to do something here that I have been, to put it mildly, reluctant to do: prepare a guiding text for couples who wish to do this work on their own. How to justify joining the ranks of those who've promised easy solutions? Two reasons, perhaps. First, I am careful to state at the outset how hard it can be to manage intimacy through its inevitable vicissitudes. Many how-to books gloss over this point. If users of the guidelines offered in these pages wobble, they would have done so anyway. Indeed what I write here anticipates that you will—and should—wobble. I predict the kinds of trouble you may expect and offer remedies for very specific ailments.

My Lover, Myself can be used in several ways. It is my belief that many—though not all—couples are capable of doing the necessary work on their own so long as they understand its nature. For them, this book will serve as a guide to help them along the way. Clearly, there are situations which will require the protection of couples therapy for all, or part, of the process. For couples and individuals already in therapy, I believe that this book will provide a useful framework upon which to base their self-explorations. Many of the insights which are here applied to couples also have proved useful to individuals seeking meaningful ways to organize and analyze their experiences.

Chapter Two

The Myth of Perfect Love

Our love stories have their beginnings in those abidingly peaceful months in perfect union with our mothers. Evolution has designed a mother's womb to perform a miracle, which is to nurture and support the life of a single cell so that it will multiply countless times until, most remarkably, it develops into a perfectly formed infant human being. Science is now finding that during these months we are perhaps more aware of the perfection of our incubating surroundings than was previously believed. We thus step into life with the innocent expectation that paradise exists and is ours simply because we too exist.

In the time immediately following birth, the illusion of pure, Edenic love persists. The mother's physical and emotional sacrifice, in safeguarding the fetus and in the unavoidable pain of birth, transforms her into a fount of unconditional love. If she doesn't completely embody such love, then certainly she is striving for it, offering her body and all of her being to ensure that her infant's world is a garden of perfect sensuality and bliss.

Small though this garden-world is, it remains supremely ful-

filling for the child, whose skin is at first the sole and consummate
locus of nurturance and sensual reception; the original source of
pure sensuality. In his or her expanding world, augmented now by
other "mothers," the infant learns the joy of physical warmth and
touch. In these encounters, he comes to depend upon the physical
and emotional sensations of love. In effect, the infant learns how
wonderful it is to have a human body and how beautiful the physical world really is. The story of unconditional love is formed in
this perfect and sensual environment. This story, that we will always have a source of perfect love, is documented in a selection of
positive memories that are both recollected and told to the child,
but experienced as a form of memory in either case.

In time, harsh reality inevitably serves up insults and injuries
to this perfect environment. Eventually, these contradictions—
illness, angers, fears, physical roughness, neglect, humiliation—
will conspire to challenge the story of perfect love, and inspire the
child first to come to terms with the imperfect nature of love and
then to tell the story of that love. From the memory of this story,
she will later go out into the world in search of the grail of Perfect
Love.

I asked a client, Rosa, to tell me her stories of perfect and imperfect love. Listen to the voices she uses. She speaks for all lovers.

Rosa's Story of Perfect Love

*My name will be Rosa when I am born. Now, I am in the
womb of darkness. All is warm, wet, mysterious, silent, dark.*

*One day I am sucked into the light. Into a new world. All con-
sciousness is sensory. My senses are out of control. This new world
is beauty and terror. I am cut off. Ripped from my viscous mother.
The parting is called birth. This is serious, my exploding body tells
me so. Bang! I cry. "Hold me, I'm falling." And they do. God's
gift, the gift of life, the gift of being, has been accomplished. I am!*

All at once, I begin to communicate with a waiting world. Nipples, breasts, succulent liquids, warm bodies, swaddlings, songs for soothing sleep, other sounds, voices, light and dark. All mine. Is this not heaven? Do I not rule this universe? In the unfolding rhythm of my needs, time flows naturally.

Days and nights are measured by my different moods and how hard "they" work to meet them, no matter yet that they may have their selfish reasons. Whatever is wrong out there remains elusive.

They are nervous about Time. Time for them is chronological, from the Greek chronos, but for me Time is what the Greeks called kairos, time as opportunity or encounter. In the battles over "schedules" and the like, Chronos and Kairos will eventually come together. Mum has a harder time with Time than Mailee, my aunt, my other mum, when she who I will call mother is away taking care of her own ailing mother who insists on dying in her own home. My mum has her eye on the clock. With Mailee, I live in the now, attuning myself to the calls of the moment, each of us listening and responding to what each moment, each hour, each situation brings. Between them I discover the rules of cooperation and co-existence.

What mum knows best is touch. When I cried in sleep before I could tell the difference between Mum, Mailee and my father, I knew them from how they touched, stroked, and wrapped their arms around me. Mum's touch spoke to my racing heart. Sssllooowww, it said, shiish. And my heart slowed down. Even the way she held my hand relaxed me and made me feel safe from all harm. By the time I was three, I couldn't wait to have my bath. My mother told me this story and though I can't say I remember it in reality, I remember it in spirit. Does the skin not have memory? Mine does. It remembers being gentled by the lightest and most comforting touch any child ever knew.

I read something recently by Brother David Steindl-Rast that took me back to my fourth year of life. "We think people are grateful because they are happy. But is this true? Look closely, and you will find that people are happy because they are grateful." I discovered what it means to be grateful in those days. When I recited my prayers of thanks as I'd been taught, especially the part at the end, ". . . God bless Mommy, Daddy, Richard, Emma . . ." and the whole string of close relatives, I cried with happiness each and every night. I have my mother to thank for this. My mother gave birth to seven children, two of whom were present at my fourth birthday party, a steamy day in July. My mother was ironing my party dress. Her smock was drenched in sweat. I asked if she hated me for making her work so hard. I'd never heard a single word of complaint from her lips, and didn't really expect a change. But what she said has stuck with me all these years: "When I was a girl your age I was very sickly. I thought I would never live to have children of my own. You and Richard and Emma are the gifts that prove my existence."

This is another birthday story. When I was five I thought I had a strange illness. For my birthday, I was taken to a zoo with my friends after the cake and ice cream. Randy, a boy I liked a lot, had found a feather outside one of the bird cages. Selina and I were gabbing as we walked from one animal house to the next. Randy and Philip were close behind, laughing maliciously. Randy was secretly feathering my neck. I said nothing. I loved it. It felt good, bad, and strangely wonderful. Randy grew tired of a trick that had failed, but I told it all to mother, not the trick so much as my sensations. Mother knew that I'd had my first hint of the swelling satisfaction of sex. She said, "You've discovered the thrill of the senses," and then went on to speak of all five senses and what each brings. "When you are just a little bit older we'll talk about sex, where all of the senses come together to sing and dance with pleasure." In the years between her promise and the telling there were times when my senses were so alive I thought they would kill me.

Father also taught me to appreciate the person I uniquely am. I am six. I have been launched at school, tentative but still confident about how smart I am. It takes no time to discover that learning comes easily. After all, my father is a professor. And that rubs off on me. But so did his swarthy skin. I am intimidated not by the genius of others, but by girls with fair skin and blue eyes. How he teased this out of me I'll never know. "Look into my eyes," he said.

"See those tears? They come from the deepest river of love for you, the most beautiful of all creatures by any standard that counts."

Starting at age seven, I became breathless with amazement at all the things there were to see and feel and do things with, even in the small part of the earth that was mine to roam. "Never forget your amazement, Rosa," my father said one day, "never let the child in you die, never neglect it, it is a precious gift."

It was father who taught me how to listen to the sounds of nature, and later to the sounds of words. What gifts! I think of him even now as I read a beautifully crafted paragraph or poem. "Put the book down and breathe it in," he'd say.

This is the Edenic story of the harmony of early years in which the expectation of unconditional love is met wholeheartedly by the child's caretakers. But, as we all know, the idyllic narrative will change. Now listen to Rosa's story of imperfect love, as she told it to me. Notice its fairy-tale sound. For years, as I listened in therapy to grown men and women telling story after childhood story, watching them retch, shudder, weep, try to hide in shame, and shrink in size before my very eyes at the inevitable denouement, the place in the plot at which betrayal, disappointment, and melancholy converge in a dramatic moment of utter powerlessness, I asked myself, "What is this like?" It was the stuff and sound of fairy tale told by adults who had almost, but not quite, lost touch with this universal tongue of childhood. I could swear the child was "in the room," along with kings, queens, giants, monsters, heroes, and other magical figures.

Rosa's Dance with a Demon

It wasn't until Rosa was eight that an exceedingly unpleasant idea invaded her mind. Her mother, a paragon of motherhood, a model of compassion and tenderness, seemed to be turning into an octopus. Year after year, one child, then another, then another seemed to grow out of her mother's sides, her torso, her hips, until there were seven, all succored by the almost hidden central figure. Her mother's hands thus occupied, Rosa rarely enjoyed her touch, which was soft and tender. She settled for her praise. "No mother ever had a better helper," her mother reiterated. Motivated by such tributes, Rosa got better and better at helping. At five, she folded diapers. At six, she hung the wash. At eight, she ironed. In those days, women bore the brunt of child-work stoically and with resignation. Rosa's mother was no exception. "He draws his circle tight, and I accept it," was how she explained her Quaker equanimity and passive refusal to test her husband's limits.

Rosa's father, Nicholas, loved his many children as a man himself raised by a kingly, kindly patriarch should. He adored each and every one, not equally—for that would not make rational sense—but deeply. He was immensely proud of everything they did, boasted about them to almost anyone who would listen at the University where he taught, and generally fussed over them in every way possible.

In return, his children both adored and had the proper fear of him, a fear fostered by his profound belief in self-discipline, strict devotion to learning and achievement, and faithful obedience to those few family rites and rules which he, with his wife's counsel, had set in place. Violations of these codes resulted in corrective actions which were taken quickly, equitably, and moderately, more as symbols than as inflictions of punishment. Yet his "raps on the knuckles" had an authority equal in power to any thunderbolt Zeus himself might fire at some disobedient, mutinous subject.

Instead of rewarding his children with treats, Nicholas fed them knowledge, information he gathered from his own studies and from the work of colleagues at the University.

"I had a talk with Athene today," he would tell Rosa and her younger siblings, when they were ready to listen. For him, Athene, the goddess of wisdom, represented the pursuit of knowledge and mastery, ideals he chose to personify in order to make them more appealing and real to his children. One day Athene would tell him something about mathematics, the next day it might be something about science, the day after that about physics or chemistry or engineering. He would rush down from Olympus, the place of higher learning where Athene resided, to pass the imparted information on, especially to Rosa, his favorite pupil, who earned much praise for hungrily devouring every particle he put on her plate.

But there was more to Rosa than obedience and a huge appetite for knowledge. She had a "wild side," which her father did not notice at first, perhaps because he, too, had another side. For when he was not stuffing his children with facts or commending them for the indulgence, or quietly surveying his rules of order, he usually retreated, book in hand, to his private fortress—"the King's Chambers," as Rosa's mother called it—his study, accessible only through the bedroom he shared with his wife. No moat ever built said more clearly, "Cross these waters at great risk," than the threshold to those two forbidden and forbidding rooms.

By the time she reached her tenth year, Rosa's appetite for learning went beyond her father's guidance. She planned a surprise for him. With her usual hunger and thirst, she read everything she could on the supernatural, with its tales of sorcery, witches, devils, evil spirits, and especially demons.

She was infatuated with demons and what they represented: Lucifer, who stood for pride, Mammon, for avarice, Asmodeus, for lechery, and Satan, for anger. They appealed to mysterious, wild urges which she could vividly feel in secret places inside herself.

Pan, worshipped in Greece as a god of fertility, was Rosa's favorite demon. He was a merry, ugly man with the horns, ears, and legs of a goat. He loved to frighten unwary travelers and was very amorous. In a famous tale, he pursued the nymph Syrinx but was foiled by her sister nymphs, who effected her escape by turning her into a reed. Rosa felt sorry for Pan, and made him a frequent visitor in her nightly imaginings. One night before falling asleep, she discovered to her amazement that if she willed it she could actually see Pan, first as a man with animal features, then as a shadow.

"Instead of fleeing," she mused, "I will dance with his shadow."
And she did.

Finally, Rosa was ready to surprise her father with her discoveries and, one evening as he sat reading his newspaper, she stood before him. To get his attention, she began, "I can dance with demons, Daddy." He peered unsmiling over his wall of print, not even trying to disguise his indifference. "Did you know that the Greek god, Pan . . ." His indifference turning to disapproval, he placed his hand over her mouth. "Useless nonsense," he declared. "You are still young, and need guidance." As she fell asleep that night, Rosa recalled that before her father concluded his brief sermon, he had conceded, "Of course, my dear, I cannot stop you from reading anything you want." Yet she felt her "mysterious urges" were being repulsed and crushed.

But not forever. Just after she reached her twelfth year, having taken the onset of menses in stride, Rosa's old curiosity about secret things involuntarily returned, and sprung free during the night she discovered the Black Box.

It was a terrible night. Rosa was awakened by a crash of thunder so loud it made her ears ring. The wind rattled the windows, and rippling shadows of the curtains danced on the wall. Rosa sat up, her knees hunched under her chin. She remembered dancing with the demon, Pan, and smiled.

Noises from below drew Rosa to the top of the stairs, from whence she caught sight of her mother and father, lit by a single light, leaning over the dining room table, the Black Box open between them. They were whispering and laughing, tipsy from the glasses of wine that they extended to each other's lips. Quietly descending, Rosa inquired in a syrupy voice, "What is in the box? May I look inside?" Her father closed it abruptly. "It is not for you, my dear," her father said, laughing again. "No, my love," added her mother, "No one may open the box," and she laughed too.

In the ensuing days, Rosa walked past the ominous bedroom doors many times, stalking the moat, as it were; tempting the irresistible pull of the Black Box, and relishing every fascinating moment. The forbidden prize was secure in its hiding place and she was secure in the safety of the parlor. But then the box's magnetic power grew. Nearing the bedroom one day, she could barely keep her balance. She felt fear. She was thrilled.

The next afternoon Rosa came home later than usual from school. Her mother was upstairs with a crying baby. It was still too soon for her father's arrival. She had decided to avoid any temptation today, but, hearing the bewitching siren's song, she took a step or two toward the bedroom door. The demon guarding the magic box reached out, and drew her toward and then across the forbidden threshold. She shuddered in the demon's grip. But tormented by desire, she wouldn't have resisted even if it had been possible.

At the very instant that her shaking hand touched the closet doorknob, it was joined by a larger one. Her father, Nicholas, had emerged unseen from his study. Both stood transfixed. As she had been led to this bewitching place in the warm grip of a demon, now she was led from it in the cool grip of a father whose instant wrath she awaited. Instead, he kept a stony silence and, tightly holding her wrist, opened the closet door with one hand, tucked the Black Box under his arm, and marched, still silent, to the parlor table, on which he set the box. "Sit," he said, just this one word, still no trace of anger in his voice. Rosa knew what was expected of her. Unbidden, she placed her hand on the box. Bidden by his own demons, one would think, Nicholas did what was expected of him. It was the first and only time Rosa "had her knuckles rapped."

Rosa's life went from happy, expansive growth to fear and contraction in an instant. Her quest for knowledge had gotten her into trouble, and her exploration of herself was cut off. Without meaning to, her father had betrayed her at this moment by making her fear herself. Her mother had betrayed her by being so distracted by the other children that she let it happen.

Rosa would later marry Victor, a man whose story of imperfect love eclipsed all reminiscence of a happy childhood. His story was of a powerful mother and a weak father: "She appropriated everything, my joys and sorrows, my accomplishments and failures. She loves me for herself. Not for me."

Victor and Rosa married quickly—too quickly, they would say later, and I agreed. Like many, they fell in love in the wrong myth. Victor is a professor, and it was his brilliant mind that excited her, as hers excited him. Note here the "presence" of Rosa's father, an academic who opened her mind to the joys of learning. In this realm, Rosa and Victor will remain forever bonded. However, in the realm of the Sexual Fantasy Myth, they were grossly mismatched. Victor feared Rosa's sexual readiness—not the thing itself but its potential. She needed a lover who would welcome its unleashing, after her early experience of repression. This was impossible for Victor because of his own past. At the stubborn root of his frozen desire, we find his own childhood tale—a story he compulsively and repeatedly told of a mother whose overpowering love translated into sexual threat. His obsession with his mother's sexuality led him to shut Rosa's sexuality down, "rapping her knuckles" whenever she threatened to unlock her own "Black Box." Rosa's Personal Myth led her to seek, from a figure similar to her father, the freedom and approval he took away from her. That moment of betrayal set her off in her search for the perfect lover. She went out into the world, as we all do, trying to rewrite the story of imperfect love, trying to make it come out right.

After a six-year sexual drought and three years of therapy, Victor and Rosa had an amicable divorce. To the (mostly) amused puzzlement of future lovers, they remained each other's guide and friend, still bonded in the Gender Myth, where their attraction had begun. Their story does have a happy ending which—in their case—means a fresh beginning to the difficult journey of love. Both have found new partners whose own mythic features make them better suited for the course. Rosa has married a man whose comfort with his own sexuality has helped her explore her own as never before. Victor has found a partner whose own stories allow her to handle his sexual restraint without serious insult to her own desires.

After a false start, Victor and Rosa were ready to join all the other "heroic lovers" described in these pages in their pursuit of desire, sex, and enduring love. In recent years, the love journey, the quest for everlasting intimacy, has been likened to the Tales of King Arthur, in which the hero has to undertake the quest for the Holy Grail in order to find again what he has lost. The rest of this book argues that what each of us has lost is a reconciliation between the first dream of happiness—the Myth of Perfect Love—with the later, inevitable, childhood story of imperfect love. The conviction that such a reconciliation is possible sustains most couples through the trials they must face in trying to repair the wound of that original tragic love story. The problems which arise between partners are a reenactment of that original betrayal in some form. Some of these wounds are invisible until they are seen in the mirror of a relationship. If a couple is able to take on the needed work that I will describe in this book, the result will be a new chance to make their love story come out right.

Chapter Three

Imperfect Love

*Always in emergencies we invent narratives. We describe
what is happening as if to confine the catastrophe. . . .
Stories are antibodies against illness and pain.*
ANATOLE BROYARD,
Intoxicated by My Illness

It is one of the many paradoxes of love that our journey toward a
life partner begins with a betrayal, an anguishing realization of our
separateness from those we cherish. It is the recollecting and
telling of that first disappointment in love that is the first step toward healing both ourselves and our partnerships.

I call these recollections of the childhood story, with all of its
characters and scenes, heroes and villains, the *Personal Myth*. The
Personal Myth contains the essence of your identity, which means
that it will affect your entire life and all of your closest relationships. Although the Personal Myth is drawn from a multitude of
individual experiences and relationships, it is often remembered as
a single event which crystallizes all the key elements of one's child-

hood, such as Rosa's encounter with the black box. Time is sub-tracted from the personal story. Across cultures, the themes are the same: loss of innocence, sudden awakening, departure from paradise. The Personal Myth is the organizing story that the child tells herself about the failure of love in her life. When a person comes to me and begins by saying, "My father was a self-made man who became a monster. To those he needed he was a snake charmer, a flatterer and a crafty businessman, but to those who had no power or influence he was a bully. I was not a person with power. When I turned to my mother all I ever saw was the back of her head. If my mother had any power, I never saw it. As a consequence, I was an unprotected target for all my father's pent-up rage. I remember the day when . . . ," he is distilling his family dynamics to one compelling story. He cannot tell all the details of his father's bullying nor of his mother's inaction. Instead, he gives me something more important: the structure of his Personal Myth, from which a fuller story will emerge over time. He is basically saying, "This is the dark side of my family. My father never gave me the love I wanted from him so badly. My mother, who tried to give that love, always failed to protect me from my father's cruelty. In a sense, I was their victim."

Within your childhood story is all the pain and betrayal, great or small, that you experienced, but also all the innocence, vulnerability, and magic of childhood. You still experience this pure love from time to time, especially when you are overcome with feelings of gratitude, nostalgia, or reconciliation, for that part of the child in you never vanishes. But it becomes obscured when you are fixed on the half-remembered betrayal and all the pain and other negative emotions that such betrayal engenders. That childhood vulnerability and sense of delight is lost to those who fail to explore their Personal Myth and, as a result, become alienated from their own feelings. Yet that childhood innocence has the power to cleanse your spirit, to make your love sacred, and to give rebirth to desire. It is with this original purity still living within you that you can heal the wounds that separate you and your lover and retrieve the desire which once united you. The recovery of this purity can turn your relationship into the greatest opportunity for growth and fulfillment you will ever have.

This condition of original innocence has been written about in every religious and mythological tradition. One of the most familiar representations is the Garden of Eden, at whose center was the Tree of Life, which offered immortality, and from which a river flowed to all points of the compass. A river that flows in four directions can only flow from the center of being, the place where all paths or all conflicts come together and are reconciled. Eden's Tree of Life and its river suggest a place beyond time and space where healing, nourishment, and renewal are given. It exists at the center of your being and awaits the moment you will choose to enter it and be restored by its healing waters. All that is true and loving within you is here.

But away from the center of the Garden of Eden stands the wall which was constructed because Adam and Eve chose to eat the fruit from the Tree of Knowledge and to learn of good and evil. It was only when God noticed that Adam and Eve had covered themselves that he understood they had eaten the forbidden fruit and were covering their shame. In childhood, the moment when we first realize that perfect love is not to be ours is also the moment when we become aware of good and evil in our world and of the shame of our unlovability. Rosa felt it for the first time when her father disapproved of her dancing with demons. As it did with our ancestors, this newfound perception of good and evil in our childhood paradise leads directly to strong emotions. As soon as we feel the presence of these emotions in adulthood, we back away from the painful memory. We repress or deny its existence, shift our focus, think about something else instead. We retreat behind the walls that block us from our inner garden. This is how our buried feelings of unlovability prevent us from examining and knowing ourselves and thus from fulfilling our desires.

When we are willing to dive into the deep, cold waters of our Personal Myths we can see that many of the desires or actions we had thought of as shameful or guilt-producing were motivated by the need for love or the desire to give love. Rosa wanted to share her gift of Pan with her father. With such an awareness we are able to forgive ourselves. Very often we find that we need no forgiveness. Parts of us that were banished are honored and reintegrated into consciousness. Rosa was eventually able to find the space in a marriage to recover this side of herself. Beneath the shame or guilt, fear or sadness are love, rebirth, and desire, all the blessings at the center of our being.

As we grow older we stop entering our Personal Myth, because it is so filled with pain, shame, and humiliation. Whenever we enter our past and encounter these feelings, we are close to the center of our being. Typically, we are frightened off from the healing waters which await us there and don't penetrate deeply enough into the story. The work that must be done is to confront the painful memories and wounds of the past, forgive the people who were involved, and reconnect with the joyful, loving child in all of us, for it is that child in you who speaks the language of love and desire. When we fall in love it is the children in each of us who are connecting and playing together. And it is when intimate partners lose that childlike openness that they begin to drift apart.

For most people, the telling of the Personal Myth is the most difficult part of reclaiming intimacy even though ultimately it is the most healing. Most people who explore their Personal Myth do so after experiencing some crisis or loss in adulthood, and especially in marriage. They need to know what led them to make the decisions which ultimately brought about the crisis. In some deep and personal way, the disappointment experienced in adulthood brings them back to their own vulnerability and even to the disappointment experienced in childhood. This leads them directly into the Personal Myth, although it often requires months or even years before many of my patients are willing to break open that dark vault and look inside. It is always a powerful moment and one which never fails to awe and move me.

Several years ago, I was conducting a session with a married couple who had long since stopped making love. I had worked with this couple for many weeks. It was clear to me that the husband, Henry, was denying his feelings and resisting the work, and I had made little headway. When he would recall incidents from his childhood in which he had suffered considerably, he wrote them off as a collection of worthless and unnecessary memories with no relevance to his present life. He made it clear that he had only come to therapy because his wife, Susan, had insisted he do it as a last attempt to save their marriage.

"He doesn't seem to have any feelings at all," Susan had complained in an early session. "He's always critical and condescending. He's very good at what he does and so he retreats into his little world and closes himself in tight and shuts me out. He doesn't hold me or touch me and we never make love anymore. It's humiliating and lonely. And he doesn't even see what he's doing. He thinks he's being perfectly nice to me. The man I married has disappeared. This one doesn't even notice me. And of course he hates for me to talk about my feelings. He doesn't want to hear I have them! Do you, Henry?" she suddenly shouted as Henry shrank into his chair.

When couples in therapy enact before me the ritual struggle they may have been playing out for years, they are accusing each other of failing to come through as the perfect lovers each thought he or she was getting; the same disappointment suffered in childhood when the presumption of a continuing perfect love is replaced by the disappointing realization that such is not to be. At these times, both are standing at the threshold of their Personal Myths and feeling again that primal disappointment in love.

In this session, Susan had been particularly shrill and challenging toward Henry. The more aggressive she became, the more Henry seemed to be disappearing. At that moment, I walked over to Susan, stood behind her chair, and placed both my hands on her shoulders. I did this so that she would understand that by turning my attention to Henry at that moment, I had not abandoned her. I was also implicitly asking her to remain open so that I could draw out her husband's story. Henry's gaze seemed intently focused on some deep inner place.

"Face Susan," I gently commanded him. He raised his suffering face and looked his wife squarely in the eye.

"Susan, I want you to look at Henry." Although for many sessions, Susan had preferred to interact with me as she voiced her complaints about Henry and their marriage, she turned and looked at her husband.

"Now, tell me the story from your childhood that is telling you how to feel and behave right now, in this moment," I said.

There was a long silence. I could feel Susan's shoulders tense.

Henry sat silent for several minutes. Susan sighed deeply and impatiently.

"I—I keep hearing my parents in another room."

"And where are you, Henry?" I asked.

"I'm at the top of the stairs listening to them."

"And what are they saying?"

"They're arguing. . . ."

"Can you hear what they're saying?"

He strained, eyes closed, to hear that long-ago conversation. Then he sighed deeply and began to speak: "They're arguing, as usual, but this time they're fighting about which one of them is going to take me after their divorce. And what they're both saying is that neither of them wants me, because I'm so out of control, and my father is saying that he never wanted a second child, and my mother is saying that I inherited all my badness from him. It's weird," he said. "I haven't really remembered that scene until this moment. I guess I must have been about ten at the time, and even though I've certainly been aware all my life that my parents didn't really like me, I had forgotten that conversation. They finally sent me to live with my grandmother until I was thirteen and then I went to military academy and stayed with my mother on vacations. I never really saw my father again until I was in my twenties and he was dying of cancer. By then he was a stranger."

As a consequence of what had happened to him in childhood, Henry was forever afraid of losing the people whom he loved and so he had hidden behind a shell of apparent indifference, afraid to love with all his heart for fear that he would be betrayed and abandoned again. This had kept him from giving himself to Susan. He had been trapped in this netherworld for most of his marriage, afraid that he would be deserted, and he had almost brought down upon himself exactly this desperately feared abandonment because of his equally strong fear of opening himself up, expressing his love, and being thrown away again.

Henry had finally dared to dive into his Personal Myth, because he had reached a point in his marriage where what was in front of him, the real possibility of abandonment through divorce, was as horrifying as what he had been guarding from his past. Although he had been vaguely aware all along that he was still protecting ancient wounds, he had steadfastly resisted revisiting them. As a result, he had been cut off from the source of his feelings and was therefore unable to feel any real love for himself or his wife. When these stories are elicited, inevitably the storyteller is trembling, because the story brings up all the emotions of the child that has never quite been left behind. And by being separated from the innocent, loving child still inside, they are also cut off from desire.

"Tell Susan what you are feeling at this moment," I said to him.

"I don't know, I don't really feel anything. Or I feel kind of empty."

"Is there anything familiar in the way you're feeling now?"

"Embarrassment, in a way, I guess. I was embarrassed when I heard my parents—or humiliated. My own parents didn't even want me."

On some level Susan had known all along that Henry was

deeply in pain, but the fact that he was admitting it to her, aloud and from a part of himself that he had long suppressed, gave her the means to accept and begin the healing process.

This day marked a new beginning in their relationship. True transformational healing, healing that will last, does not happen all at once. It requires consistent work to incorporate what we have learned and to develop new behaviors and new ways of looking at life. In a sense, we must reprogram ourselves. The story which surfaces or is elicited by a therapist when a couple is engaged in one of their ritual battles is only the beginning. It's not the whole story by any means. That will evolve over time. It is the structure of the story that is important, because that structure, buried in the Personal Myth, repeats itself every time the couple does battle.

Susan and Henry were able to build on this beginning and develop a wonderful marriage. They were able to identify and reconnect with what had drawn them together in the first place, and to become conscious of the unfulfillable contracts each had dropped at the other's feet. Henry had fallen in love with Susan's steadiness and her strength. He was awed by the way Susan had pulled herself up by her bootstraps, taught herself a great deal about medicine, and started a company which made medical training films. She seemed like a woman who would always be there for him. Susan, who had grown up in a household under the pall of her adored father's chronic illness, and the financial and emotional insecurities that came with it, loved Henry's competence. She felt she could relax at last, because Henry always seemed to know what to do and he made a good living. For the first time, she felt protected and cared for. The loneliness of her parents' household seemed to retreat into the past. As they explored each other's Personal Myths and the needs each had brought to the marriage, the emphasis in their relationship shifted from trying to change each other to understanding and accepting each other's differences and enjoying their many similarities.

In order to understand the connection between the deep needs which we project upon others as adults in search of love and first need to understand the nature of childhood love.

Children are born *innocent* in the root sense of the word: they are free of injury or hurt, and above all they are vulnerable. In this primal innocence, every child believes that the contract between himself and his parents ensures unconditional love—that all of his needs will be met and that he will meet all of his parents' need for love. The child is capable, for a time, in the sincerity of childhood love, of fulfilling her side of the contract, but no parent—no matter how loving or well-meaning—can be all things to a child and still function in the adult world. Nor of course can even the most loving and sensitive parents be certain of the unique and often unstated needs of their child. Thus the parents, whom the trusting child views as omnipotent, even godlike, cannot help but betray this expectation of perfect love.

Betrayal awakens the child to the family dynamics and her place within those dynamics. It also reveals the specific issues that are implicit within the family, issues that will give the child's life definition and direction but that will also have to be coped with in adulthood. Disappointment and betrayal establish a gulf between ourselves and those we love, and create a longing for love, harmony, and intimacy which we carry into later life. All of this exists within us as part of our Personal Myth. Thus, when one of my clients remembers asking such questions as "Why is Mommy sad?" or "How can I make Daddy happy?" she is standing at the threshold of her myth.

In most cases, the betrayal is innocent—the single mother who is forced to leave her son at a day care center each morning is not deliberately betraying her child. The father who gently laughs at his daughter's insistence on watching the football game with him is not knowingly wounding her. Yet, in these moments of separation, the child realizes that he or she is not really understood and is not therefore perfectly loved. The very person or people upon whom she depends for love have unknowingly robbed her of her innocent expectation that they can be all things to her and she to them. At that moment, the child is filled with feelings of grievous disappointment. His world has changed forever, and even though such small wounds, often not even recognized by the parent, are inevitable in the process of growing up and becoming an individual, an unconscious crusade has begun: to find that person who will love him unconditionally in the way that he yearns to be understood and loved. It is at this moment that the child begins the journey to adulthood and, eventually, partnership.

For many children, of course, children like Henry, the betrayal is not innocent at all: the alcoholic parents who terrify with the sounds of their fighting; the parent who hides from life in a series of feigned illnesses, rejecting the role of caregiver so as to be cared for by the family; the narcissistic parent who uses her child to bring attention to herself. Other forms of betrayal abound. Many children are verbally, physically, or sexually abused by a parent. Some are sabotaged by a jealous parent who envies the child's beauty or intelligence or his or her relationship with the other parent.

And to the child, who still believes that her parents, by their mere existence, are perfect beings, only one explanation of their failure is possible: "These grown-ups have disappointed me because I am unlovable, and it is something bad in me which makes me unlovable to them whom I love so much." The revelation of your unlovability brings with it strong emotions which are your way of responding to Eden's gate being slammed in your face. These emotions exist along a continuum:

> Guilt............... Shame
> Anger.............. Rage
> Fear................. Anxiety
> Sadness........... Grief

"What is wrong with me that you don't love me the way I love you?" the child asks. It is a question which remains with us for life, buried at the our center and frequently resurfacing, unless we return, think deeply, and locate its source. In effect, the buried mem-

ory of that betrayal which revealed the impossibility of perfect
love—in my work, I call the memory the *shadow*—cuts you off
from many of the natural impulses you had as a child and still have
as an adult. These emotions that arose so long ago in response to
feeling unloved still exist within each of us as a barrier to our deepest desires and motivations. The strength of your shadow in the
Personal Myth depends upon where the psyche positions itself
along each continuum. For example, a shadow born of shame is
more destructive than one born of guilt. Someone whose Personal
Myth places him on more than one continuum is said to have a
more powerful shadow. Still seeking proof of love from those
around you, in adulthood your shadow makes you act like that disappointed child, desperate to feel loved but also revisiting these
strong emotions which cause you to act in ways that are guaranteed to keep you from seeming lovable to your partner.

We are all familiar with the look of undisguised anguish on a
child's face when his world has failed to measure up. A child retains the capacity for shock and suffering each time the adult world
displays its lack of grace. Thus, to a child, many experiences feel
catastrophic. Until he does something about the large and small
catastrophes that undermine his faith in the adult world, the child
inhabits a maelstrom of uncertainty.

If you have children of your own, you may be able to glimpse
in their body language moments of melancholy, in which they are
making it as loud and clear as possible that you have let them
down. Watch a child's eyes in the presence of an adult who is misreading her and you will glimpse the yearning for someone who
truly sees and understands. Desire, the yearning for the perfect
other, is born in sulking, tears, and childhood melancholy.

At that moment of great pain and disappointment, the child
does what all children do when confronted with a situation over
which they have no influence. He begins to create a story in which
all conflicts are resolved and the needed love is given. Central to
that childhood story is a hero, a being of mythic power and authority, who will protect the child and who will love her even

though she "knows," from her parents' reaction to her needs, that she is unworthy of love. This longed-for rescuer is a fixture in many fairy tales. Just when a figure of superhuman powers is needed most, he or she arrives in the form of Prince Charming or a magician or a wise animal. One of the reasons that fairy tales are so powerful and evocative of the depths of the human psyche is that they articulate this Personal Myth that every child invents and every adult holds within.

Alas, in real life the child's invented hero doesn't arrive when needed most, but the child continues to hope and to refine the image of the magical *other* who possesses the characteristics she deems essential for her survival. They may be compassion, wisdom, the strength to endure pain, or the power to hold the family together despite its difficulties. The culture surrounding the child also contributes detail to the longed-for hero. Movies, television, and stories read by parents all contain stock heroes which are available as raw materials to use in the construction of a rescuer.

This long-buried hero-rescuer figure is so important in our adult love relationships because no matter what our age, we carry deep inside us the scars of childhood, and also that long-ago wish for the right person to come along and intuit what we need to feel loved, and then provide it. The adult's longing for a mate with particular characteristics derives from the small and large betrayals of childhood. If the truant hero were to arrive in time, he or she would do, say, and even look like whatever the child's imagination constructed for her salvation. These then become the characteristics of the perfect mate. It is this shadowy figure who influences our selection of an intimate partner. By adolescence, we have written and revised and rewritten the romantic lead in our love stories. In adulthood, we will audition people who seem to have these qualities, and it is those who seem to have "the right stuff" with whom we will fall in love.

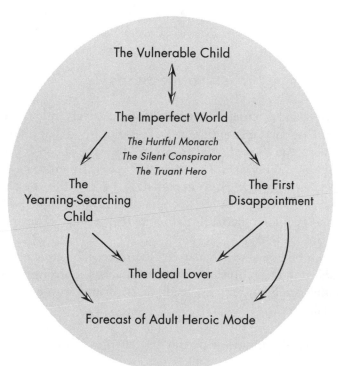

The Vulnerable Child

The Imperfect World

The Hurtful Monarch
The Silent Conspirator
The Truant Hero

The
Yearning-Searching
Child

The First
Disappointment

The Ideal Lover

Forecast of Adult Heroic Mode

The Universal Character of the Personal Myth

I suspect that no quest for intimacy can be sustained or successfully completed without a return to the roots from which we grow our capacity to give and receive love. Every lover, and every professional who tries to help with failing love, can only gain from understanding love's basic structure. Relatively early in my experience, listening to story after story, it came to me one day that they all seemed to follow a similar storyline which unfolded within a simple format whose seven features took on a universal character.

Setting the Stage

I am weak and defenseless compared to them (Everychild thinks). I know that once, a long time ago, I was truly loved, but it is only a memory. Am I loved now? How can I be sure? There! It's happened again. Why, when I cry at night because I want to be with them longer, do they get so impatient and angry? (To the child, even trivial affronts can be experienced as major assaults.) They hate me. (Children naturally dramatize their claims.) They probably want me to die.

Each offense—whether trivial, outrageous, or atrocious—is stockpiled in an archive of complaints against the stronger, more powerful family authorities, ready to be shaped into a story of betrayal.

THE SEVEN RECURRING FEATURES OF THE PERSONAL MYTH

1. The Hurtful Monarch
2. The Silent Conspirator
3. The Truant Hero
4. Melancholic Disappointment
5. Specific Themes of Betrayal
6. Longing and Yearning for the Future Lover
7. The "When I Grow Up" Hero

The prevalence of these compelling childhood stories and the quality and scale of the energy devoted to their telling in adulthood are indicative of their irrevocable place in the establishment of love. When this storytelling is intelligently probed, the stories' nature is strikingly revealed. They are, primarily, stories of lost love. They are also a child's art form, and a child's revenge, whereby she gets even in narrative if not in fact. Their themes of betrayal come in many degrees of intensity and many shades of emotion. They also contain the seeds of redemption, implicitly pointing the way to deliverance and the recovery of lost love.

As we saw with Henry and Susan, it is only when we can dare to re-explore this early disappointment and loss, and its source in that original betrayal, innocent or devastating as it may have been, that we can begin to see the shadowy outline of that secret rescuer which continues to shape our yearning for a perfect love, and which is also the basis for sexual desire. This is the pathway back to finding and giving the love of which you were originally capable.

The teasing out and retelling of the stories of these childhood turning points is a task which must be undertaken by both partners, either separately or together. The reason is clear: just as your childhood disappointment has led to the creation of an idealized other half and then to the choice of a partner to fill that role as well as possible, so has your partner's past led him to the same point. Just as you have cast him as the lead in your unpublished script, he has cast you in a similar role. Each of you has holes that the relationship can't repair. Until these unspoken expectations, and the stories which gave rise to them, are brought into the light, you will both eventually fall short. You will have little chance of remaining heroic or desirable in each other's eyes once the blindness of the initial passion is removed. At worst, you will find yourselves at war, each of you the other's enemy. Or, you will find that the vitality and promise of your courtship are missing; that your horizons have shrunk and you are living a smaller life than you had planned together.

But how much truth can we expect to find within these personal narratives? Do Personal Myths deliver fact or metaphor? "How can that be true?" a shocked seventy-year-old mother demanded, when confronted at last with the stunning particulars of her middle-aged daughter's story. This sort of question—*Are these the facts? How can this be?*—are unavoidable in daily life, but next to useless in psychology. For the therapist or for the partners exploring their personal pasts, the more important question is, "What purpose do the stories serve?" The stories are a means by which we all compensate for our vulnerability and empower ourselves to grapple with reality. Every recollected story has redemptive and transcendent possibilities. Thus, we should not too quickly disown the fictive elements in our myths; they provide essential material for the construction of ideals. As Thomas Moore says in his book, *Soul Mates,* "From a deeper perspective, the *images* we have of our parents may be more important than any observable direct influence. . . . Stories about our parents are not only actual memories, but also stories that tell the myths we live by and that account for our feelings."

Here I want to tell the Personal Myth of Rosa's husband, Victor, because, as we will see later, its fictive elements lose none of their power for being fictional, and it shows clearly how the memories of the Personal Myth affect our later intimacies.

Victor, a software engineer in his mid-thirties, grew up in a small town outside Düsseldorf, Germany. As Victor was growing up, he had a carefully guarded secret. Late at night, when there was no possibility of one of his parents walking in on him, Victor wrote poetry. Not even his best friends knew, and he would rather have swum to Denmark with a stone tied to each ankle than share even his best poems with his mother.

Victor's father was a simple man who loved his wife and son, but he had a peculiar way of showing it. If his wife was irrational and seemed on the verge of careening off into the deep end, he humored her as if she was someone in an asylum of whom nothing could be expected. If he displeased her, she would let him know it in no uncertain terms and he would cower like a beaten dog. He liked spending time with his son, but at home he kept his distance. Victor always felt as if he were a piece of territory to which his mother had staked a claim; that he was hers alone and that her husband had better keep his hands off their son.

This theory came to Victor one day when he was especially eager to spend time with his father and his mother noticed. "I love you, Victor," she said. "My love for you and all I want to do for you are greater even than the hatred I have for my father, for all he did to me." (When she was sixteen, her father had turned her out of the house to fend for herself.) Victor realized that he was being asked to meet love with love, but he felt only hatred. His mother's words made his blood boil. His heart pounded his ribcage like someone beating on the doors of a cathedral until he feared the sound would give him and his feelings away.

"I would like to go to my room," he said quietly.

"Don't go yet," she said, ignoring or failing to notice that his fair-skinned cheeks had turned crimson. "I have only you and without you I am lost. You are more important to me than life itself."

"Then you are lost," he thought to himself, "because I can't look at you except with hatred."

One evening, after a very good dinner served on the family's best china, Victor's mother said to his father, "I have a surprise for Victor, and I want you to see it too." She disappeared into her bedroom. His father shrugged and smiled sheepishly, more puzzled than Victor, who always expected the worst. When his mother returned, she appeared in a see-through macramé dress, a relic of her wilder days in the 1960s. Without a word of explanation, she put on a tape and began to dance freely, glancing from time to time at the small assembly as if for their approval. As she glided around the room, her long hair waved loosely and she began to sing or chant. When Victor made out the words, his eyes began to water, but not with joy. The words were fragments from one of his poems. He felt humiliated, robbed, and forced into a world of his mother's creation. He felt her theft as a seizure of control.

Seeing the look of utter distress on his son's face, Victor's father groped for words. "Your mother is beautiful," he said. Victor thought his mother had lost her mind. Then, without warning, she reached out for her husband's hand and dragged him into her wild dance. But he was unprepared and, knocking over a chair, he spun free and collapsed onto the sofa.

"Leave it, leave it!" she screeched in high-pitched laughter. She seemed immersed in her rapture and incapable of stopping. Her whole body began to undulate as she swept around the room. Victor was mesmerized with disgust, but in a moment when his guard was down, his mother locked his wrists in a vise-grip and pulled her stunned son to his feet. Feeling that he would go mad if he did not instantly stop this frantic scene, Victor shot his own leg between his mother's legs and they both fell to the floor in a tangle. Victor screamed, "*Stop it!*" in a voice he did not recognize. His father turned the tape player off and there was silence.

Victor felt as if he was dying. Even as he fled, sobbing, through the halls, his lifeblood seemed to flow out of him. By the time he reached his room he was cold, colder than he had ever been before. Tears spilled from his eyes as he tried to erase the memory of his humiliation. "I could kill her," he thought. "I could avenge myself by taking a hammer and striking her dead. I wish she had been a Vestal Virgin so that I would never have been born to her." In that moment, Victor decided never to write another poem.

Some time after Victor and Rosa first came to me because of difficulties they were having in their intimate relationship, I had occasion to meet Victor's parents. In front of me Victor recalled the scene to his parents. Neither parent, neither then nor in a private session with me, could remember such an occurrence. I believed them then and do to this day. But that is not to say that Victor was not telling the truth, for he was. Victor was giving me the structure of his personal mythology, revealing to me the dark side of his family life. He saw his father as weak and incapable of fending off a woman who was dominating and possessive in the extreme. Later we will see how this story continued to play out in his life with Rosa.

Not every childhood story will be as dramatic as Henry's or

Victor's. As I have said, the seminal childhood disappointment in
love is usually innocent, perhaps no more than a parental over-
sight or a series of them, for all families are imperfect. Even if there
were such a thing as a perfect family, the child would discover—
would embody, if necessary—their particular Achilles heel. This
first experience of imperfection is crucial to the forging of identity.
It is what leads the child into the adult world where, with the help
of the right person, he or she hopes to do a better job. This sense
of disconnection and separateness, while necessary for growth, becomes loneliness, isolation, and abandonment: the forge in which
dramas of love solidify.

For my client Gordon, the decisive and memorable event, the
one which became central to his story, occurred when he was
twelve or thirteen. As Gordon tells it:

"There was no talking about feelings in my family. I knew feelings existed. They washed over me all the time, but I didn't have
a vocabulary for them. I hadn't been taught their names. I lacked
the example of family members saying things like, 'Oh, I'm sad
right now.' Or 'I'm happy now: what you did just made me happy.'
I had no way of knowing if anyone else in the family felt emotions
or knew anything about warmth, love, or happiness.

"It wasn't so hard to recognize anger and tension. They were
constants. One night, as we were seated at the dining room table,
it was worse than usual. My sister wouldn't look up from her food.
My father was bristly, fidgety, completely ill at ease.

"I tried some chitchat about my grades in school. No response.
Then my father barked, 'Your mother is really upset. You need to
be quiet and careful right now.' At this, my mother leapt up and
ran from the table. Dead silence while she hid upstairs in the bedroom and cried. When she came downstairs again, she apologized
as she always did. But for what? For being upset!

"That night I suddenly understood that having feelings and
wanting to be honest about them made me different from everyone else in my family and particularly from my father. I felt separate from them all, and so sad. I understood the importance of

emotion, but it made me lonelier than before. That night at the table my heart shut down."

Gordon's story contains the breakaway point, the crucial moment of transition to self-awareness. In recounting stories such as this, children become archivists of family memory, but the child's story points forward as well, to a future dedicated, above all, to the proposition that the past will not be repeated. No matter what else happens, he tells himself that "what happened then" will not happen all over again.

"But nothing terrible ever happened to me," many clients say. "I'm just bored with my marriage. I'm not into sex the way I used to be. I don't see what that has to do with my childhood. I don't have any terrible secrets to dredge up. I wasn't abused, I'm not crazy. My parents loved me and each other, and I had a secure and happy childhood. So how can all this soul-searching possibly help now?"

This is a common refrain in my practice, and although some patients, like Henry, are denying and suppressing humiliating or painful memories that are now blocking their feelings and cutting them off from the pleasure-loving child within, for others the loss of innocence seems quite harmless in retrospect. Even so, its effect is long-lasting and powerful.

Early in my career, I saw a Harvard senior who complained of mild depression which turned out, really, to be a case of aggravated boredom. Sinclair felt hollow, dull, indifferent to his success and good fortune. Extremely good-looking, he easily attracted the women of his choice; schoolwork and popularity in the fashionable set also came easily. When Sinclair had been admitted to Harvard, his parents, who were rich, successful, and intelligent—in short, perfect—celebrated, but Sinclair did not participate in the rejoicing. He had expected admission into Harvard. Success had been the natural order of things. When he came to me, having just been admitted to Yale Medical School, his first choice, he again felt no sense of elation. Getting what he wanted was customary. Success was routine. Life was unexciting.

As we came to see in our work together, success was for Sinclair not a goal, but an obstacle. Perfection had enveloped him as a child; it had to be shed, and imperfection courted, before he could achieve identity. My impulse was to slap him on the wrist and take him on a tour of ghetto streets; show him the back wards of a mental hospital. In fact, Sinclair took such a tour on his own initiative. Impressed by genuine suffering, he chose to pursue a career in psychiatry. And, although he was endlessly pursued by a procession of sleek debutantes, Sinclair chose to marry Joanne, a feisty newspaper reporter from a working class Irish background.

When I encountered Sinclair years later at a professional meeting, he told me about his training at a psychoanalytic institute where he had discovered an anger at his parents—more "profound vexation" than rage—that had been buried for years under his composure and equilibrium. He described himself as "coasting, spoiled silly," and his drives as "dead muscle." His marriage had suffered, he told me, somewhat embarrassed, when Joanne, his wife, had grown intolerant of their tepid sex. Sinclair was also somewhat embarrassed to admit that he ran true to psychological form: uncovering his anger at his parents had given him more energy for love.

Sinclair was awakened to and stimulated by imperfection after a delay, unlike Henry, who was robbed of the fundamental rights of childhood: the right to be loved for his own sake, the right to two parents who were present, and the right to the safety of an undivided home. Disappointment was far less blatant in Sinclair's world, and identifying it was more difficult.

I learned more when Sinclair and Joanne came in several years later for a consultation. Joanne's complaint, particularly difficult for her to air given their outwardly harmonious relationship, had forced the visit. "His fear of displeasing me makes him, well, boring in bed," she complained. "Real lovemaking, sex with passion, takes some getting *down*, some being *dirty*. Good sex doesn't happen if you're always thinking about staying neat and clean!"

After I discussed with them the role of childhood stories and images in the origins of desire, Joanne and Sinclair went home and did some hard work together. One day, Sinclair dredged up a memory that he called "The Case of the Dirty Fingernails." As a boy, Sinclair had liked helping his mother in her garden. One day, eager to please her, he had planted a plant in exactly the spot for which it was destined. He was proud, expectant, competent, independent. He was a man, her man.

At the table, his mother noticed that he had failed to change his clothes and wash up, which was unusual for him. Was he showing off his newfound dirtiness and independence, making it impossible for her not to notice, or had he merely forgotten? As an adult he could no longer vouch for what his motives had been at the time, but he had no trouble at all recalling his mother's crushing response. No notice was made of the good job he had done in the garden. "Change those filthy clothes," she scolded. "Wash up and for God's sake, Sinclair, scrub those repulsive fingernails!"

It was a charged moment for Sinclair. He could have rebelled. He could have fought, stamped his feet, cried and criticized his mother's insensitivity. Instead, he forgave her as usual, on the grounds of his general good fortune, thereby disowning an anger it would take years of life and considerable work to reclaim.

In Joanne, Sinclair had made a good choice. Deep inside, he yearned for a partner who would force him to get his hands dirty, in the fullest sense of the term. As Jean-Paul Sartre asserted in his play *Les Mains Sales* (*The Dirty Hands*): "*Si l'on veux fricoter, il faut salir les mains*" ("If you want to cook, you have to get your hands dirty"). Joanne showed Sinclair a new world. In effect, she was saying to him: "Don't worry that things aren't perfect out there! You don't have to be bored, because there's a lot to be done. Let's roll up our sleeves, meet it head-on and have fun doing it. Come on, Sinclair, dare to get your hands dirty!"

And while Sinclair and Joanne did have fun together, and Joanne did get Sinclair out into the wider world, there was still something lacking, and it showed up in bed. Joanne's childhood story led her to Sinclair, because she needed to escape the poverty

and chaos that had reigned at home. She was attracted to Sinclair's
assurance and ease. She needed him to provide a safe haven from
which to go out into the world and right its wrongs. But what she
needed in bed was a man who would pin her arms behind her head
and ravish her. Sinclair found it too embarrassing even to try to
summon up such animal passion.

If Joanne had not held out for what she needed and forced
Sinclair, with my help at first, to look into his past and find the
memory that was cutting him off from his own sexuality, they
would probably have settled, at least for a while, for the sanitized
sexuality dictated by Sinclair's past which whispered: "A lovable
man isn't dirty. A lovable man is perfect. Keep it clean, keep it
safe."

Sinclair and Joanne's story again underscores the impoverish-
ment of intimacy and desire which can occur when we censor our
own childhood stories. To have lasting and deepening intimacy
over a lifetime, we must not shy away from the pain of our initial
disappointments, but instead dig out what it was that gave birth to
the heroes we and our partners expect each other to be. Until we
do, that primal sense of unlovability and shame, of falling short,
will arise again and again. And, as long as we expect our partners
to rescue the forgotten child within us, they too can't help but fall
short. Neither of you is meaning to withhold the needed love; the
problem is that neither partner, with his or her parallel needs, can
be exactly what the other needs. Your story was written long ago.
Your partner arrived too late in your drama to rewrite it from the
beginning for you. It is the child in you who must come to terms
with her own pain and learn how to love herself.

If both partners remember and share their stories, there is
room for magic, because the deep knowing and acceptance of one
another's Personal Myths is the door to self-love. The beauty of relationship, and especially sexual relationship, is that it can lead us
back to the paradise of childhood purity, and also force us to confront old patterns and wounds that originated then and are causing each of us to behave in ways that bring about conflict in the

relationship now. Those patterns are often hard to see, and we need our partners to point them out so that we can grow beyond them. In fact, if a relationship is to be successful, it must lead you both back to these places within yourselves. For only there can we find the fountain of love, our heroic aspirations, and the sexual attraction within our marriages. The key to entering the condition of original purity is to explore the feelings within the Personal Myth. To truly experience these feelings is to transcend all judgment of yourself and to re-experience the pure and beautiful child whose only desire was to love and be loved. That love which you will find for yourself, and your desire to love your mate are the basis of renewal. Once we give ourselves the love we deserve, our partners are also able to give more. The promises of the early days of courtship are fulfilled, and intimacy and desire continue to grow.

Unfortunately, we often deny the criticisms or revelations our mate offers, telling ourselves that he or she is trying to manipulate us. "My partner is trying to get me to behave in ways that will make her happy, but that will not necessarily make me happy," we may tell ourselves. Here we reach an impasse, because neither partner is behaving in a such a way as to help the other heal the old wounds. He or she is merely pointing out those wounds' reverberations within the couple's daily life. The fact is that we must each go back and do our own "work," using the mirror our partner offers us as a guide, but not expecting the other to make things right for us. Alas, this is the unstated contract in most marriages. When the *other* fails to heal you, you feel let down and polarized from your spouse. Desire diminishes and the two of you are left separate and alone. Each is saying to the other in whatever words, "Why aren't you loving me? Why aren't you being what I need you to be? Why have you broken the promises we made together at the beginning?" If you are to heal this inevitable crisis, you must both be willing to explore your Personal Myths.

The question emerges, then: how do we enter the Personal Myth and find that lost childhood? Our mythology, fairy tales, and religious traditions suggest that in order to heal ourselves, we must occasionally change our perspective. In the Gospel of Matthew, Jesus is quoted as saying: "Except ye be converted and become as little children, ye shall not enter the Kingdom of Heaven." These words mean, of course, that we must drop our adult armor—our pride, pretension, and shame.

Sometimes being a child is as simple as saying, "I don't know." Healing in marriage begins with the words, "Perhaps my mate is seeing something about me that I am not seeing. Perhaps things about me are causing the problems in our relationship, or at least contributing to them. Perhaps I can change these things and make our relationship better." At that moment, you are able to embrace the power of innocence. This little statement to yourself makes surrender possible. At this point, you can begin to allow your partner's words to have meaning and importance which, until this moment, you may have been denying. The walls that have kept you from growing are thereby weakened and even made permeable.

Discovering Your Personal Myth

The feelings and memories you are searching for may be very vivid and may come to mind quickly. You may think of them often. Or, it may take some time for memories to surface once you have asked yourself the questions. Search your dreams, and pay attention to your thoughts; the Personal Myth will reveal itself slowly, often in indirect ways. Looking at photographs is often a good way to reconnect with memories and feelings. Another is having conversations with family members. Give the process time. These questions are designed to get you started. Other questions may occur to you. Ask them of yourself and wait patiently for the answers. Keep a journal or notebook handy, as they may arrive at inopportune times, including during sleep.

1. What are your earliest memories? What feelings accompany these memories?
2. Can you remember your mother's scent? Your father's? What memories and feelings arise for you when you remember them?
3. Try to remember the first time you felt lonely or sad, angry or embarrassed. What was happening to you?
4. Are there fears and other feelings which have lasted in your life since childhood? Can you trace them back to particular incidents or times in your life?
5. Look at photographs from your childhood. Can you remember what you were feeling when they were taken? Looking at them now, what can you discern about yourself or your family?

Chapter Four

The Gender Myth and the Search for the Ideal Lover

Just as our childhood disappointments form the basis for sexual desire in adulthood by sending us out into the world in search of that perfect *other* who will see us as we truly are, we create another myth later in childhood and adolescence to draw others to us. I call this the *Gender Myth*. It is the flag we fly in the world, the persona we piece together and then project to inform others of the kind of man or woman we are, in relationship to society and particularly to potential mates. Your profession, the way you speak and dress, and your politics and hobbies are all part of your Gender Myth. Much as the Personal Myth is the unconscious basis of desire, the Gender Myth is usually the conscious basis, at least initially, for attraction between two people. When you meet a person and find him or her appealing or sexy it is usually, though not always, due to a harmony between your respective Gender Myths.

In childhood, you responded to your need for unconditional love by creating the image of a magical *other* who would restore you to the paradise that was lost when you were robbed, however innocently, of the illusion of perfect love. This truant hero of childhood—who never came when needed; and for whom some part of you never ceases to wait and hope—fuels sexual desire in adulthood. As you grow up and spend more time in the world around you, your focus changes from finding an *other*, who can give unconditional love, to your *self* as someone who can attract the love you need. By now the yearning for unconditional love has been replaced by the understanding that love is, by nature, conditional. It is conditional upon your projecting an image that will appeal to another whose Gender Myth is harmonious with your own. Thus you begin quite consciously to mold your gender image. This consciously created image offers the maturing young person a lodestar by which to navigate her path toward becoming the adult she dreams of being. It tells her how to behave in order to become that person. This is a process which continues, to some degree, throughout life, but is primarily a task of later childhood and adolescence.

In constructing your gender image, you are asking yourself "What kind of person do I want to be seen as, and how, therefore, shall I act?" and, "What kind of person do I admire and want to emulate?" While the hero of the Personal Myth is a result of the developmental imperative of becoming separate from one's parents, the hero of the Gender Myth is part of the process of differentiation whereby you embrace your uniqueness and separateness rather than lament them. There are dreams within you yearning to be expressed. Now you have begun the process of becoming one of the leads in your own life drama.

The Development of Your Gender Myth

Your Gender Myth is rich in detail and unique to you. Nevertheless, you have pieced together this persona from many influences and role models in the outer world. The culture, in the form of books, movies, art, and television, has offered you an endless array of gender heroes to help you draw a clearer picture of yourself. Celebrities and others who are larger than life have played this essential role in all societies, past and present. In a sense, they are mythic heroes and heroines whose real importance lies in helping us to articulate our own longings to achieve heroic status and thus to be loved as fully as we secretly dream we can be.

If you were lucky enough to have had a teacher, family member, or other mentor who took an active interest in you or who noticed or encouraged you in a special talent, this guidance may have played a strong influence in the creation of your Gender Myth. Another common formative experience is a key conversation, or a number of conversations, with an important friend who offered you an image of how he saw you; an image that was accurate and made you proud. Jobs, clubs, church, or athletics can all provide the opportunity to experience your power and talents, your unique contribution.

Raymond, a client of mine to whom I will refer throughout this book, developed a strong gender image early in life. As we will come to see later, Raymond lives primarily from his Gender Myth, a way of being which has brought him to the top of his profession, but which has had predictable consequences in his love life.

Raymond, in his early fifties, is a striking-looking man, tall and fit with a headful of wavy salt and pepper hair. He is a professor of one of the sciences at MIT and is considered a leading thinker in his discipline. Not only is Raymond a hero within his own field, but he is also a personal hero to a number of women friends, women to whom he is constantly providing support, guidance, and assistance in one area of their lives or another.

Raymond's Gender Myth began to emerge in grammar school. Throughout his student years Raymond was singled out for his academic achievements, particularly in science and math, but in other academic fields as well. His array of talents was such that he could as easily have been a writer or historian as a scientist or mathematician. In his junior year of high school, he came under the spell of his chemistry teacher, a passionate young man with Coke-bottle glasses and unruly hair who pounded his fist on table tops for emphasis and even sometimes let tears stand in his eyes as he described the chemical reactions that constitute life itself. This teacher had decided against a research career in favor of teaching science to the next generation. At one point Raymond submitted an assigned essay to this teacher, who, after reading the piece, called Raymond into his office. "You belong in science," he said. "That essay was beautiful, I mean really topflight—work a college student would be proud of." If Raymond had been unclear until then which of his many talents to pursue, this moment was a turning point. His Gender Myth was fast emerging and was now validated by someone he deeply respected.

Whenever Raymond faced a particularly challenging situation, he used to think of how one of his heroes—Werner von Braun, who pioneered the U.S. space program, or Friedrich Nietzsche, the philosopher—would have handled the situation. While these were Raymond's real-life heroes, the mythical figure with whom Raymond most identified was the most celebrated of King Arthur's Knights of the Round Table, Sir Lancelot. Such admiration had a certain clairvoyance, for Raymond, like Sir Lancelot, would perform many heroic deeds and meet with great success in life, but his relationship with his one true love would also be marked by triangles and betrayal.

Raymond's first meeting with his second wife, Samantha, was like a chemical reaction between Gender Myths. Samantha, a talented writer and editor, was working with a professor at Stanford on some writing projects. One evening, the professor invited her to a lecture which he said was going to be given by an extraordinary iconoclast, a man who had radically changed the existing thinking in his field. Although this field wasn't of great interest to Samantha, her employer insisted she come just to witness history in the making. The moment Raymond strode to the podium, she was riveted by his leonine presence. She couldn't take her eyes off him even though the paper he was giving soon spiraled off into realms of science she couldn't follow. After the lecture, her em-

ployer invited her to dine with Raymond and him. By the time
they had reached coffee, the air between Raymond and Samantha
was charged. Samantha is an unnervingly beautiful woman. She
has the serenity and coloring of a Botticelli Madonna with
wheaten hair and teal-blue eyes. To this day, I am somewhat unclear on many of the particulars of her background, because
Samantha has guarded many of her mysteries, but she has about
her the air of a natural aristocrat. She sits in perfect stillness, her
eyes placidly watching and clearly missing little. Samantha is careful to downplay her physical brilliance. Modesty about her surface
elegance calls attention to her inner grace. This modesty will be
important later, as we follow Raymond's and Samantha's course
from that first meeting. Raymond, who was a collector of women,
would not rest until he possessed her beauty and her reticence. The
very next day, as he was about to leave for the airport, he dropped
by her office and said, "I want you to come East and work for me."

Gender Masks

Just as outside influences can help us develop our Gender Myths,
they can also confuse us as to our true gender ideal. Rather than
doing the self-analysis necessary to understand our true natures,
many of us, particularly when we are young, instead mimic the persona of a mentor, cultural icon, or celebrity. In adolescence, many
of us experiment with various personalities in our quest to find the
one which best suits our nature. But our true Gender Myths are always in harmony with our talents and our inner nature. The per-
sonae which do not really fit are masks. If you adopt a gender mask
not in harmony with your deepest nature, you set yourself up for a
crisis which will ultimately force you to discard the mask and find
the truth. If you fail to recognize the discord and do not discard the
mask, you will probably never feel fulfilled in your life work.

I frequently see people in therapy who have come to me after discovering that their jobs no longer satisfy them, which is often an indication that their Gender Myths are changing or were only masks. It often turns out that these people have chosen careers out of family pressure. For example, I briefly saw a man whom I will call Murray, whose mother should have been the doctor she told Murray, from the age of six, that he would be. His father, a medical supply salesman, had wanted to go to medical school and hadn't been able to, and his wife had transferred her ambitions from him to their son, who was a gifted writer. Murray became "my son, the doctor." This bright, disciplined, and obedient son suffered throughout a twenty-year career in radiology. In his late forties, after much agonizing, he walked out on a profession and a lifestyle which had never suited him. Alas, that lifestyle suited his wife just fine. So he left her with the house, two cars, a vacation home, and all but a small part of his retirement portfolio and moved to Montana, where he worked to become the writer he had always wanted to be.

George, a corporate lawyer earning more than half a million dollars a year, was really a social activist by nature. He had followed his father and brothers into the law firm his grandfather had started. But George found the greed of his fellow attorneys and the acts of the corporate clients he was forced to defend morally repugnant. Over the years he developed various strategies to cope with this rift between his inner self and the mask he was forced to wear. He donated his entire bonus to charities, he did pro bono work for many causes which had been harmed by the various clients he was defending, and he volunteered on the local ambulance on weekends. But these activities merely emphasized for him the split between his true nature and the man he appeared to be in the world. Finally, he could no longer bear the lie he was living and walked out of his office forever. When I next heard from him, he was in London, working as a lawyer for Oxfam.

Very often in life we feel forced to wear masks because we cannot find a place in society which allows us to live from our true Gender Myths. Instead, we live as chameleons, trying to fit in but never quite feeling at home. Some unfortunate people live their entire lives stifled by a vague sense of not quite having found a soul-satisfying place in society. Others, the luckier ones like Murray and George, find that they are unable to continue the lie, and have the courage to tear apart the structure of their lives to retrieve and pursue their true Gender Myth.

Immature Gender Myths

Another common problem occurs when one or both partners in a relationship commit to each other before the hero of their Gender Myth has fully formed. This was the case with Sally and Steve, two high-school sweethearts. These two grew up in a small Midwestern town. Sally's father ran the local hardware store and Steve's father ran a tractor dealership. Both mothers were homemakers with large families. Sally was the prettiest of her three sisters. In fact, she was considered one of the prettiest girls in the town. Sally's major dream at that point was to find a good-looking man, settle down near her parents, and start what she hoped would be a large, happy family—something like the Brady Bunch. She made the cheerleading squad and soon attracted the school's number one dreamboat, Steve, a star athlete and big man on campus. The ideal couple, the two represented gender heroes for the whole school, even the town—Sally with her blue eyes and brunette flip, and All-American Steve with his broad shoulders and Midwestern wholesomeness. Two weeks after high school graduation, they walked up yet another aisle and into what both expected would be a fairytale life.

Unfortunately, high school heroics were no preparation for real life. Once Steve hung up his uniforms and Sally put down her pompoms, they needed to start to grow and to learn about themselves and one another. Sally was willing to make the voyage of self-discovery that would give them deepening intimacy and love.

In fact, Sally had an instinctual sense of what was needed to make a marriage work. Without knowing why, she found herself wondering why she was always angry with her mother and a little bit afraid of her father, and why she always wanted to save people from their problems. She started to ask herself why she always felt compelled to be sweet and supportive to everyone around her. Sally knew that she wanted to have children, but something inside also told her that she needed to know herself better in order to be a good mother. Although Steve would have preferred for her to stay home like his own mother had, Sally got a part-time job at the library. Still madly in love with Steve, she felt herself growing and wondering about the world and her own place in it.

Steve, on the other hand, was still holding on to his outdated Gender Myth—that of all-around athlete and high school heartthrob. He got a job at the local recreation department and earned a small salary while living off memories of his playing-field heroics. Secretly, however, he feared that his best days were behind him. Terrified to discover that this might be true, he refused to enter his inner domain where he would have been forced to face the little boy inside himself, a little boy who was afraid to grow up and leave his glory days behind. Stronger voices were telling him that a "real man" doesn't express his feelings or his doubts, especially not about himself. A real man is bold, knowing and sure—all things that Steve was not, outside the gymnasium. By resisting exploring his Personal Myth and refusing to allow his Gender Myth to grow and develop into new areas where he might shine, Steve allowed his immature Gender Myth to repress and limit his psychological development. Sadder still, he didn't realize that his wife could have helped him, because she wanted to have the kind of conversations that could answer his unacknowledged questions and permit his inchoate Gender Myth to expand. Unfortunately, Steve refused to engage in this process. "I can't understand you when you talk like that, Sally," he'd say in frustration when she would try to talk about their childhoods. The conversation would end as soon as it had started.

As the early years of their marriage went by, Sally and Steve had a daughter and were relegated to the sort of low-income lifestyle that Sally had hoped to avoid by marrying the hero her unformed Gender Myth had told her was right for the girl she was at that time. When she became pregnant again, Steve insisted she have an abortion because they couldn't afford another child. The abortion was a serious mistake for their relationship, although it marked a turning point in Sally's life. Raised Catholic, Sally had many unexamined feelings about the subject of abortion, but she went along with Steve's request. As she lay on a gurney in the doctor's office recovering from the procedure, she wept bitterly. She could forgive neither her husband nor herself, and at that point she started to turn away from him.

She applied to the nearby state university and was accepted on a full scholarship. Secretly threatened, Steve made little effort to help. Sally dropped her young child off at her parents' house each day, commuted to school, and then came home and cared for her family. Meanwhile, Steve acted as though nothing had changed in their lives. He was still one of the boys, still a local legend among the guys at the bar, and still unwilling to address his growing doubts about himself or his future.

During this time, Sally's Gender Myth began to change radically. For the first time she was exposed to men and women with lofty ambitions and a fundamental belief in their (and her) ability to achieve dreams. Four years later, Sally emerged with a degree in political science and wondered what she was going to do with the rest of her life. A professor recommended that she apply to the University of Chicago Law School. Figuring she had nothing to lose, Sally applied and, much to her surprise, was accepted. Once she was there, her Gender Myth continued to expand as she met women with dreams of attaining important posts in government and in the legal profession. Her world opened up, and with it her image of herself.

Steve stayed in the same place and clung to his high school Gender Myth. He went camping and fishing with his friends, played recreational softball and watched a lot of television. He was bewildered. His cheerleader was gone and in her place was a new woman with a new Gender Myth. Her new myth told her that she was an intelligent, capable, hardworking woman, one who could earn a good living and take care of herself and her child. This Gender Myth also contained an image of a man who was every bit her equal or even better than she, a man who could take care of her and master the world. Sally's and Steve's Gender Myths were now completely at odds. Steve was frightened by Sally's ambition and the likelihood that she would realize it. She no longer made him feel good about himself. She, on the other hand, found him distant, repressed, and hidden. He took out his anxieties in a variety of passive-aggressive maneuvers designed to put small roadblocks in front of her every day. He'd laugh if she overcooked the dinner because she was studying, or he'd "forget" to pick their daughter up from band practice. Steve had absolutely no desire to change, and his buddies and his family backed him up; to them, Sally was too big for her britches. Eventually they stopped talking about anything except the logistics of the shared parts of their lives. Intimate discourse had died. Sally begged Steve to go to couples therapy with her, but he mockingly refused. If he was like a foreigner to her, he said, it was her fault for no longer speaking his language. "You sold me a bucket of suds," he said. "You're not the girl I married." "And you're not eighteen anymore," she replied bitterly. Soon after they reached this impasse, they divorced and Sally moved to Boston where she got a job in a large law firm.

Attraction Within the Gender Myth

While the hero-rescuer which you created out of your childhood wounds still functions within you and forms the unconscious basis for desire and, eventually, union, you yourself are the hero of your Gender Myth. Although it is unique to you and, with luck or hard work, true to your real self, it is a starring role that you have written for yourself in the belief that the characteristics you project will bring you the love you desire. You fall in love with those who have the characteristics which elicit and strengthen your own Gender Myth. When two people whose Gender Myths are in harmony encounter one another, there is a feeling of tremendous energy and power, in part because each offers the other hope that their partnership will bring them closer to becoming the people they have always wanted to become. When two people recognize such a match of gender ideals, which usually occurs unconsciously, there may be an overwhelming sexual attraction. Each feels heroic in his own eyes and in the other's, and each sees a future filled with promise. The two realize that they are in love with each other, but also with themselves, because of the way each supports the other's dreams. This love takes firmer hold after the two have their first deep conversation. Two aspects of this conversation stand out as important. First, you find yourself talking more openly and freely, the exchange taking you more deeply into yourself than any conversation you've had before with others.

In this first Gender Myth conversation, you find out who the other's mythic heroes are. You mention a book you're reading and he responds, "Oh, he sounds like Raskolnikov, one of the most fascinating characters in literature for my money. Think how far ahead of Freud Dostoevsky really was. He just didn't label things." You then ask him who his favorite writer is and tell him that you're deep into Beryl Markham at the moment. To which he replies, "I've only read some of her short stories about flying and horse racing. As a pilot, I can tell you she has an amazing sense of what flying is really about." "I've read those stories too," you say, an image of him sitting in the cockpit of a plane flitting across your mind—he's talking to the tower, competent and sexy beyond belief—"and I'm a rider and she really understands the minds of horses." You hope he's visualizing you on a magnificent horse jumping huge fences. "She was an extraordinary woman. She and Isak Dinesen. Those are lives I would love to have lived."

Most couples never forget this first conversation. It is a bench-mark and sets a standard you never want to lose. Indeed, when things cool down and trouble begins to show up here and there, you may remember this conversation with longing because you seem to have lost the ability to have a good conversation in the domain of the Gender Myth. Even couples who are violently at war can come into my office, drop their weapons, and recall in fond detail what was said at that time.

Let us watch as this archetypal encounter plays out between two strong and harmonious Gender Myths. To the outside ob-server, their initial meeting took place under the most ordinary of circumstances. Rick and Ruth were both coming out of the same college lecture hall, where they had been attending a talk called "False Patriots: The Rise of Right-Wing Hate Groups." As Rick walked down the corridor, he glided alongside of Ruth so that she had to look up at him. He smiled and said, "Hi, my name's Rick. I've been wanting to meet you. You're Ruth, right?"

"That's right," she said with a laugh. "I'm Ruth." She had heard from friends that he had been making inquiries about her, and she was glad that he had finally gotten around to introducing himself. She liked his looks. It wasn't that he was extraordinarily handsome; there was just something pleasant about his face and manner. And she was impressed that he had organized a volunteer paralegal group to aid the impoverished neighborhood surround-ing the university. Rick seemed to possess a thoughtfulness that was lacking in so many of the men she knew.

Momentarily thrown off-balance by Ruth's playfulness, Rick recovered and said, "So . . . what do you think of this course? I think it's good stuff. My father was a member of SDS during the sixties, registered voters down South, marched on Washington. My mother too. They thought they had changed the world forever and look where we are. These hate groups and militias really frighten me. It's made me realize I want to go on and get a law de-gree so I can go out and fight them with serious weapons like

Morris Dees and the Southern Poverty Law Center. He's one of my real heroes."

Embedded within the subtext of Rick's words is a very clear statement which flows from his Gender Myth as he attempts to define himself to Ruth. He is saying: "I am a bright man, bright enough to go to law school, but not just so I can become a fat cat. My goal is to help others who have no power. I come from the kind of family which has always cared about the underdog and has tried to help. That is one of the best parts of myself that I want you to know about."

Then it was Ruth's turn to reply from her Gender Myth. "My parents were conservatives during the sixties, still are, actually. It's hard to believe that anyone could have been during the Vietnam War and the civil rights movement, but they were proud of it. They had immigrated here from Ireland, and they believed in their adopted country—right or wrong. My brother died in Vietnam, but my parents still believed in what we were trying to do over there. The more I learn, the more I disagree with them, but I respect them for standing by their principles. I just try to avoid discussing politics with them."

Implicit within Ruth's words is the statement that she comes from loyal stock, the bedrock of the nation, but that she has visions of her own. She is telling Rick that she embodies traditional values and at the same time can think for herself. She is saying, in essence, "You will have to be your best self to attract me. Although I come from a different background, I, too, have a vision of a better world and could work with you to realize it if you're the right man for me."

"I was on my way to the snack bar," Rick said. "Can I buy you a cup of coffee?" He moved just a little bit closer to her. Her scent seemed to draw him into her aura. Suddenly all his antennae were up. Seeing her up close for the first time, he marveled at her smooth skin, the black flecks in her green eyes, her lustrous copper hair. Rick's senses were so heightened by the excitement of this moment that he seemed to have shifted into a different reality. He felt as if he could take in every bit of energy which radiated from this woman who stood before him.

"I've got an hour till my next class. I'd love to," she said. "This is a really interesting guy," she was thinking to herself. "There's something almost familiar about him. I feel very comfortable with him. He fits me somehow."

Our Gender Myths inform us not only of our own best selves—the selves we wish to show the rest of the world, and especially to prospective lovers—but also of the kind of mates who will fit into our own Gender Mythology and reinforce our ideal images of ourselves. Our beloved's looks, manner, values, even the way he or she dresses, are all absorbed and processed and then embraced or rejected. "This is the kind of person I've been looking for," our Gender Myth informs us. "I want this person because he or she makes precisely the right statement about her/himself, a statement that I have been searching for as a counterpart to my own."

Though neither Rick nor Ruth would have used the term, both understood, if only unconsciously, that they had just experienced a meeting of two matching Gender Myths. As often happens when these myths collide, time seemed to stand still. Two hours later, Ruth's class missed and over, they were still talking with all the excitement of two people who have experienced that earthshaking recognition inherent in such a meeting.

When the Gender Myths Are in Balance

When the Gender Myth is balanced within two people who are also able to talk about their personal mythologies, it is capable of conferring real magic. A year after their initial encounter in the college hallway, Rick and Ruth were married. While they, like all other couples, withstood some conflict before they really started to share each other's Personal Myths, they remained excited by the allure created by each other's Gender Myths.

After he finished law school, Rick kept to his ideal of eschewing corporate law in favor of helping disadvantaged people. He joined a firm which specialized in poverty law and discrimination cases. Ruth started a human resources consulting business.

One afternoon, the two planned to meet for lunch. At the appointed hour, Ruth showed up at Rick's office and found him still in a meeting with two other lawyers, who Rick had told her were there to discuss a settlement with him. Rick's office was glass-enclosed so that Ruth could see what was going on but not hear the words being spoken. Clearly an argument was in progress. One of the other men looked downright violent. Ruth sat down at a desk in the reception area and made some calls, all the while watching the scene in Rick's office. Ruth could only see Rick's face, but the other two men seemed to be voicing opposing opinions and there was much gesturing and finger-pointing. All the while Rick listened attentively to both of them, his face impassive. His composure and his obvious air of nobility was in sharp contrast to the manner of the others. Gradually, the two lawyers appeared to be drawn into Rick's calm aura. The angry energy was obviously dissipating. Meanwhile, Rick's demeanor had not changed at all. Now he was talking, his manner calm and assured. As her husband spoke, Ruth could almost feel the power gathering around him. The two men nodded almost sheepishly. Still talking calmly, Rick rose from his seat and walked over to the men. He placed a hand on each man's shoulder and continued to speak calmly. The three then walked to the door of the office. "Today gives us a good starting point for discussion. Let's mull this over and talk again on Friday," Rick said. The two men shook hands with Rick and left, apparently somewhat mollified.

To Ruth, witnessing the scene, this was such a display of competence and power by *her man* that a wave of sexual hunger coursed through her body. She wanted to make love to Rick right there on his desk.

Meanwhile, the phone at the desk Ruth was using rang. It was for her, and her attention slipped away from Rick. For the first time Rick noticed that Ruth had arrived and was on the telephone. He opened his door to listen to Ruth; she was speaking with someone from her office. Clearly one of her clients was having some sort of crisis. As always, he marveled at his wife's intelligence, her command of information, and her ability to handle difficult situations. The way she talked, she seemed to know more about her client's business than the client did. She was establishing a set of priorities for the person she was talking to, telling him the order in which to proceed and the steps he would have to take over the next two weeks. As Rick listened, he realized his appetite for lunch was gone, replaced with a hunger for her body.

"Let's go home and cuddle," he said, putting his arm around her. It was just what Ruth wanted to hear.

"Let's."

When two people like Rick and Ruth experience attraction between their Gender Myths, they find themselves aflame with sexual desire for each other. It's as if each were witnessing his hero in fullest glory. Suddenly, the partner who stands before you is the embodiment of your Sexual Fantasy Myth and the person toward whom all your sexual desires are directed.

Overreliance on the Gender Myth

There are endless variations on what happens when our lives rest disproportionately on the Gender Myth, especially one that is not in harmony with your Personal Myth. Many married people grow up thinking that a man behaves in a certain way and a woman behaves in another way, and both are locked into their stereotypes. After perhaps half a dozen years of marriage, these couples stop talking about anything personal and recognize, if only superficially, that it has become increasingly difficult to share the concerns each might have about life or about themselves. As the years go by, they accept the barriers that develop between them as taboos never to be breached. Eventually, they retreat to their respective places in the house and remain there except on the regular occasions when they bicker with one another or explode into full-scale arguments. Neither ever admits to doubts or failures. Neither says "I'm sorry." They are as distant as strangers. At some point they stop having sex. Many avoid sex for the remainder of their marriages. In short, they are dead long before they are in the grave. All such a couple—all anyone who is stuck exclusively in his or her Gender Myth—can hope for is a crisis. A crisis is nearly inevitable, because the psyche, in its insistence on wholeness and integration, brings about a situation which forces the couple to choose between life and death. At that point, we must relinquish our Gender Myths in their current form. The crisis looks like misfortune on the outside, but it's really the mind's way of bringing health and rebirth back to the couple. If they respond to the crisis by getting help or by exploring their Personal Myths, they have begun the process of restoring love and desire to their marriage. The crisis looks (and feels) terrible, but is really a kind of grace, because it leads the partners to their Personal Myths and the possibility of rebirth. As we saw with Sally, the former cheerleader, and Steve, such a crisis may not bring about reconciliation or a lasting marriage if both partners don't want to do the needed exploration of the Personal Myth.

Sally Finds a Match in Both the Gender and the Personal Myths

After moving to Boston with her young daughter, Sally remained single for several years. She was busy establishing her law practice and helping her daughter grow up. When she did meet a man who seemed right, he was an entirely different type from Steve. Bob was a man whose Gender Myth complemented Sally's mature vision of herself. He is an engineer who invests in real estate. He owns several apartment buildings in the Boston area, where he serves as a kind of benevolent landlord to people who range from the wealthy to the underprivileged. Bob can afford to be generous when one of his tenants calls to say the rent will be late. His generosity is a central part of his Gender Myth. He sees himself as a protector of less fortunate people; a strong man who has made his own fortune and who is capable of helping out people who have drawn more difficult lots in life. Being able to help people gives him tremendous satisfaction and reinforces his gender image. Sally supports Bob's myth as well. Not only does she hold the same principles and politics as Bob, but, unbeknownst to most people who know them, Sally herself comes from the stratum of society whose members Bob so often finds himself helping. But perhaps even more important for a full and intimate marriage, Bob was well acquainted with his Personal Myth, and its dark side, because he too had been married before and, in the wake of his divorce, had worked with me in individual therapy.

"I didn't want to leave any stone unturned," he told me. "I spent a lot of time really coming to know myself before I even thought about another woman. This time I wanted someone I could share both ideas and feelings with."

Bob is right. The anonymous and purposeful energy of the Gender Myth alone is not enough to sustain a love relationship. Until partners can share both gender conversation and emotional conversation arising from the Personal Myth, they don't yet have the most important elements for building, sustaining, or rebuilding desire. While most attractions begin in the Gender and/or Sexual Fantasy realms, if our relationships are to last and deepen, they must include deep, intimate conversation. In actual fact, most couples don't really acquire the ability to have this conversation until its lack has caused a gradual loss of desire, an interpersonal dreariness, or perhaps a crisis important enough to make both partners take notice.

Discovering Your Gender Myth

Whether we are conscious of all of it or not, our Gender Myth is the part of us that tells the world what kind of mate we want and what kind of mate we would be. Here are some questions to ask yourself so that you can see more clearly the kind of message you send to a potential lover. Understanding your Gender Myth can help you clarify that message.

1. What are the stories you tell from your childhood, adolescence, and young adulthood? What are the common themes which link them? They are about your Gender Myth in its formation.
2. What are the heroic stories your close friends tell about you from adolescence? What are the themes that link them?
3. What are some of the defining qualities or capacities that other key figures in your past (teachers, family friends, mentors) recognized in you—kindness, determination, open-mindedness, vision? It may have seemed to you that they were recognizing things you did not yet see about yourself but about which you felt proud, as you resonated with the positive identity that they represented.
4. What were the qualities for which you were, and are, recognized and rewarded? Employers and institutions recognize in us those attributes which they need, and by rewarding us for our heroic qualities, they reinforce them.
5. Who are the famous figures in history, mythology, and literature whom you admire? Whenever we reflect on these figures we see our own heroic qualities more clearly.
6. Ask your partner's opinion. He or she usually has recognized your Gender Myth qualities even when you haven't made them explicit.

Chapter Five

Three Heroes Within

Men and women shape their Gender Myths around three hero archetypes. Each gives love and experiences life in a unique way. Our heroic modes determine our habitual reactions to events, how we cope with anxiety, and what we do to feel safe in the world. When two people understand each other's heroic modes, they have an important key to communication. While there are, of course, an unlimited number of unique personalities playing out their individual stories, our heroic natures can be distilled into three basic types: the Survivor, the Fixer, and the Protector. Although each of us carries parts of all three heroes within our natures, and our goal is to integrate all three, we tend to express ourselves predominantly through one, or perhaps two, heroic modes. No one type is better, healthier, or more adaptive. Each is simply different, with a different way of relating to the world, processing experience, and giving love.

Each of these three heroic types has its ascendant aspect, its zone where its highest qualities reside. Each type needs to experience its ascendant qualities in order to feel vital, authentic, and fully alive. Experiencing your heroic characteristics in their light zone is a kind of peak experience. Self-love animates you and you feel capable of all that you want to do in the world, whether it be to endure, to fix, or to help. When your heroic nature emerges in all its plumage, no matter whether you are a man or a woman, there is an erotic thrill to it as if you are experiencing all of your sexual attractiveness.

However, embedded in these hero types are darker sides where a gray zone shades into the blackest black, which is that hero's shadow. Like the Shadow of the Personal Myth, the voice from childhood which tells us we are unlovable, which is the mother of all shadows, the shadow of each Gender Myth hero is a ghostly demon which whispers to us of our unlovability and the likelihood of our falling short. The shadow is a vast inner domain where each of us, no matter what heroic type we embody, holds all our biases, doubts, and fears, and which causes us to project them onto people and situations which we do not understand. The voice of our hero's shadow comes to us straight from our Personal Myth. It reminds us again and again of the painful moment when we understood that perfect love was not to be ours. The shadow is the dark side of our heroic natures, a side that lives in fear and feels powerless and victimized in the face of those fears. When our heroic natures or our actions are questioned, rejected, or simply not understood in a high-stakes situation, without knowing why, we are plunged back into our failed childhood love stories and the powerlessness we felt as children unable to get our deepest needs met. Not only do our shadows whisper to us that we are unlovable, they also make our gender heroes behave and speak in ways which guarantee that we will not be heard correctly and that we will not be loved. The voice of our deepest Shadows is terrifying to our partners, because it is so unfamiliar to those who believe they know us. The voices arising from our shadows are those of the betrayed child trying to cope with the world as she perceives it—not the mother, artist, or corporate lawyer your partner knows you as.

We will discuss the shadow and its poisonous effect on our

intimate communication, as well as its ability to heal us, in greater depth later on. For the moment it is enough to know that along with the strengths inherent in its unique view, each heroic mode has a corresponding and unique dark side where the childhood tragedy dominates and darkens that hero's world view. It is important, also, to understand that the shadow moves in and out of a person's awareness so that one minute he or she can be plunged into self-hatred and a few hours later be back in a state of balance and self-appreciation. When we operate from our shadows it is as if we are possessed. We act out of an underlying belief that we are unloved and unworthy of love, yet desperate for our loved one to contradict the shadow, to tell us that we *are* loved. When, because of the terrible ways we speak and behave when possessed by the shadow, our partners make no attempt to give us the love we are begging for albeit in the voice of the betrayed child, we invariably become enraged at him or her for failing to appreciate our viewpoint, our plan of action—in short, our heroic offering. Thus the shadow repeatedly defeats our efforts to receive love. Its message is a sort of self-fulfilling prophecy about our unlovability. *"You're not worthy of anyone's love,"* it whispers. *"And I'll make sure you speak and act in such a manner that you'll see that I am right again and again and again."*

The Survivor: *I Endure and Overcome*

The Survivor's great strength is endurance and perseverance. The Survivor hero type carries her pain as if it didn't exist. Survivors are the quintessential "copers." She will never let you see her suffering, because Survivors rarely let others inside willingly. Of course, like all of us, the Survivor carries around her own share of pain from her childhood story, but she gets through life by keeping it and her vulnerability well-hidden. Survivors suffer in silence, cutting themselves off from others, because, to this type, the pain

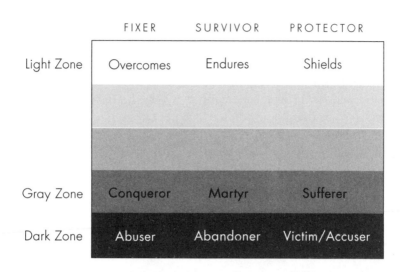

	FIXER	SURVIVOR	PROTECTOR
Light Zone	Overcomes	Endures	Shields
Gray Zone	Conqueror	Martyr	Sufferer
Dark Zone	Abuser	Abandoner	Victim/Accuser

seems less agonizing if unwitnessed, even by their innermost selves. Survivors may even deny physical pain. I have seen Survivors facing major surgery or chemotherapy as blithely as if it were part of their daily routine. Although the Survivor type behaves in a rather macho manner, there are as many female as male Survivors.

During his 1992 presidential campaign, George Bush, a classic Survivor, was asked about his feelings when his fighter plane had been shot down during World War II. Bush thought about it for a moment and then said that the thing that came immediately to mind as he bobbed in the water awaiting capture by the enemy or rescue by friendly forces was the importance of the separation between Church and State.

A woman I know, an arch-Survivor, whom I will call Nancy, recently lost her father to cancer. Nancy, a well-educated financial advisor, is on good terms with everyone she knows because she is unperturbed by any crisis. She positions herself at just the right emotional distance to help others find their way out of their own difficulties. A friend of Nancy's, hearing of her loss, offered condolences. She then asked Nancy how she was holding up. The friend's questions brought a tinge of sadness into Nancy's consciousness. At that moment, another type, a Protector able to embrace her own suffering, might have spoken of her pain or cried, but the rising emotions made Nancy extremely uncomfortable. Suddenly, she shifted gears, made a throw away gesture with her hand, and said in an upbeat manner, "Oh well, what are you gonna do?" It's not that Nancy didn't love her father. Nancy suppresses her feelings because, as a Survivor, she believes that it's wrong to allow feelings of sadness, loss, or betrayal to surface in her mind and affect her outward behavior.

Survivors have difficulty responding to questions about their feelings because they spend so much of their lives avoiding them. Their own feelings are a mysterious realm, but they don't know how out of touch with these feelings they really are. Ask any Survivor if he's in touch with his feelings and he'll say "Of course." At the same time, Survivors are discomfited by others' feelings of vulnerability as well, because they hit too close to the pain that the Survivor must wall off in order to function. If a spouse or friend, or even a co-worker, tells a Survivor "I'm upset," or "I'm feeling depressed," the Survivor distances himself in order to seal off emotions of his own which could rise and threaten his equanimity.

Most, if not all, Survivors live by a code. Many military men and women are Survivors and adopt the code of the warrior. Others adopt the code of their profession, be it doctor, lawyer, or banker. For other Survivors the code may be no more specific than to maintain at all costs a certain outer image: "I'm a hard worker" . . . "I'm a very orderly person" . . . "I'm wise" . . . or "I'm a WASP." Living by a code is very attractive to those who wish to appear invulnerable. Codes also provide a general outline of what is appropriate behavior, and leave little doubt of how the Survivor should act in any situation. Many Survivors are extremely polite, and use their manners to maintain a barrier between themselves and others. This barrier protects them from having to reveal their inner feelings, and from encouraging others to feel comfortable enough to reveal theirs.

Survivors frequently use humor to keep their own and others' pain at bay. Mention some tender or personal issue of your own, and the Survivor may turn it into a joke. It's probably not intended to wound you—although it's likely to feel that way. Its intent is to keep your pain and the Survivor's under the rug. By the same token, if you do manage to get a Survivor to share her feelings, you'll often notice she does so with a smile on her face, or she may laugh or intellectualize about them. The Survivor wants you to believe that he or she is as composed and balanced inwardly as he or she appears to be outwardly. Thus, the Survivor's outwardly projected image is often a statement to the effect that "what you see is what you get." "There's no pain in my life that I can't handle comfortably," says the Survivor. " I can't even understand that concept. I'm content. I don't cry. Nor do I experience depression or anxiety or worry about death."

Popular American culture promotes the creation of Survivors, because we like to appear as though we have all the answers and that our lives make perfect sense. We like to feel that all problems can be solved by a thirty-minute manager or by the perseverance of the strong silent type. As a nation of pilgrims and pioneers, we have been served well by the gender image of the heroic Survivor, but it can also limit our ability to find love and fulfillment in the world if we do not examine how it tells us to react. The unexamined Survivor is shielded from pain, but also from the deeper levels of her psyche.

The Survivor's Shadow: The Abandoner

What is essentially adaptive behavior in the Survivor's light zone—the ability to carry on and adapt to circumstances—becomes maladaptive in the shadows. The Survivor goes completely underground. When faced with powerful emotions, he goes rigid like a mouse transfixed by a cobra. He turns to stone, disowning his feelings and not acknowledging yours, because all deep feelings are a threat to his way of being heroic, which is to be stoic, to *survive* at all costs. At a shallow depth—the gateway to the shadow—is the Survivor's tendency to emphasize the martyr in her or himself. He or she perseveres uncomplainingly.

The deeper pit of darkness into which virtually all Survivors who have not faced their shadows fall is abandonment of self and others. In order for the Survivor to endure the hardships of life she must live like a chameleon, suppressing her own needs or desires if they don't fit the circumstances. In the process, she abandons herself and her emotional and psychological pain. She abandons those who would make her enter her pain and vulnerability by expressing their own. As a result, Survivors with deep shadows often leave their partners feeling unloved, unappreciated, and unnoticed. And, by abandoning their own feelings and not discussing them, they rob the relationship of the tools for change.

The Survivor in the Personal Myth

Survivors who, as children, were punished for weakness or for expressing vulnerability often do not want social situations or personal encounters to become too intimate or heavy, which means that Survivors, by their nature, avoid the Personal Myth. Personal encounters can easily slip into intimacy and the Personal Myth, where so much old and unresolved pain lives on. Such Survivors want to keep their encounters rooted in the Gender Myth, where they can avoid talking about deeply personal issues. As soon as a Survivor's friend or mate begins to descend into the Personal Myth, the Survivor begins to distance himself from the person sharing the story. He abandons that person for making him feel things he'd rather not feel or even think about. Yet one cannot abandon someone else without abandoning one's self. When the Survivor states (in one way or another) "I don't want to talk about that," he is really saying, "I don't want to experience my own pain and suffering which you are making me feel by your words or actions." This is why Survivors often come across as very forgiving. Indeed, in their light zone, it is one of their best qualities. Forgiveness is the language of love for this type. He or she wants to move beyond the past: "Let's not get caught up in it," the Survivor wants to say. "Don't worry. Be optimistic about the future like I am and let it go." Because Survivors don't want to become tangled in emotions, they are often regarded as people who can be reasoned with. Survivors are the most forgiving of the three heroic modes, because they don't want to dwell at all on personal issues, old wounds, or psychic pain. The only problem with such ready forgiveness is that the Survivor may forgive automatically without really acknowledging the grievance or pain. When this happens, he may end up unwittingly punishing the wrong people in his life. When the Survivor is denying and covering up her feelings, rather than truly forgiving, unacknowledged anger from the Personal Myth can emerge elsewhere and damage partners and friends without the Survivor's even noticing it.

Ask a Survivor about his mother and he will likely describe a saint without a shadow. Those Survivors who did not have wonderful mothers will either avoid the question entirely as being irrelevant to the present or they will give scant details that will be expressed with utter objectivity, as if they are reporting the details of someone else's life. Ask a Survivor about his childhood and he'll tell you how great it was. A Survivor can lose both parents early on and be on her own long before others, and she'll still tell you how happy her childhood was. If pressed about the difficulty of being orphaned, she'll reply, "Yes, but it taught me how to survive, so it wasn't that bad." Survivors prefer to focus on the cup that is half full and to deny their problems. If a Survivor does talk about past sorrows, she doesn't go too far up or down in the emotional register. She remains emotionally neutral, neither giving herself over to the pain nor to the elation she might feel about something else.

Despite their aversion to emotions, Survivors are often great listeners. They have a detachment that makes them non-judgmental. This can be infuriating for some people because they often look for compassion and a greater closeness than the Survivor wants to provide. This is not to say that Survivors aren't compassionate. Many are, but in a detached way. They will listen and tell you they understand, but they express their empathy within the same narrow band of emotion from which they might discuss the minor accident that slowed traffic on the way home.

At some point, a Survivor will open the door to his Personal Myth. He or she will say something like: "I remember when I was a kid and my parents always turned their backs on me if I was afraid or sad, and that made me feel all the more frightened." Or, "I remember all the drunken fights and watching my mother slowly destroy my father. I was ashamed because nothing I could do would make her stop destroying him." At that moment, the Survivor has just begun the process of healing. She awakens to the part of her psyche which was betrayed and is still in pain. By creating walls around his Personal Myth, the Survivor has prevented himself from healing his emotional and psychological wounds. The denial of these wounds shapes her personality and directly affects her character and her capacity to love and be loved.

The Survivor in the Gender Myth

Survivors shine in the Gender Myth. They love the infusion of energy and direction which the Gender Myth provides. In relationships, it also provides clear boundaries which the Survivor needs to feel secure and not about to be swallowed in emotions. When the Survivor speaks about something from her Gender Myth she is full of purpose and direction. She knows what she wants. She sees the goal ahead with great clarity. All of her desire is focused upon it as if it were the only thing in her sights. Her words have balance and integrity. As in the Personal Myth, her words are delivered in the same emotional register, giving people faith and security in her judgment. The Survivor's discussions lean toward the abstract and the intellectual. The sheer purposefulness and competence of the Survivor in the Gender Myth makes him or her highly attractive, even beautiful and, to many, highly sexual.

The Fixer: *I Will Solve the Problem and Rescue You*

In every situation, the Fixer's mantra is "I will" as in "I will solve the problem and restore harmony." Fixers want to make things all right for themselves and those they love. Their vision may extend to the larger world as well. Fixers are goal-oriented, with their eyes on the prize, and not necessarily aware of others' needs and other obstacles on the way. Fixers provide energy and new insights or sheer force in overcoming barriers. It could be said that Fixers have trouble acknowledging the randomness of the universe. They prefer to feel competent to fix whatever is thrown their way. They put themselves into situations which require solutions, often solutions which have eluded others. When they are feeling really inspired, nothing seems impossible to them. At their best and most developed, they confront and solve problems and correct injustices. They are true visionaries. At their worst, they are fiddlers.

Judge Thurgood Marshall, the first African-American to sit on the U.S. Supreme Court, was a true Fixer without a deep shadow. He was able to hold his goal in mind and to persevere in his vision, despite the heinous treatment he was given at many points along the way.

A Fixer makes her loved ones feel safe and protected, because she will see what needs to be done, design a solution, and then *follow through*, whereas a Survivor might claim endurance and the capacity to survive but not stay around to experience or witness vulnerability. He may survive by leaving the scene while the Fixer stays and fights. If a blizzard is coming, inside the Fixer's home the wood will be stacked by the fireplace, the tubs and sinks filled with water, and candles and provisions will be at the ready. Next door, the Survivor may well be downplaying the situation, telling everyone the storm is headed out to sea. If it does hit and he and his family are cold and hungry, he'll endure without a whimper and may well feel pleased with himself that he survived rough times so well, and scornful that his family are such complainers.

The Fixer's Shadow: The Abuser

When the Fixer descends into his shadow zones, he inevitably responds with power. He goes through a continuum from coercion to abusiveness. He focuses outward and attempts to overcome or, failing that, to conquer elements in his environment that he perceives to be the cause of his being denied appreciation or love. In intimate relationships, such unexamined Fixers become so bent upon fulfilling their own desires—especially that of fixing their partners—that they can lose sight of the fact that their mates have feelings and desires of their own and may resist being fixed. It is precisely at these moments that the indomitable Fixer slips into the shadow and becomes abusive. People must adhere to his vision, he tells them. If they don't see things his way and get behind him, he gets angry. The reason is simply that he has difficulty hearing another's point of view if it contrasts with his own. A conversation with a Fixer in her shadow will be loud, fierce, and sometimes threatening.

The reason a Fixer can easily be engulfed by her shadow is that she sees the function of creating new avenues, righting wrongs, and solving problems as her reason for being. It is her way of giving love. But there is a fine line between constructively finding solutions and rearranging a situation or a person's life when it doesn't need rearranging, just to satisfy the Fixer's urge to have something to fix. If the Fixer's partner speaks up and says, "Go away. I don't agree that *I'm* the one who needs fixing, and I don't want your help," the Fixer hears that her love is not being understood or accepted and her heroic vision of herself is being negated. The shadow descends, and she becomes enraged and more insistent, behaving in a way that will guarantee her partner will see her as The Enemy—at least until her shadow passes. The Fixer is most vulnerable to slipping into her shadow when she spends too much time looking outward rather than inward for problems and solutions. When the Fixer is deeply in his shadow, it's often better to leave him to his demons for the time being until the shadow passes, not unlike giving an angry child a "time-out," because in the deepest shadows of the Fixer still resides the child who is reacting to imperfect love by throwing a tantrum or pounding his fist against his mother's leg.

The Fixer in the Personal Myth

When the Fixer is in the domain of the Personal Myth, he or she tackles inner conflicts and wounds quickly and fearlessly, even impatiently. If Fixers experience any pain at all, they don't spend much time with it. Something cranks up in their brains and comes up with a menu of solutions. Fixers, like Survivors, are optimists. But while the Survivor expects that Fate will be kind, the Fixer has no such illusions. She is simply supremely confident of her ability to overcome problems on her own. Fixers believe that everything can be easily fixed, even the ancient wounds of the Personal Myth. Their vision is usually directed toward a brighter future, because they envision all problems being solved. Fixers do not like to feel their own powerlessness. When they are faced with it, they experience tremendous frustration which may call up their shadows. Once in the shadow, the Fixer faces self-condemnation and tries to conquer it as quickly as possible. For some that can mean accomplishing their purposes by any means available. If you share a problem with a frustrated Fixer, you may find yourself being viewed as the problem. Fixers with less-aggressive shadows can listen and even feel compassion, but their compassion moves them to find answers for you. You don't go to a Fixer just to be held. You go for answers, and the more talented the Fixer, the more likely you are to get excellent results.

Fixers in the Gender Myth

The Gender Myth is often the arena in which Fixers thrive. They are courageous, energetic, and visionary. They need to feel ahead of their time and to bring about innovative solutions. In some bedrock place within the Fixer's psyche is the belief that she can find an answer to any problem she confronts. Fixers need challenges, because it is in this way that they experience their heroic natures. Part of the way a Fixer feels loved and loving, desired and desiring, is by changing his environment. If a Fixer doesn't have challenges to face she may feel bored and aimless. She wants to experience her heroic potential and be celebrated for it. If a Fixer cannot find a true solution to a problem, he may adopt a cosmetic one, because to him any solution is better than none. This allows him to look good and avoid his own shadow.

Like Survivors, Fixers can be found in all professions. There are Fixer plumbers, therapists, professors, housewives, nurses, writers, doctors, and grocers. Among the more well-known Fixers are Bill Gates, Newt Gingrich, Gloria Steinem, and Ralph Nader. Fixers tend to be reformers, warriors, and visionaries no matter what field they are in. They push the limits of old beliefs and break new ground. They bring their own perspectives and typically unflagging optimism to whatever issue is at hand.

Fixers bring these same qualities to interpersonal relationships. They are constantly looking for ways to make their relationships better, to achieve new heights of love, emotion, intensity. Unfortunately, they often presume to improve their relationships by changing others rather than themselves. This is es-

pecially true of Fixers who are cut off from experiencing the
Survivor and the Protector within themselves. Without being able
to shift from Fixer to another heroic mode, the Fixer is stuck in the
role of problem-solver.

Raymond, the scientist, is a good example of someone who,
prior to entering therapy, was stuck in the role of Fixer, unable to
experience his own ability to endure as a Survivor or his own inner
suffering. As a result, he related to his wife by trying to fix her,
change their situation, or bring new life to their lovemaking.
Rebuffed in lovemaking by Samantha, his Survivor wife who, like
so many Survivors, never expressed her real needs, Raymond
sought out other women whom he could save. He basked in the attention they gave him and the opportunity to correct some imbalance or problem in their lives. Alas, he couldn't save his wife,
who resisted his efforts to fix her—an unpleasant reprise of life
with his depressed mother who resisted his boyish efforts to set her
life, and thus his, to rights. When Raymond discovers the Survivor
and the Protector within himself he will find the source of his pain
and the reason he is trying so desperately to look outside and fix
his wife and others.

A Fixer often describes what she wants as being "what is best"
for the couple or the family. Relating to your Fixer-lover when she
feels under pressure to prove something in her Gender Myth will
be like relating to your tax accountant, travel agent, personal
trainer, shrink, and priest or rabbi all at once. He or she will be
planning your future, solving your problems, getting you in shape,
and paving your way to heaven all in a single evening. By the time
the two of you are ready to go to bed—assuming you're not ready
to strangle him or her—you'll be exhausted.

Fixers are impatient and restless, even during times of relative
interpersonal peace. If a Fixer doesn't have an outlet for his desire
to fix, he may invent a problem or cause an argument with his
spouse just to have a crisis that needs repair. People with opposing
viewpoints are often seen by the Fixer as obstacles in the path.
Rather than seeing opposing viewpoints as complementary and

therefore needing synthesis, Fixers are often frustrated by people with ideas contrary to their own. Such frustration can lead to incorrect perceptions of the situation or the other person. This can prevent the Fixer from really hearing the other person because he's too busy trying to figure out how to get the other to fall in step with his own vision.

The Protector: *I Feel The World's Pain and My Own*

The Protector's mantra is "I will not," as in "I will not stand by idly, experiencing my own suffering, or yours, and pretend it doesn't exist." The Protector is far more willing than the two other heroes to admit to personal limits; to say "I cannot go on. There is danger here that you, the persevering Survivor, or you, the willful Fixer, do not see." The Protector is conscious of his own pain and needs, and of yours, too. One of his greatest gifts is the ability to identify areas of pain within himself and others—a truly rare gift—and to empathize with it. Hence the Protector talks with great familiarity of his own inner world or that of others around him. Archetypal Protectors are guardians of the heart. Sympathetic souls, they help others bear their pain. They are often spokespeople for the sick, the downtrodden, the poor, weak, and abused. Mother Teresa of Calcutta was an archetypal healthy Protector without a deep shadow. She cared for the horribly diseased for whom there was no cure—only the giving of love and physical comfort until they finally succumbed. Such work would be impossible for a Fixer, who would search tirelessly for a cure, or for a Survivor who would rebuild the hospital and maintain its order, efficiently but without empathy. Only a beneficent Protector can carry the burdens of the sick with compassion, grace, and dignity, without asking them to get better or be brave. The Protector's compassion and empathy even extend to the physical environment and the planet, as in the case of many committed environmentalists.

Protectors are essential in any relationship or group of people, because they realize where the problems are in advance of Survivors. They are also able to provide Fixers with the information needed to correct imbalances or disharmonies, either in relationships or in group settings.

The Shadow of the Protector: The Victim/Accuser

As the Protector slips into the shadow, he or she can become the maudlin victim. Life feels bleak and overwhelming. Effort seems pointless. The Protector's shadow exists in degrees. In its more shallow manifestations, the Protector simply gives up. She identifies too much with her own needs and sense of powerlessness, even when she is physically capable of continuing. This is a kind of gray zone within the Protector's shadow, and it may mean only that the Protector needs rest.

As the shadow of the Protector deepens and begins to engulf her, she perceives only weakness and sorrow. She sees the tenderness of human existence but very often fails to perceive the strength in herself and others. In such instances, the Protector can become overwhelmed by her own pain and the world's. Deeper into the shadow, the Protector feels herself a powerless victim, too weak to overcome oppression. In her deepest shadows, she becomes an accusatory child shrieking at her parents: "*You*, who have all the power, are preventing me from getting the love I need." She may not be helpless at all. She may have law or medical degrees and children of her own, but in the shadow she is plunged right back to the helplessness of childhood. Protectors in their shadows are Sufferers, unleavened by any sense of humor or even of irony.

This unbalanced view of life eliminates all possibility for creativity and resolution. The victimized Protector is doomed—not by any outside force or enemy but by his own fecklessness. The Survivor in him could endure and find a way to overcome. The Fixer could create and carry out a plan. But the Protector who is trapped inside his own shadow is all too aware of his vulnerability and his status as a victim. So what does he do? He rails against the injustice of the world. He is ever vigilant for any evidence of wrongdoing, and so sees wrongdoing in many of his mate's actions. One of the most common ways Protectors trapped within their shadows cope with their victim status is by retreating into infantile behavior and wailing endlessly about the bad behavior of those around them. Protectors in their shadow invariably act as if the world is withholding what they deserve, which, of course, only serves to further alienate those around them. Meanwhile, they resist going into the real pain which exists in the darkness of their being. Ultimately, a Protector who is trapped by his shadow is not penetrating his own psyche sufficiently to understand the nature of his pain and its source. He is refusing to know himself well enough to know why he is so filled with pain. The victimized Protector resists the real work of going deeper into the darkness and finding the light of understanding, which brings with it the strength to contain her suffering. However, this may not be altogether apparent at first, because the Protector seems so intimate with her feelings, so unashamed of her vulnerability.

The Protector in the Personal Myth

The Personal Myth is the Protector's domain. He is fluent in its highly nuanced information. Protectors express and honor betrayal, disappointment, and original purity, in themselves and in others. Because of their intimacy with their own Personal Myths, Protectors know how to create relationships founded on conversation about the most heartfelt issues in life. A Protector doesn't want to conduct relationships solely in the intellect. It's not that ideas and world issues are not of interest to Protectors; they are often of paramount concern. It's the tone in which they are discussed. Like Fixers and Survivors, Protectors communicate their tone within their words. Their voices have a softness which beckons others into the tender areas of life. They gently probe and listen carefully, offering compassion as if it were an open door to a pleasant little cottage in one's soul. "Rest, have some tea. Tell me how you're doing," is the message in the tone, even when the words are merely "How's it going?"

Their compassion and empathic powers give Protectors tremendous intuition. They can sense when someone is troubled or out of sorts long before anyone else can. Such sensitivity, however, also makes them susceptible to being buffeted by people with strong emotions, especially negative ones.

Whenever you want to be heard without being fixed or treated objectively, you want to talk to a Protector. The Protector firmly believes in Buddha's First Noble Truth: Life is sorrow. The best we can do is to be kind.

The Protector in the Gender Myth

The Protector hero is the champion of the downtrodden, the sick, the disadvantaged. Protectors stand up for the rights of children, animals, the elderly, and the environment. Without Protectors, we would have no Greenpeace, no Red Cross, no CARE, no ASPCA, nor any of the literally thousands of organizations founded solely to protect the disadvantaged. When you talk to a Protector in his Gender Myth you are faced with someone who passionately believes in his or her cause. Protectors espouse their beliefs with the courage of lions bolstered by encyclopedic knowledge. Highly evolved Protectors without deep victim/accuser shadows become great leaders and often make important contributions to the world's consciousness.

However, it is in the Gender Myth that Protectors walk a dangerous line, because they can easily slip into the shadows. The

Protector who takes up a cause in the Gender Myth can identify too closely with victims and their powerlessness. When possessed by their shadows, Protectors simply cannot abide the conditions of the earth. They see the world and everyone in it as corrupt and cruel. At this point their shadows can become utterly insufferable, because their personal wounds are mingling with the larger social issues and giving them an excuse to bludgeon people with their anger.

How We Choose Our Heroic Modes

People invariably ask me, "How did I choose to be a Survivor, Fixer, or Protector?" This question cannot be fully answered. As every parent who has had more than one child knows, each has a unique nature, one he or she seemed to bring to the world. Each child is predisposed, to some extent, to express one or another of the heroic modes. Your dominant heroic mode is probably determined early in life and is at least partly genetic and biological. The hero you embody will be the one which best serves as your vehicle for reducing existential anxiety, and you will accomplish this partly by getting and giving love.

Nevertheless, family patterns definitely influence the child's development as one or another heroic type. This is especially true if one or two of the heroic modes clearly dominates in a family, because one of the children is almost forced to assume the missing role. For example, a family of Survivors will likely refuse to express their individual and collective pain. They may attempt to project to the world a picture of a balanced, happy, and integrated family grinning from their annual Christmas card, when in fact they are engaged in a soul-depleting effort to suppress every dark emotion and secret. In that case, one of the children may become a Protector, expressing the pain or the secrets the family refuses to express. Another child in the family may become a Fixer and attempt to elicit the Protectors from within the family. That child may work to correct family patterns that may be preventing such expression. In a family of Protectors, one child may become a Survivor, simply refusing to let the prevailing sense of victimhood possess him or her. Another might become a Fixer, trying to save the family from whatever torments it may be experiencing. Many of the so-called "wounded healers" come from families in which one or both parents is alcoholic. In these situations, the child becomes the Fixer, trying to save his or her parents. In the process, he oversteps any number of boundaries, especially his own, and must relearn in adulthood what it means to take care of himself rather than spend his life fixing everyone else.

Many people also wonder whether the heroic mode we end up operating from is derived from the truant hero of our childhoods. Does a child who dreamt of a Protector always become one as an effort to become whole? Did Raymond, who so desperately wanted to fix his broken family and repair his mother, end up a Fixer in adult life for this reason? Again, humans being as complex as they are, it's not always neat and linear. In many cases there seems to be no correlation between the longed-for hero of childhood and the adult gender hero. The search for the truant hero, the perfect lover who is about to appear around the next corner, gives rise to desire—the yearning which propels the self out into the world in search of that perfect other. But the hero of the Gender Myth is the self, which is constructed in such a way as to attract the perfect love.

The Heroes in Love

These three types of hero experience and project love very differently. Without an understanding of the heroic modes, mates can easily reject each other's gifts of love. Understanding your and your partner's heroic modes makes it possible for you to understand how each of you views and interprets reality and how each of you most commonly expresses your respective interpretations. I do not want to give the impression that all those who operate from their Gender Myth as a particular type will also operate from that same heroic mode in the realm of sexual fantasy—what I call the Sexual Fantasy Myth. People are more complex and contradictory than that.

The Survivor

Survivors keep their more vulnerable or weaker feelings out of the bedroom. They expect themselves to be strong, to endure, and to satisfy their lovers sexually. They want to give pleasure. They emphasize the physical pleasures of sex over emotional expression or involvement in lovemaking. Even when making love, Survivors look to their partners for cues. They do not lead. Survivor men tend to endure sexually for long periods. They are happy to postpone their own pleasure if they think it's what their partner wants. Survivor women will serve their partners in much the same way, abandoning any thought of their needs in favor of their partner's.

But when Survivors are in their shadows they can easily make their lovers feel abandoned and invisible. They often make love with their eyes closed. They will be so deep into their own shells that lovemaking will feel to their partners more like masturbation—just friction with all emotion withdrawn.

The Fixer

Fixers are often sexual explorers. Most prefer to lead while making love, with the intention of surpassing old limits, bringing their lovers to new heights, and hoping to transform her or him through sex. Unlike Survivors, they are searching for emotions in their partners, the tender places where the person holds his or her feelings of vulnerability, joy, and sadness. The Fixer wants to penetrate the soul of his or her partner during sex, leading him or her into hidden feelings. They are constantly testing the barriers and limits. Consequently, Fixers are usually the first to try new positions, sex toys, or pornography. They'll usually try anything at least once in order to achieve some new level of sexual excitement which will make sex special for the partner. They believe in sexual healing.

The Protector

Protectors want to express the Personal Myth when making love, which is to say they want to have sex with great tenderness, purity, and emotional intensity. They want to be held and comforted in the most intimate way when they are most vulnerable. There are much stricter rules for making love with Protectors. They want sex to be gentle, tender, and intimate. Oils, massage, and scented candles are parts of the Protector's worshipful and caretaking way of making love.

Attractions Between the Heroes

One might assume that Survivors who avoid the Personal Myth would tend to be sexually attracted to other Survivors, at least initially. However, the relationship between two Survivors can become boring in large measure, because neither stimulates the other to grow. In a short while each appears shallow and uninspiring to the other. There's no dynamism, no really exciting demands are made. There are few conflicts to work out, and thus little or no passion or growth. After a few years, two Survivors often find themselves saying that the charge has gone out of their sex lives.

The brightest sparks fly between two people who love each other and require each other to venture into the dangerous areas of each other's psyches. Such a relationship can't help but evoke the deeper elements of each person which renews and reinspires the relationship. Two people who are growing in this fashion find their sex life being reanimated continually, because life itself is exciting for such a couple.

This is why Survivors often find themselves in long-term relationships with Protectors, because a Protector offers the Survivor the possibility of dealing with his or her inner conflicts and wounds, rather than just glossing them over as the Survivor might prefer. Yet, the human psyche searches for wholeness. On some level even the Survivor is searching for safe ways to reconcile the old conflicts, heal the childhood scars, and move on to a more balanced condition. In short, the Survivor unconsciously longs to explore and become more comfortable with the Personal Myth and in the process release some of the pressure that has built from constantly suppressing it. The Protector offers such an opportunity by leading the Survivor into that myth and forcing him or her to become more than just a Survivor; to become truly courageous.

The Survivor is tempted to criticize the Protector for expressing so many feelings. What the Survivor must learn is to become conscious of what she is feeling when the Protector is talking about his pain. At first, the Survivor's only reactions may be dismissal and annoyance. Later, anger becomes the second line of defense when the partner, whose emotions the Survivor is trying to shut out, persists. It may help the Survivor to say: "It makes me feel angry when you talk about that subject." However, the Survivor must also commit to expressing what she feels after the anger passes.

Fixers often marry Survivors or Protectors. All goes well for a time while the attraction is still largely occurring in the Gender Myth. But, when Eros departs, the couple is left with their contradictory languages which they must use to understand their respective Personal Myths and heroic modes. Soon, the wife starts acting, speaking and making love like a Survivor and the husband does these things like a Fixer. They are speaking very different languages and have very different needs.

Couples Speaking Different Languages

Mario and Cynthia:
A Survivor and a Protector

Mario and Cynthia also speak from different heroic archetypes, jeopardizing the very real happiness they bring to each other's lives except when their shadows are in control.

Mario is the CEO of a *Fortune* 500 company. He arrived in America from Palermo, Sicily, as a teenager with less than a thousand dollars to his name and rose to the top of one of the nation's great industries. As you might expect, Mario struggled and suffered many difficulties, but you would never know this by talking to him. He's charismatic and sincere. "I'm one of the luckiest people I know," he'll tell you. "Good luck has always found me." Asked about any difficulties he might have experienced on the way to the top, he dismisses the notion with a wave of his hand. "There really wasn't that much, and why think about it now?"

One of the ways he has gotten to the top is through his ability to discern between projects that are working and deserve continued support, and others which are weak or in trouble—which he abandons quickly and efficiently. Meanwhile, he appears positive about everything. He's always moving forward, chasing new horizons, oblivious to the past. By now, you may have gathered that Mario is an inexhaustible Survivor. The way he expresses his love is to tolerate difficulties and carry on without complaint, focusing on the positive and ignoring the rest. This is what attracts would-be lovers to the Survivor, and it is certainly what attracted his wife, Cynthia. Cynthia found Mario's strength and stability, his grace under pressure, magnetic and sexual. Cynthia, as we will come to see, is a Protector, and one who is not expressing either of her other heroic modes.

Cynthia and Mario had been married for twenty-one years

when they first came to me. Because Cynthia has always found Mario supremely attractive, she imagines that every other woman in the world does as well. The two have come to therapy partly to deal with Cynthia's nearly incapacitating fear that Mario is secretly and perpetually unfaithful to her. Mario cannot go to the newsstand in the morning without his wife's worrying that during the few extra minutes he takes, he has made a telephone call to another woman from a pay phone. When the two sit in a restaurant, Cynthia is always on the alert for any sign that Mario's eye might be wandering. "You saw that beautiful woman, didn't you? She looked at you like she knows you. Do you know her for some reason?" When Mario makes one of his frequent business trips, Cynthia is in a frenzy over the women he might have in other ports. She quizzes him relentlessly, questions credit card charges, and examines the telephone bills, but no matter how much he tries to reassure her, his words fail to give her lasting peace. Two days later she's afraid and untrusting again.

In private sessions, I have probed Mario as to the possibility that he has been unfaithful to Cynthia or given her grounds for suspicion. No, he assures me. He loves his wife and is absolutely committed to her, even though he finds her endless paranoia very trying. I am convinced he is telling the truth. "Sure, I've been guilty a few times of flirting. What man doesn't? I'm alive. I enjoy women and I like to be flattered. But my wife is beautiful too. I've never been seriously tempted to stray—not even once, actually. It's this dark side that she occasionally slips into that drives me absolutely crazy. I can't convince her. What can I do?"

"I'm completely ashamed of myself as the words are leaving my mouth," Cynthia tells me in a private session. "One part of me knows I'm probably acting crazy, and I'm humiliated, but when the fears start to arise they seem to take over, and I just can't control them." Each new woman, each new situation this couple encounters requires a new reassurance. "But why do I always feel that his mind is elsewhere? He doesn't give me enough of himself. How do I know the rest doesn't get spread around? I know I have a problem that's all mine, but if he was more loving, more open with me, I think I'd trust his love; the fact that it's me he sees when he does look at me."

Her destructive inquisitions contrast dramatically with all the good that Cynthia, the Protector, brings to her husband and which he delights in. Cynthia leads Mario into worlds of delight that he would otherwise be blind to. She directs her husband's attention to beauty, art, tenderness, and innocence. As a Protector, Cynthia's heart is open to the world of emotion from which Mario is cut off. When she is in her light zone she is able to direct Mario into his own inner world of feeling and nostalgia. Often she does this by bringing him into the natural world on long walks in a nearby forest or vacations on a chartered sail boat. When she's not on his case, she makes their home a sensuous haven with fresh flowers scenting the rooms, luxurious bed linens that are stored with lavender bouquets, satisfying food and wine.

Unlike her husband, Cynthia feels her pain. She expresses and experiences love by empathizing and supporting people in their emotional and psychological needs. She wants Mario to feel and acknowledge her pain and his own. For Cynthia, love means two people sharing one another's inner worlds. Unfortunately, Mario denies his pain and his wife's. He slams the door in the face of emotional issues. That's part of what it means to be a Survivor. For Cynthia who holds the world of emotions as the paramount expression of love, Mario's denial of emotions is experienced as a denial of love. Her reaction to his walled-off emotional nature is to try to batter down his walls. In the attempt she becomes frustrated, frightened and uncertain about his feelings toward her which often leads her straight into her shadow where her worst fears about being unloved reign. As she descends to the depths of that dark side she becomes the powerless victim, the angry sufferer, which lies in the shadows of the Protector archetype. Mario's shadow, which is brought up in response to Cynthia's own, immediately jumps ship and withdraws his emotions even more. Instead of reaching out to his wife, he stays in a superficial emotional realm and tries to ignore the needy feelings within himself.

My work with this couple is directed at helping them to see these light and dark parts of themselves, and to recognize how each unconsciously surrenders to his or her shadow and creates a vicious cycle in which each becomes less and less appealing to the other.

Cynthia and Mario push each other into corners by refusing to acknowledge other aspects of themselves and by each insisting on their own singular perspectives on life. If Mario opened up and shared his fears, sadness, and losses, Cynthia would feel closer to him. But for Mario the experience of feelings is extremely uncomfortable, because the minute he becomes aware of his emotional life he re-experiences all the pain he has been denying for so long. So he changes the subject or focuses on the television or drifts off within himself, abandoning his wife. This is the distance that Cynthia is experiencing, and which she interprets as proof of his having an affair. This feeling puts Cynthia right into her shadow, where she becomes a powerless child, too weak to overcome the omnipotent oppressor. Cynthia needs to evoke the Survivor and the Fixer in herself. The Survivor could find a way to endure while the Fixer could come up with a plan. When Cynthia is sufficiently angry, she can muster the power and determination of the Fixer, but she often expresses this part of herself with too much anger, which forces her Survivor husband to run from her.

Raymond and Samantha: A Fixer and a Survivor

How this problem in communication, if not examined, can affect a couple's love life is well illustrated by Raymond, the Fixer-scientist, and his wife, Samantha, an arch-Survivor. Samantha lived within their marriage for many years like a typical chameleon-Survivor, abandoning her own sexual preferences and desires because they didn't fit in with Raymond's clear interests.

As a typical Fixer, Raymond wanted sex to be a peak experience for his partner, and he thought that pornography, esoteric positions, and, later, scenes with third parties, would make sex special for Samantha. In the absence of any input from Samantha, he assumed that she shared his tastes. As far as he knew, she certainly seemed to.

I first met this couple when they were trying to get back together after Samantha had discovered that, for the second time in their marriage, Raymond was conducting a serious, long-term affair. This time, Samantha had left and gone to heal herself in Maine. They worked with me in both joint and separate sessions, Raymond trying to understand how as a Fixer he had strayed over the line into abusiveness against Samantha. One of the most tender points was Raymond's insistence that Samantha must have been sexually abused in childhood and that she needed to work it through with him as her guide. This contention upset and angered Samantha and made her feel manipulated and victimized by Raymond, for whom she lost all sexual desire.

"Isn't it enough for two bodies to crave each other, to long to touch? Those X-rated films with slimy men masturbating ten feet away literally nauseated me. I once threw up leaving the theater, but you didn't even notice!"

"How did you manage to survive?" I asked her.

"Raymond had the ability to set my senses afire. Every time he entered a room I felt the thrill of his body. The rest—Raymond's pornography—my body just edited it out just as I'd do with a short story." She turned to Raymond. "Your rapacious craving for smut, your sex toys and pornographic videos gave me nightmares, but I didn't speak up because I didn't want to risk losing you. Instead, I all but lost myself. I left when I found out about Maggie so as not to lose myself completely," she went on. "At that point, my body-editing no longer worked for me."

This interaction shows the chameleon nature of the Survivor extremely well. They are willing to abandon themselves and their needs by putting up with whatever is thrown their way, until finally one straw—in this case the uncovering of Raymond's second affair—causes a crisis which brings the chance for repair and redemption.

But both shadows danced here. At the same time that Samantha was hiding in her shadow and not feeling worthy of having her needs met, Raymond was the abusive Fixer. He had meager knowledge of Samantha's Personal Myth because she was stingy with details. His hypothesis about her childhood abuse was actually way off the mark, but Raymond continued to try to fix her. At the same time, he strutted his sexual fantasies, past experiences, and wildest desires in a humiliating daily parade from which his wife shrank further and further. Later, in therapy, he became more aware of how his shadow had such a terrible impact on his wife's sexual integrity. However, by remaining silent about her own feelings through all the years of marriage and separation, Samantha did Raymond, but even more her own self, a major disservice.

The oneness of deep relationship is awe-inspiring. So united are two people who enter into a committed relationship that each equilibrates with the other. Neither Cynthia nor Mario nor Raymond nor Samantha is a pure hero type. But the more emotions are denied by Mario and Samantha, the more deeply entrenched Cynthia will be in her Protector's victim/accuser shadow and Raymond will be in his Fixer's abuser shadow. When Mario embraces the Protector within himself, Cynthia will be able to shift out of her Protector-sufferer mode and into her own Fixer or Survivor. The more Samantha learns to ask for what she needs, the less Raymond will annoy her with misguided attempts to fix her.

This is not to suggest that either partner is responsible for the other's imbalance. Each has a long history, prior to this relationship, which has shaped their choices. Once they entered into partnership, they bonded in a deeply psychological and spiritual way.

In this context they can bring out the balanced best in one another.

Becoming Whole

In any committed relationship, people unconsciously work together to make each other more complete. Couples' members do this, in part, by embodying those aspects of human nature their mates need to embrace. In fact, what couples rarely realize, but must come to understand, is that each partner tends to exaggerate those aspects that the other denies. When your spouse brings up issues or behaves in a way which makes you uncomfortable, you must go within and ask yourself why this is so troubling for you. Try to experience that mode yourself and express the feelings that come up for you from within that mode.

We must also become acquainted with our shadow and how it influences our self-image. We must understand that while we are lost in the shadow calling for love, we are in fact pushing away those we love. This is a hard paradox to fathom at first, even though our partners are invariably telling us as much. We must also come to understand that the Shadow censors the information we are receiving from our psyches. It blocks out self-love because self-love is inconsistent with the shadow's message to us.

The psyche is always struggling for integration and wholeness. Ideally we need to be in touch with all three heroic modes within ourselves. To neglect one or another is to divorce ourselves from an essential part of our being. The Fixer in each of us gives us the ability to solve problems; the Survivor gives us the strength to endure when a solution is not immediately apparent, or when certain issues are better dealt with by tolerating them; and the Protector gives us an open heart and compassion so that we can experience our vulnerability and that of others.

Discovering Your Heroic Mode

1. *If you were at Mother Teresa's hospital would your preferred role be:*
    a. to comfort and care for the ill and dying?
    b. to work in the laboratory searching for cures and solutions?
    c. to take over the hospital's administration, making long-term plans to improve patient care but never mixing with patients?

2. *When someone comes to you with problems or fears, do you:*
    a. listen well at the same time that the person's complaining and emotions make you uncomfortable?
    b. want the person to listen to you as you devise the correct solution and how to implement it?
    c. want to listen to the person's words, spoken and unspoken, and to comfort the person?

3. *Which do you pride yourself on the most?*
    a. your ability to cope and survive
    b. your ability to analyze a problem and then devise and apply the correct solution
    c. your ability to feel; your empathy

4. *Do you surprise people with your insight into their feelings or those of others? Can you tell by someone's voice or expression when something is wrong or when they are lying? (Protector)*

5. *Are you good at deferring short-term gains or pleasures to reach a long-term goal? (Survivor)*

6. *Do you think the end justifies the means? (Fixer)*

7. *Do you rarely feel vulnerable, and does it make you uncomfortable when others show their vulnerabilities? (Survivor)*

8. *Do you always try to act appropriately in a situation, even if it means ignoring your own feelings? (Survivor)*

8a. *Do you prefer to have your partner take the lead in lovemaking? (Survivor)*

9. *Do you feel competent to find solutions to most problems which come your way, and do you enjoy doing so? (Fixer)*

10. *Do you feel bored or aimless if you don't face a challenge? (Fixer)*

11. *Do you prefer wild or experimental lovemaking designed to lead your partner to new heights? (Fixer)*

12. *Are you able to talk easily about your emotions and those of others? (Protector)*

13. *Do you have a natural affinity for helping those who cannot help themselves? (Protector)*

14. *Do you prefer lovemaking to be gentle and tender, perhaps even mystical? (Protector)*

Chapter Six

The Sexual Fantasy Myth

*In sex, the sublime and the vulgar are separated by a
hair's breadth. That hair's breadth, like the atom, contains
enormous amounts of energy and tension. Sexual
tension is thus one of the secrets of desire.*
ALBERT SZENT-GYÖRGYI

Why is sexual fulfillment so difficult to maintain over time? Is it
possible to be in love with the same person for a lifetime and be
truly fulfilled sexually? The short answer to the latter question is
an unequivocal *yes*, but only if the sexual journey is undertaken.
Boredom reflects only the failure to deepen the sexual dialogue, to
honor the mystery of love, and to know yourself and your partner.

When the excitement of sex leaves a relationship and stays
gone for an extended period, its absence is felt. At that point it's
time to look more deeply at your relationship and, even more important, at yourself. Now is not the time to blame yourself or your
mate. Throughout this book, I have emphasized the importance of
sharing our myths with our partners. This is true for the Personal

Myth. Intimate discourse in the Personal Myth is essential for the deepening of knowing, which will preserve or restore desire and sexuality. Gender Myth conversation is essential for excitement and attraction, but sexual dialogue, the language of the Sexual Fantasy Myth, may be internal. What is essential is that you each come to know the contents of your own Sexual Fantasy Myths.

In your mind, consider whether you feel satisfied with how each of you touch and behave during lovemaking. Are one or both of you more preoccupied with your own pleasure than with your partner's? What would you like your partner to do to you? What would you like to do? What were your sexual fantasies when you were an adolescent, and which of them have you maintained? Sex inevitably leads us ever deeper into tender realms, even into childhood patterns and desires. Ultimately, it reunites us with vital, creative, or wounded parts of ourselves and helps to make us whole again.

You can turn away from this inward journey, of course, and a great many of us do. Hollywood's mythology informs us that sex should automatically be thrilling and fulfilling. In other words, you can deny that sex is an expression of the deeper aspects of the soul and, in the process, insist that sex be fantastic without ever doing the inner work. Thus we let fate or luck decide whether or not our sexual relationships will be satisfying. Yet, as every adult who is honest with himself discovers, the consequence of ignoring the inner world and its mysteries is a protracted journey through one unsatisfying relationship after another. It is to be doomed in relationships and deprived of love. Few fates in life are more terrible.

At its most basic level, sex is the instinctual act by which the human race sustains itself. The power of sexual desire to lead us to seek a sexual partner is a genetic and instinctual urge whose roots reach back over three billion years. Driven by the primordial memories of both our human and non-human ancestors, whose collective will to survive still throbs in our loins, we are relentlessly propelled by the singular imperative to go forth and procreate.

The Swiss psychiatrist Carl Jung likened the sex drive to the

Leviathan, a great and powerful beast which exists in the waters of the unconscious. From the depths, it rises as it wills, according to its own proclivities, and awakens us to the need to conjugate. The Leviathan, which is symbolic of the awesome power of the sex drive, as well as of the human will to survive, was never meant by nature to be ignored or denied. Indeed, those who would deny their sexual nature often become somehow deformed. For us to live in civilization this nature must not be denied, but it must be tamed. Many people have the capacity to tap into the vast storehouse of sexual energy which lies in the shoals of their unconscious mind. Untamed, it can be destructive.

What tames it, as Freud made clear, is love. Indeed, love plays a key role in the way families, states, and even our civilizations conduct themselves. The heinous sexual crimes committed against women by soldiers is a result of a militant hatred of the enemy which transforms men into beasts.

Recently I sat mesmerized as one of my clients, a Vietnam War veteran told me about returning to Southeast Asia on business. For years after the war he had had no interest in returning, because he was only capable of seeing the Vietnamese people as "gooks"—as the enemy; people he had to hate in order to kill them. But recently he has fallen in love and married, after a smorgasbord of empty relationships in which sex was only a way of having orgasms with female objects, and was completely divorced from love. "And do you know," he told me, "as soon as I got off the plane and saw their faces again after all those years, I realized I didn't hate them. In fact I found I loved them. I could see their beauty, and I could see the tragedies they had suffered, some of them at my own hands. But it's only because I've found Lynn and have finally understood and felt love for a woman that I could even see the Vietnamese as humans." Indeed, sexual crimes are common when love and compassion don't exist. Long before the Greeks, women were considered spoils of war. The rape of strangers and family incest both originate from the same pathetic and pathological place—lovelessness. The gang of boys out "wilding" who raped and mercilessly beat a young woman who had been jogging in New York's Central Park in 1988 were able to do this because, in the words of Robert Bly, they "never learned to shudder." For the rest of us civilized people, were it not for love, the untamed sexual drive would be capable of much damage. Love channels the sex drive through story. The Personal Myth, the Gender Myth, and the Sexual Fantasy Myth—three love stories—are the channels through which love tames the sheer force of unbridled sexual energy. The child's story of imperfect love, and the adult's story of love-me-as-the-hero-I-am, are the raw materials that are fired in the kilns of all our sexual fantasies.

What Is the Sexual Fantasy Myth?

When our instinctual sex drive is tamed by our consciousness and shaped by our mythologies, it automatically takes on particular characteristics which define our sexual desires. If the sex drive, or libido, is analogous to a great sea-beast, then the Sexual Fantasy Myth defines the Leviathan's destination. The Sexual Fantasy Myth is the means by which we carry out two essential functions. First, through it we tap into and call forth desire when we want to make love or are invited to do so. It is the silken curtain into the exciting world of sexual pleasures, accessible only when we pass a threshold into that erotic sunlit garden or mysterious dark cave or splendid palace.

The narrative that informs the Sexual Fantasy Myth is not written until after adolescence. But it is not preposterous to propose that the seeds of sexuality take hold in the womb. For in that pulsating warm darkness, the sense of touch, which the anthropologist Ashley Montague has termed "the mother of the senses," first comes to life. It is the first of the five senses to develop—and usually the last to depart at the other end of life. Sexual experiences and feelings come slowly after birth, but eventually build toward adulthood until you have accumulated a significant body of experiences within your psyche. Some of that experience is un-examined, some of it is forgotten or repressed, and some is simply prevented from ever entering your inner world. We can think of the psyche as a container for your vast sexual life which includes experiences, thoughts, and emotions. From that container, you se-lectively draw upon certain experiences, beliefs, and feelings to create a story which is the Sexual Fantasy Myth.

As you mature, your sexual feelings begin to rouse the slum-bering Leviathan, but the sexual drive needs an explicit means of self-expression. It needs to be taught how to direct its energies. The Leviathan needs to be told what is beautiful, what is sexually al-luring, and what kind of experiences you will find erotic. That which informs the libido of its desires is the Sexual Fantasy Myth. Without this myth, the libido is a blind force which exists only in our genitals and the most primitive part of the brain. But with the Sexual Fantasy Myth, the sheer unconscious power of sex is united with the conscious mind, which automatically translates the sex-ual urge into a story, the details of which define the kind of part-ner you desire and the kind of circumstances which would satisfy you sexually. This story is a set of creative fantasies which arise when sexual energy and imagination mingle. It is the rich store-house of all your sexual yearnings, lustful fantasies, and sexual ad-ventures—both those experienced and those only fantasized about. The Sexual Fantasy Myth contains all the ways you can have sex and all the possibilities for ecstasy and fulfillment that sex offers you. The stories in our Sexual Fantasy Myths are neither true nor false; they are the fruits of the imagination. Our Sexual Fantasy Myths allow us to recognize and preserve the sexual mystery through the power of the imagination. They are, ultimately, pre-scriptions for the survival of sexual desire. By exploring this myth on your own, you can come to understand yourself in new ways and enrich your sex life, which in turn enriches your entire life.

Through the Sexual Fantasy Myth you contain and frame de-sire, channeling it into one of three domains: the body, the mind, or real life. These domains are the places where we access desire. We do this through narrative. I have made much of the purpose and power of story in this book, because I believe that we are defined by the images and stories of our lifetimes, from our earliest days of life to the ever-present moment. Our stories, both those from the past and those we spin in the present, are essential ways of focusing the imagination, which is like a switch that we use to arouse ourselves and access desire in one or more of the three domains. Some people fantasize and make love in only one domain, while others can make love or feel desire in more than one or in all three.

The *body domain* involves the senses directly and is experienced almost entirely within the body. The sense of touch dominates and awakens all the other senses as well. Lovers whose preferred domain is the body rely on the feel, the scent, the taste, and even the sounds of their and their partner's bodies for arousal.

Lovers who prefer the *domain of mind* are aroused by their imaginations. Their desire is stimulated by exciting mental images or detailed stories, which may resemble movies playing in their minds.

The *real-life domain* refers to arrangements in real life which afford the opportunity for a sexual encounter between two or more people. Their "public" aspect is what distinguishes them from fantasies that are confined to the mind or body. We would also include in this class of Sexual Fantasy Myths pairs of couples who are turned on by "playing" with the idea of swapping partners and then, aroused by the naughtiness, retreat to separate bedrooms perhaps playing mental movies of lustful sex with their friends while they make love with their own partners. Also included here are those couples who do switch for an evening and then return to their own partners, their lust highly amplified.

As with all typologies, some people fix on one domain only, some settle on a favorite, and some can find pleasure in all three locales, depending upon their partner or upon their own mood. It is highly personal, and you are not less sexual or "healthy" if you prefer one domain and have no interest in the others. It has been suggested that any differences in preferred domain fall along male-female lines, but everything I have learned about men and women over the past thirty years of listening to thousands of stories has convinced me otherwise. Where once the conventional understanding was that all women needed to be romanced into bed and that, as a rule, they preferred tender sex and rarely developed fetishes, what I have seen has convinced me that these rules were based on a superficial understanding of men and women. The differences we may heretofore have observed have been cultural biases. Now, as the Gender Myths permitted men and women are blurring so that women can become astronauts and men can stay home with the children, the heroic modes they choose are changing and so is their sexuality. Many women I know enjoy and script real life scenes with third parties or complicated sex toys, while many men, now that they are allowed to express such needs, find that their desire is best aroused with romance, scented candles, and long loving massages.

Ashley and Gio: Sexual Desire in All Three Domains

Gio and Ashley are reading next to a warm wood stove. The resiny scent of burning locust wood envelops the room. Outside, the wind rages, and flakes of snow flitter at the windows. They are listening to Chopin's Nocturnes. It is almost too much for Ashley—good music, Rilke. She is "stirred," a code word they have for arousal. She lays her book open on her lap. "Let's make love," she says. She comes over and nuzzles Gio. "Chopin does this to me sometimes. I'm glad you're here, not anyone else. I could do something bad."

This is her way of challenging him, Gio knows. Still, taken just a little by surprise, but delighted, somewhere in him arises the question, "But where is my desire?" Gio's answer comes from his Sexual Fantasy Myth. It is here that he goes to summon desire and answer his lover's call.

Gio and Ashley are versatile lovers. Their sexual relationship succeeds because each can summon desire in all three domains. On this evening, Gio chooses to go into the realm of the mind. Unprepared for lovemaking that evening, but very open to it, Gio feels a rush of love for Ashley—the true source of his pleasure. Scores of moments in which Ashley gave him more joy than he had ever expected to receive in a lifetime revisit him. His mind goes to work. Now visual stories parade across his mental screen. Inwardly he smiles; he loves these stories he has created over time not just for occasions such as this. They are stories of sexual naughtiness and sexual loyalty, which define him as a man who is in love with Ashley.

Rick and Ruth: The Domains of Body and Mind

We have met Rick and Ruth Perlman in previous chapters where they were shown to be an excellent match in the Gender Myth. I first met this young couple when they began to experience mild sexual difficulties which were based on the fact that their Sexual Fantasy Myths manifested themselves in very different domains. Rick was instantly arousable and ready for lovemaking, while Ruth needed a longer time to marshall her desire to the point where lovemaking would be as exquisite for her as she knew it could be. Ruth described Rick's sex drive as a machine that could be turned on with the flip of a switch. Much of the time her mere presence is that switch. As we talked, it became clear that Rick's sex drive was centered completely in the body. For Rick, Ruth's entire body had erotic potential.

People who focus their desire on the body and find the body itself an unlimited source of desire are probably more sensual than those of us who turn to scenarios in the mind or in real life. Rick's strongest sense was smell, with touch running a close second. For him, there was nothing headier than Ruth's musky smell when her body was moist with sweat from exercise or vigorous sex on a summer afternoon. Not surprisingly, Rick enjoyed oral sex. Touching Ruth between her legs with finger or tongue after lovemaking and putting his fingers to his nostrils was, for him, "like being transported back to post-orgasmic heaven."

Ruth, on the other hand, needed a gradual accretion of intimacy and mental stimulation to prepare her body for sex. Once the pair understood this difference between them, they were able to make small changes which made an enormous difference. Often when Rick comes home from work or a business trip and is eager, more than eager, to make love, Ruth will delay him with some wine and a long talk. Meanwhile, she is warming herself with her own inner stories so that when the two finally do fall into each other's arms, they are equally passionate and hungry for each other. In this way they respect each other's differences, and each takes responsibility for his or her needs.

Raymond and Samantha: The Domains of Real Life and the Body

As we saw in the previous chapter, as Fixer and Survivor this couple spoke different languages in the Gender Myth. Samantha's way was to go along with whatever Raymond asked of her, while Raymond, like most Fixers, was desperate to give his wife peak sexual experiences. However, this couple also operated from different domains within the Sexual Fantasy Myth. Samantha was a sensual woman who could have an orgasm just by the feel of sun and a warm wind on her body as she tended her garden. Raymond, on the other hand, turned to scenes of the mind that spilled over into real life for his sexual inspiration. His Sexual Fantasy Myth ranged from wanting Samantha to watch porn movies with him, at the mildest, to wanting to watch her make love with one of their friends. Indeed, in one period, relationships with some other couples and one male colleague were so sexually charged (under

Raymond's guiding hand) that Samantha's allegation, made in therapy years later, that "we were into mate-swapping" did not seem far off. Alas, because the two also operated from different heroic modes, Samantha was not the sort who would speak up for her own needs and desires. She abandoned herself and went along with his desires. But in so doing, she abandoned her husband as well, because she did not clue him in to what pleased or displeased her. It wasn't Raymond's way in those days to wonder why she asked so little of him; why her pleasure was tied so perfectly to his. Thus, for years Raymond acted on his untested assumptions, taking her only into his Sexual Fantasy Myth and real-life scenes, but never engaging in a sensitive sexual dialogue which might have brought him closer to understanding how she needed to make love.

Rebecca and Carlton: The Domains of Body and Mind

I worked with Rebecca and Carlton for many years. Like Rick, Carlton was virtually priapic and insatiable; Rebecca's desire required more mental stimulation. Carlton was an insensitive and inexperienced lover. Capable of orgasm on a moment's notice, he was also able to make up for his sexual explosion by his ability to become hard again after only a few minutes to "satisfy" Rebecca. Strangely, Carlton was a virgin when the two met. Rebecca was clearly not, although he never questioned her. Indeed, Carlton was grateful for Rebecca's experience and the fact that in the early years of their relationship she was the more sexually liberated in every way. That "look in her eye" meant that she would soon seek out his erection, the quickness of which was, at first, a source of pride and arousal in her. At the opera, in a dark theater or movie house, or on a plane, she would "brighten his day" by deftly unzipping his fly while nonchalantly playing with him. They still roar with laughter at Carlton's occasional "accidents."

Alas, Carlton had no idea that a year into their marriage

Rebecca's need and desire had waned. Later, she even resorted to taking a long-term lover who was capable of including her own sexual needs in their lovemaking. But until that point, Rebecca handled Carlton's "just stick it in" type of lovemaking with a fantasy. This scene, played out in her mind, inspired her desire but still left her needs unmet. It allowed her to be in the sexual experience for Carlton and to be faithful to him and his needs. Without it, she felt she would have had to face the implications of a marriage that was unhappy in several other areas, as we shall see, and to fake orgasm or endure her husband's insatiable pounding. None of these options was acceptable.

In Rebecca's fantasy, she is on her knees in the bed, having transformed reality, for Carlton only makes love in the missionary position. Carlton enters the room naked, having just showered. Her backside facing him, she turns her head to watch his advance. (In reality, Carlton has probably already come once by now.) She hears a thunderous noise as an enormous bull bursts through the door. Carlton backs off in surprise and then disappears. Sometimes he is swatted away by the bull who, on every occasion, has only one thing on his mind—entering her from the rear. She is entranced by his penis, which is huge and pulsing, but also repelled by the sight of it. She tries to lock her knees to deny entry, but then changes her mind. When the bull, who is big enough to fill the room, straddles her, she changes her mind again. She surprises herself with how willing her orifice is to stretch and receive this inhuman instrument of revulsion and pleasure. By this time, her husband is on her again. She will time Carlton's second orgasm to the bull's first and also to her own. In a paroxysm of ecstasy she opens herself to the bull's hugeness. Only then, in a mixture of satiety and disgust, does she erase the bull from her mind and return to her husband, who is up and about before she wishes him to leave.

We will revisit Carlton and Rebecca in more detail later. I describe them here as an example of two people who make love in different domains yet whose sexual dialogue is so undeveloped that Carlton provides his wife with little pleasure and doesn't even know it. Eventually, after she and her lover broke up, Rebecca's bull fantasy stopped working and she could no longer manage to stay sexual with her husband. When I first met them they had all but stopped making love for eight years.

Sexual Dialogue: Why There's No Such Thing as a "Good Lover"

Sexual Dialogue is not perforce about conversation. At its best it is improvisation. Sexual dialogue bridges two partners' mythologies in a language called lovemaking. Without sexual dialogue, a couple can "have sex." They may even be able to make love *to* each other. But without sexual dialogue, they can't make love *with* each other.

"Lovemaking is an interpretive loop in which the language is not only words but kisses and caresses, and the meaning conveyed is intimacy and affection and pleasure," writes philosopher David Grudin in *On Dialogue: An Essay in Free Thought*: "Lovemaking is thus a dialogue, with each new statement changing both stater and statee, with each excited response becoming a newly exciting statement, all spiraling into a vortex of intensity. What love-makers create is a four-dimensional work of dialogic art, impermanent and yet unforgettable. What love-makers create is a reciprocal symmetry, corporeal yet formally superior to most philosophy and art."

The philosopher Robert Nozick echoes Grudin in his book *The Examined Life*: "Sexual partners are engaged in a dialogue, partly scored, partly improvised, where each attentively responds to the statements and the bodily motions of [the] other."

This comparison of lovemaking at its best to a jazz improvisation shows precisely what I mean about sexual dialogue. Sexual dialogue is the currency with which we transform two separate

Sexual Fantasy Myths into a joint *mysterium tremendum* whereby the two become one.

For many years, sex manuals, puritanical in their message of the importance of mentally healthy sex, have warned us of the dire consequences to each partner and to the relationship if we don't tell each other what turns us on and exactly where and how we want to be touched, and bring the contents of our most secret fantasies up into the light of day where they can become sanitized, integrated—and lose what I feel is a necessary mystery. To my way of thinking, too much talking about sex kills off too much of the power and magic. The Sexual Fantasy Myth—that place you go to summon desire—should be part of your internal milieu. Indeed, in my office I have seen many people who took the advice of these well-meaning sexual psychology books and lost their ability to make love—either because one partner wanted to preserve the mystery and tension or because one didn't want to hear the contents of the other's sexual fantasy. Yet they were admonished by the books—and often bullied by their partners—to shed their "inhibitions" and enjoy healthy lusty sex.

As I see it, the sexual dialogue is a sensuous reconnaissance mission into your partner's body and soul. There is no need to verbalize about this journey unless that foray leads you and your partner to an understanding that words are desired, that certain types of talking might add excitement. If you listen with your inner ear you will be able to hear just how much talking your partner wants. If you can feel your partner saying "No, not yet" or "Not quite so hard" or "Over here but not there," you have no need of words. If your partner touches you in the wrong way at the wrong time, there's a better way to redirect her than by talking—unless talking turns both of you on. It's a matter of developing your sexual dialogue—your shared body language of lovemaking.

Sexual dialogue is the means by which we communicate our Sexual Fantasy Myths to our lovers. It is made up of the acts we perform together, the passion and enjoyment each communicates to the other, and the feelings of love, intimacy, trust, and surrender that each offers up to the other. In the nuances of our move-ments, in the moments of stillness when movement is expected, in answering our partner's emotional excitement with building emo-tional excitement of our own, we spin out sexual narratives which we hope will be understood. When they are, we are encouraged by a sense that our partner has read us intimately and can intuit what we would like. In the final analysis, sexual dialogue is two people knowing the language of their own body and that of their lover. Ultimately it is two bodies conversing. At its best, sexual dialogue is as close as we can come to the longed-for perfect love of child-hood, where our needs are intuited and met completely, and where we are capable of giving perfect love.

The quality of sex between two people depends upon the ef-fectiveness of their sexual dialogue. That is why there is no such thing as a good lover. Lovemaking is only as good as the sexual di-alogue spanning the two mythologies. Certainly there are those who are more or less adept at sexual conversation, but in general good lovers are made, not born. Desire departs when we are cut off from our own Sexual Fantasy Myths and the sexual dialogue breaks down. We can see the breakdown in the story of Samantha and Raymond, in which case Raymond had no idea that his sexuality was threatening, even repulsive to his wife. Samantha, as a deeply shadowed Survivor, martyred and abandoned herself by not speak-ing up for her needs and going along with Raymond. Raymond's way of being heroic was to make sex wild and over-the-top, which he assumed would please his wife as much as it did him. He never thought to become aware of how his Survivor wife was respond-ing, because he sincerely believed that he knew how to give her pleasure and she never disabused him of this assumption. Another such case is that of Rebecca, a Protector wearing a Survivor's mask and abandoning her marriage to Carlton. For Carlton, sex was es-sentially masturbation. He did not gain an understanding of his own Sexual Fantasy Myth until much later, because his ever-ready erection seemed to require no guidance. Victor is another exam-ple: his mind was so dominated by his Personal Myth that he couldn't hear his own sexual desires for many years, and certainly didn't want to see his women as sexual.

Fantasy and Fidelity

The Sexual Fantasy Myth is the guarantor of freedom and control. Because it is private, it assures us control over our desires. It allows us to pursue the tantalizing and secret nature of sex without restraints. In the Sexual Fantasy Myth all is permitted so long as the secret is kept to ourselves or rejected when we disclose it to our partner in the sexual dialogue.

Some people resist the idea of fantasy as a prescription for keeping desire alive. It's like being unfaithful, many say. To fantasize is to separate oneself from one's lover, perhaps even to make love with someone else or many others. I would suggest that the opposite is also true: that living within one's thoughts or pictures during lovemaking can connect fantasy and reality. If my desire ebbs and I inspire it through fantasy, I am being faithful to my desire to please. If my spouse has lost the "beauty" of youth, I can imagine her essence as it was and always will be and embellish this essence in an internal narrative if I choose. Is this not being faithful?

Sexual Darkness

Just as our Personal Myths and our Gender Myths have shadow realms where demon voices hold forth, our Sexual Fantasy Myths also have their dark side. This particular shadow is derived from an early sexual story in the Personal Myth, and it too relates to imperfect love, although it does not appear until later when a person becomes or tries to become sexual.

Sex, because it bridges our Personal Myths and our Gender

Myths, is the most powerful arena in which we act out our betrayal in the Personal Myth. In most cases, the sexual darkness is not deep. An understanding of one's Personal Myth will usually reveal a story or an image which will shed light on peculiarities of sexual behavior. The deepest sexual shadows occur in cases in which there has been incest in the Personal Myth—the ultimate betrayal. But, occasionally, I meet someone whose Personal Myth is dominated by a less-sexual experience in childhood which nevertheless translates into a dark shadow in their adult sexuality. For example, Victor, whom we met in the chapter on the Personal Myth, lives under such a deep sexual shadow derived from his Personal Myth that he is able to make love only under the strictest, most controlled circumstances.

Victor's Sexual Shadow: Obsession with the Personal Myth

As we saw, Victor's Personal Myth was structured around a voracious and controlling mother who terrified Victor with her sexuality and her stealing of his secrets—namely his poetry. As I said previously, in this instance I actually met both parents in Victor's presence and heard the other side of the story. Both parents denied—and I believe them without question—that the mad dancing scene which Victor so vividly remembers ever occurred in real life. But that recollected scene serves to illustrate the terrain of Victor's perception of his mother as he experienced it. The identity of the storyteller naturally determines which story will be told. It is entirely possible that Victor spun his complicated tale because he once saw his mother naked or because her breasts showed in one of her dresses or because he saw her sitting seductively on his father's lap. Another child in the family might have had an entirely different take on the family story. But to Victor, his mother's actions could be read only as attempts to control, dominate, and finally humiliate him, while his father was only a passive onlooker, unable to play a strong role in the boy's life. Victor's mother, a heroic Survivor, told me that because her father had turned her out into the streets where she had to fend off the depredations of drunken Nazis, hunger, and homelessness, she was determined to give her only child all she could. To her, Victor represented all that she loved in life; all that was truly her own. Yet Victor experienced her only as invasive and frightening. Despite the parents' denials in front of Victor in my office, I did not call into question the veracity of Victor's memory because his recollection symbolized his experience of his mother.

In later life, Victor fell in love with an exotic Italian beauty named Rosa. Rosa, who had grown up under the repressive thumb of a father who did everything he could to stamp out and negate her burgeoning sexuality, expected that once she met the right man her interior "black box," the sexuality she knew lay hidden deep within, could finally be opened and safely explored, and she couldn't wait. She and Victor were a perfect match in the Gender Myth, a true meeting of minds. Both held important jobs in the rarefied atmosphere of the high-tech companies springing up on the perimeter of Boston. Although in somewhat different areas of computer science, each was impressed by the other's professional standing. The ease with which they could converse about everything was just a further sign to them that they belonged together. Soon after they became engaged, they went skiing for the weekend. Knowing that she was soon to be married, and excited that at last she, the good Italian Catholic, would have a husband with whom to explore all the sexual delights she had been imagining, Rosa decided to rid herself of her virginity that weekend. Although Victor had checked them into separate rooms, Rosa lingered in Victor's. When Victor went down the hall to get some ice for a final nightcap, Rosa prepared her surprise. When he returned to the room, she ripped open her silk blouse, displaying her ripe breasts in all their glory, and cried, "Fuck me!" Victor blushed deeply and looked away. "Please get dressed," he said, recoiling in horror, images of his mother dancing crowding his mind. "I'm not ready for this yet." Sadly, he was never ready for the next eight years. The opening of Rosa's black box and the sexual delights she knew to be awaiting her would have to be postponed until her second marriage. Despite their utter mismatch in the domain of the Sexual Fantasy Myth, their perfect pairing in the domain of the Gender Myth has kept them best friends. Victor, for his part, finally found another woman. But his sexuality is still completely constrained by his resolute insistence on dwelling in the horror of his Personal Myth. Indeed, Victor cannot make love with a woman who is on top. Even an unsolicited kiss by Clare, his current girlfriend, makes him freeze and withdraw. Extraordinarily, on one occasion Clare made the same mistake as Victor's mother had: in an effort to arouse him, she decided to dance wildly in front of him. One wonders how the relationship survived! Recently, she put her hands on his shoulders, a bold move which occasioned a two-day argument between them. Victor is exceptional in that exploration of his Personal Myth has proved futile. This is so because it is the only myth he will visit. His obsession with it, his inability to escape it, and its effect on his adult life has all but destroyed his sexuality.

Recently Victor has found a Sexual Fantasy Myth which works for him. In it he is a cock pheasant and his lover a beautiful white dove. He fluffs his feathers and drums as mating birds do, calling her to him. When his white dove comes to him, he enfolds her in his wings and makes love to her. He is in control, he is strong and male, and his lover is enveloped in his wings, demure and white and chaste.

Adrian and Nicole: Childhood Sexual Shadows That Work Together in Adult Life

Adrian is another example of a man with a deeper than normal sexual shadow. Adrian, however, is blessed with having found a partner whose story dovetails perfectly with his own. Adrian is the son of a famous stage actress who had been through several husbands by the time Adrian was born. Soon enough she tired of Adrian's father, a union set carpenter from one of her plays, and sent him on his way with a generous payoff, never to be seen again. Adrian grew up surrounded by a bohemian family of theater people and artists. For a time in the sixties, his mother was at the fringe of Andy Warhol's circle. Times were wild, drugs were everywhere, but his mother was the toast of Broadway. While she might indulge in marijuana, cocaine, and casual sex between plays, when she was working, she worked hard. She saw little of Adrian during the months of a big production and she felt guilty for shortchanging him. But she found a way to make some of it up to him which she thought would make him feel warm and loved. When she would arrive home in the middle of the night after having dined out with critics and admirers, she would come into Adrian's bedroom and climb in bed with him. She would then commence to tickle him until he shrieked in that quasi-orgasmic combination of pain and pleasure that only tickling brings.

In our conversations, Adrian doesn't remember that there were sexual overtones to these late-night sessions with his mother, although he does remember often having erections during their tussles. Usually his mother would end her visits with a soothing back-rub and then she would tuck him in and proceed to her own bed.

Nicole also grew up in a virtually fatherless family. It was during the Korean War, and her father was a surgeon who completed several tours of duty. It was a hard time for her mother and their large Irish Catholic family. Nicole, one of the oldest, was sent to a Catholic boarding school where she was surrounded by extremely strict and devout nuns. Of all the things she learned at that convent, the one which stuck most clearly in her mind was: "*Never touch yourself!*" For the longest time Nicole thought this grim edict applied to all parts of her body, but then she came to understand that only her "naughty bits," as Sister Bertha called them, fell under this rubric. Accordingly, Nicole was twenty-three before she realized she could masturbate, and she was a virgin for several more years. Anxious finally to have sex with a partner with whom to share the exquisite sensations she could now produce between her legs, she finally allowed herself to be picked up at a bar by a boy who clearly intended the evening to end in bed. And end it did, but not in a torrent of ecstasy, because Nicole found the feelings of another naked body next to her own impossibly unpleasant, both physically and mentally. The guilt was too overpowering. She got up abruptly, dressed and fled, leaving behind an annoyed young man.

Confused by her conflicts, Nicole began to read everything she could about sex. In the course of her reading she came across a practice the books referred to as fetishism. Although the book said that fetishism was fairly rare and almost always the domain of males, Nicole found herself highly aroused by the photographs of rubber fetishists. Here were people fully clothed in rubber suits, even their penises encased in condoms, while others wore only rubber raincoats or made love on rubber sheets. Some wore masks, a greater anonymity which also appealed to Nicole. Gradually she began to experiment. She began by masturbating while wearing her scuba diving wet suit. The smell of the latex, the sounds it made, the feel against her skin, aroused her more intensely than ever before. What she didn't know was how to go about finding a partner with whom to share her secret.

At the same time, in a Back Bay apartment, Adrian, now in graduate school, was having sexual problems of his own. While he had been sexually active since the age of seventeen, most of his encounters had been spoiled, because he couldn't allow a woman to see his naked body or to touch his penis. Otherwise, like any young male, he was highly arousable. He certainly didn't need to be touched in order to have an erection. In fact, he was constantly walking around the campus, trousers tented embarrassingly. He was particularly drawn to somewhat older women. Although he was happy to sleep with women his own age, and usually did, he felt that women only became more sexual as they aged. He often fantasized about making love to a woman in her fifties, one who hadn't been seduced in many years, one who no longer felt sexy. He would bring her joy and she'd be grateful to him for his instant and hard erection which would prove him eager and desirous of her without her even having to touch him, so unlike the men of her own age.

There is a saying, "God makes them and they find each other." And this is what happened for Adrian and Nicole. They met when both were working for a political candidate. Over time, as they stuffed envelopes and canvassed neighborhoods together, they found they had much in common. Both were in advertising, both liked scuba diving, and both liked to cook gourmet feasts and drink of good wine. Nicole was exactly what Adrian had dreamt of. She was twelve years older and seemed hungry. They didn't tell me the particulars of how they each discovered that the other's way of making love worked perfectly. But the man who didn't want to be touched eagerly complied with making love in a rubber suit or one of the many other latex and neoprene garments in Nicole's closet, and Nicole *was* delighted by his youthful, ever-ready erection.

Thus, while each person's family stories cast shadows on his or her adult sexuality, unlike Victor and Rosa, these two found in each other the perfect mate in both the Gender Myth and the Sexual Fantasy Myth. When later in their relationship they came to me because the initial fireworks seemed to be slacking off, we did some work in the Personal Myth and Adrian and Nicole were able to find the origins of their sexual desires. This couple was very easy to work with. They made diligent efforts and soon developed a marriage which worked in all three myths.

In earlier times, Adrian and Nicole and quite possibly Raymond, who enjoyed watching other people make love to his wife, would have been pathologized, probably even labeled deviant. Although there would have been a caveat that very few women even develop paraphilias such as fetishism, attempts to explain Nicole's fetishism might have centered on her having been aroused as a child to sights, smells, or sounds created by rubber

sheets or other rubber she had encountered in earliest childhood.
Adrian would be written off as a repressed homosexual or at least
a man who had been severely damaged by his mother, and even
Raymond might be seen by some as showing evidence of repressed
homosexual desires in which he was identifying with his wife receiving pleasure from other men.

My own feeling is that these psychoanalytic explanations
don't take into account the richness and complexity of individual
human beings and their childhood stories. When considered in
this light, no one seems deviant, except perhaps the loveless souls
who rape, commit sex murders, or molest children. Our sexual
needs and fantasies arise from the way in which we view and unconsciously interpret our family stories—not because of problems
in potty training or penis envy or an inability to let go of our mothers—even though family stories may sometimes give rise to people whose Personal Myths bear scars from potty training, or
feelings that they'd be better loved if they were a different sex, or
disordered boundaries with a parent.

Discovering Your Sexual Fantasy Myth

1. *What are your memories of your earliest childhood sexual fantasies?
What made you fantasize about these things?*

2. *To what extent are you turned on via your senses (touch, taste,
smell, sight, hearing), your imagination, or by scenes in real life?*

3. *What sexual encounters in your life have you found most exciting,
and why?*

4. *Do you remember the first time you masturbated and what your feelings were? What fantasies occurred (and still occur) to you when you
masturbate?*

5. *Are there things you haven't tried but perhaps want to do (or think you want to do?)*

6. *What happens inside your mind when you make love?*

7. *What were the attitudes in your family regarding sex?*

8. *What really turns you off? Do you know why?*

Because the Sexual Fantasy Myth can be kept private, anything goes if it doesn't harm you or another. The goal is to discover your own myth, your own desires and, if they differ from your partner's, to find a way to turn those differences into the magic of sexual dialogue.

Chapter Seven

Making Love

In man and woman are found all the materials and experiences
of the world. When they unite, these experiences and materials
can be distilled into a vision of and a harmonization with
the dynamic unity underlying all of reality.
NIK DOUGLAS AND PENNY SLINGER,
Sexual Secrets

There are as many ways of making love as there are people. Each
of us brings to the sexual union our unique combination of myths
and stories, heroic modes and cultural influences. When fully developed, the sexual dialogue between two people is as original and
as distinct as a piece of music.

Just as each of the myths defines a particular part of your identity and your life story, gives rise to a particular element of desire, and leads you to look for a particular type of interaction
with love partners, so too does each myth donate a specific type
of energy to lovemaking. The different myths have different
powers to arouse desire. When we are aware of these powers, we

may mix different elements of desire from the three myths in a single act of lovemaking, although many people make love in only one myth—usually the Gender Myth or the Sexual Fantasy Myth.

Love in the Gender Myth

The quality of lovemaking in the Gender Myth is impersonal, even anonymous. It is here that the erotic influences of the three hero types are most distinct. Whether you are a Survivor, Fixer, or Protector determines to a great extent the way you are able to communicate sexually if your lovemaking is primarily centered in the Gender Myth. Again, I wish to underscore that there is no one most healthy, most appropriate, or most fulfilling way to make love. The person you are making love with and where your relationship stands in its development both influence lovemaking. My goal is to introduce you to the unlimited ways available for you and your partner to make love.

Since the Gender Myth is the myth in which most people realize their initial attraction, in a way it is the most superficial way of making love simply because you are both in your heroic modes. These heroes are created in part to attract another person; to show you off at your best. Accordingly, lovemaking in the Gender Myth may lack some of the deeper truth and tenderness of lovemaking in the Personal Myth. It is more likely to be an exercise in which each partner is trying to let his hero speak and speak his or her best words. As two lovers come to know their respective myths and shadows, their lovemaking repertoires can expand so that they have more latitude in how they make love. Then, it is likely that they will be able to incorporate lovemaking in the Personal Myth when or if each needs or desires that type of lovemaking. When you have access to the sexual energy of both the Personal Myth and the Gender Myth in your relationship, your Sexual Fantasy

Myth cannot help but be engaged and your sexual dialogue will be better than all right.

Since most sexual dialogue between two people begins in the Gender Myth, let us look at how the heroes make love from within this myth.

The Survivor's Sexual Style

The Survivor's sexual style is to please his or her lover endlessly, to endure endlessly. In the Survivor's light zone this endurance may manifest itself as a man's ability to hold back his pleasure until his partner reaches orgasm—or the woman's ability to hang in as long as is needed to arouse her aging husband. However, in sex, shadowed Survivors can also be master-manipulators. Knowing that there is glamor in distance, they know how to keep their partners at just the right distance, waiting to be engaged. In the gray zone, the Survivor's apparent endurance may in fact be sexual martyrdom, the beginning of the long slide into the deepest part of the Survivor's shadow: the Abandoner. We have seen this with Samantha, an arch-Survivor who anesthetized her mind and body from the pain caused by Raymond's insensitive behavior and thus tacitly participated in a sexual monologue scripted solely by her Fixer husband. Her psyche justified her simply "tuning out" and denying her feelings as a way of avoiding pain.

The Fixer's Sexual Style

Raymond, Samantha's husband, is an excellent example of the Fixer-lover. Making love with a Fixer highlights the grand, passionate, sweeping emotions and gestures of erotic love. The Fixer's intense sexual moods can blow the roof off of lovemaking when she or he is teamed with another Fixer-lover. Ideal? Who knows? Teamed with a courageous Survivor who is quite aware of what turns her on (and it's often Fixer-type wild sex), and lets her desires be known, the Fixer-lover may be fascinated. With this type of Survivor's preprimed willingness to "survive the dangers" or "be taken to the edge," the Fixer may be able to plumb depths two Fixers who both want to lead the way cannot plumb.

As a Fixer, Raymond wanted to go to the edge with his wife, but he proceeded without acknowledging the love he had for her. If he had, he would have had to take responsibility for the pain he caused her. Instead, he allowed himself to work from the Fixer's shadow mode and to become sexually abusive in the scenes where he forced her to act out his real-life fantasies. Unfortunately, until he had lost her and sought help in therapy, Raymond lacked even the slightest bit of self-reflection. Certainly he never questioned Samantha's seeming perfect acquiescence in his fantasy life. His certainty that his needs were their needs accurately displays the abusive side of the Fixer in sex. He was walled off from his own Personal Myth and the Protector in himself, which meant that he was divorced from both his own tenderness and his wife's need to share in it. His sexual repertoire was thus limited to his Gender Myth, dominated by the Fixer hero, and his Sexual Fantasy Myth, which he gave free rein.

The Protector's Sexual Style

In general, the Protector's preferred way of making love has more of the tender quality of love in the Personal Myth. It is more likely to be reverential, caretaking, and sensual. These are the lovers for whom cooking a fine meal, opening great bottles of wine, and creating an atmosphere of pleasure and nurture are erotic. In this sense, lovemaking between two Protectors without deep shadows may be ideal for them both. However, in the shadows of the Protector lies the fearful victim who may be overcritical or try, out of fear, to inhibit the expression of sexual behaviors which could be pleasurable. Again, depending upon the individuals involved, their myths and their shadows, a Protector might find the wild, over-the-top love-making of many Fixers terrifying. Or, it might titillate and even empower the Protector by taking him or her even farther away from the shadows where he or she is overly childlike and victimized.

Dr. No: The Danger of Love in the Gender Myth and Sexual Fantasy Myth Alone

Not long ago, in the course of changing health insurance, I went to see a young doctor for a checkup. When he asked me about my work I explained that I specialized in family and couples therapy. The doctor proceeded to tell me that he had no intention of getting married.

"Why?" I asked him.

"Because," he said, "the best sex is anonymous sex. For me it's much better if I've just met the person or don't know her very well or if she's seriously involved with someone else."

The doctor feels this way because he overemphasizes his Gender Myth and his Sexual Fantasy Myth while completely avoiding his Personal Myth. This allows him to have sex without the involvement of deeper feelings and the growth that such feelings demand. He cannot receive love from the women who briefly cross his path, since he hardly sees or hears them. Nor does he offer them anything more than his carefully painted mask. These are the people of whom Freud wrote in his essay, "On the Universal Tendency to Debasement in Love," "Where they love they do not desire and where they desire they cannot love."

Because I have been a therapist for a long time now, and have seen people in various stages of life, I know where this combination of weak Personal Myth and total reliance upon Gender and Sexual Fantasy Myths takes a person. The gaping hole that such people fall into is time and aging. Those people who indulge in an endless string of anonymous relationships miss the opportunity for intimacy with themselves and others. They never come to know themselves or anyone else. Meanwhile time is passing and they are getting older. As they age, their psyches demand deeper and more lasting relationships, but because they have neglected this aspect of their life, they don't understand that what is really missing is love, understanding, and constancy. They are rootless in themselves and in the world, and they have no clue how to go about establishing these roots because they have avoided the painful trip home to childhood. Their habit of drifting from relationship to relationship, often well-armed with rationalizations about why each wasn't quite right, is so ingrained that it's difficult to change. Their fear of entering their Personal Myths is magnified by the sure knowledge that they have accumulated great poisonous wastepiles of pain over the years from discarding so many relationships.

Nowhere is this piteously empty destiny better portrayed than in the film *Carnal Knowledge*, in which Jack Nicholson's character is rendered impotent—indeed is destroyed—by his unrestricted and destructive sexual profligacy. Like Nicholson's character, the doctor who examined me is setting himself up for a crisis, in part because his Gender Myth will never be able to satisfy the needs of his Personal Myth, which will eventually rear up and engulf him— perhaps when he's least expecting it. If he's lucky, the crisis will teach him that his life is empty of what he most needs: to love and be loved. Love is what sustains us. Unfortunately, too many of us never make that realization, or come to it too late to be saved from loneliness, bitterness, and despair.

Loving and Making Love
in the Personal Myth

To experience love in the Personal Myth is to feel raw longing for another human being. You are asking to give and receive love. Your heart is wide open, tender and vulnerable. At its best, love in the Personal Myth is nostalgic. You are once again the vulnerable child, innocent and hopeful, as he stands before his parents expectant that his needs for love will be met. A common desire among those making love in the Personal Myth is to be held protectively and touched. It is perhaps a stirring of distant memories of being held in that way by larger-than-life figures who made you feel physically and emotionally secure. And if, in adulthood, your love is returned, all the yearnings which still exist within that child who lives on in your Personal Myth are satisfied and completed. You are aware of both the burning excitement of your desire and the gentle inner glow of Edenic happiness.

At its worst, lovemaking in the Personal Myth is a melancholic reminder of childhood's romantic tragedy. Many people shy away from love in the Personal Myth, because of their fear of stripping away the adult defenses that protect that child and all its pain. To confront the Personal Myth means to wrestle with the fundamental questions of love. Whenever we begin an important relationship, or confront a new opportunity to more fully express ourselves, we bring with us all the fears of betrayal that exist in this myth. *"Do I give my love unconditionally, knowing full well that I could be hurt?"* we ask ourselves. *"Do I allow myself to hope, or do I pull back, play it safe and cool, never giving too much of myself, never allowing myself too much hope because I am afraid my love and hope will be spurned? I could be made a fool just as I was as a child. I could be forced again to feel that terrible shame, that utter dejected embarrassment at finding out from this person I so yearn for that I am unloved and, worse yet, unlovable."*

When partners make love entirely in the Personal Myth, love-making is typically less sexually charged, since it involves making love in the same way again and again with the same partner. But, curiously, each time is different. Like a painter painting the same scene again and again, it becomes a study in truth. The "next" painting is never the same. It is a revelation.

The erotic element in the Personal Myth has a rare quality which is derived from mining truths and deep meanings from your two pasts. Gio, whom we met in the last chapter, once said, "Every day with Ashley is like turning another page in her story. One day you discover another twist in the sweetness of her nature. Making love on that day might make you feel joyous. On another page you are fascinated by a weakness or ugliness. If your fascination is held in compassion rather than contempt, these uglier truths can be erotic because they are intimate. Making love on that day might be rapturous, like being carried to another sphere of existence or like coming home."

Charles and Dorothea: A Couple Who Make Love Primarily in the Personal Myth

Charles and Dorothea seemed to be brought together by benevolent forces which sought to heal each of them of old wounds, broken dreams, and lingering betrayals. Charles, nearly sixty at the time they met, had lost his first wife to a particularly painful and lingering cancer. Charles was devastated by the loss, not only because he loved Anita but because her death made it inescapably clear how he had neglected her during their life together. It was at this point that he found his way to me.

Like so many men, Charles had sworn to himself that he would be a better father to their two children than his father had been to him, but the demands and opportunities of his career kept taking him away. "Somehow it always seemed like *now* was never the right time to really be with the family," he told me in one of our early sessions. "My job was constantly grabbing my attention, even when there was nothing I could do about the problems on the job."

His father, successful in the same field, was a selfish, mean-spirited philanderer, also inaccessible to his wife and children. Charles's mother suffered her husband's absence openly and badly. She lapsed into depressions and fits of tears which, although he loved her deeply, turned Charles, the Survivor, away from her. "Why can't she just endure like I do?" he recalled thinking as a child. Charles endured and escaped the pain of his Personal Myth by entering ever more deeply into his Gender Myth, and by abandoning his mother's pain. He was extremely talented and was singled out by his teachers as a boy with a bright future. Then, when he was seventeen, his mother died. What was even more painful for Charles than her death was the recognition that he had abandoned her long ago. In hindsight, she seemed so tender, so sad. All he wanted to do was give her a hug, but now he had missed his chance for that. Thus, as always, betrayal was at the center of Charles's Personal Myth—but in his case, the betrayals were large and cast a deep shadow: Charles's father's betrayal of the family and Charles's betrayal of his mother.

When Charles's wife Anita died, all this history reared up and nearly snuffed out his life when he realized that, once again, he had betrayed and abandoned a woman in his life. Anita had not suffered in silence before she died. She criticized Charles regularly for not paying attention to her and to the family, and her words carried all the agony of a woman facing the end, in mortal psychic and physical pain, and telling the undisguised truth. Charles did not try to deny her accusations. On the contrary, he actually heard them, and suffered all the more from the understanding that there would be no second chance. After having failed his mother and let her go to her grave alone and lonely, he had let it happen again.

The fact was that Charles had suffered so many unaddressed wounds in his Personal Myth that he had always had trouble being with his wife and children. They reminded him too much of his own painful childhood. He wanted to give them so much that every encounter with them was stressful for him. He told himself that everything he did was inadequate and all that he had not done was unbearable even to think about. For Charles, in those years, family life was a confrontation with too much anxiety, pain, and guilt from both the past and the present. It was easier just to drift away to his work than to stay and fight for his family—which also meant fighting for his own right to happiness. After Anita died, Charles made sure that his children had the best therapists and other help he could buy them, but as much as he tried to avoid condemning himself he couldn't deny how much of his father still existed in him.

Dorothea was twenty-five when she met Charles. She was the eldest of five children who were raised in a highly cultured Jewish family. Her father was a successful lawyer who had been blessed with an imperturbable equanimity. "Anything short of a second Holocaust isn't worth losing sleep over," he used to say, and he meant it. Dorothea was steeped in good music and surrounded by some of the brightest and most accomplished people in New York City. As she grew older she became beautiful. She was also blessed with her father's temperament, which meant that she was more curious than afraid. This gave her a self-possession that intimidated many, but which attracted strong men, many of whom were older friends of the family. As this began to happen more frequently, Dorothea's mother, who had always been envious of her daughter's beauty and self-assurance, became even more jealous. But Dorothea was her father's daughter and had every bit of his strength. Nothing her mother had ever said or done could keep Dorothea from embracing life. At seventeen, when she entered Harvard, she had already developed a preference for older men, and had several affairs over the next four years. "I realized early on that having sex with boys my age was not what love was all about," she told me.

She wasn't looking for anything in particular when she met Charles, but the minute the two encountered each other, they could feel the pull of each other's gravitational fields.

Right from the start of their work with me, I wanted to know what attracted them to each other. Specifically, I wanted to know whether their relationship was more than the stereotypical stuff of a father-daughter redux. But what if it was only that, a reworking of old issues between father and daughter? True love is always healing. My job is not to judge another person's needs, only to help him or her fulfill those needs within the confines of what we, together, define as healthy and life-supporting. I learned quickly that there was none of the father-daughter dynamic between them. In fact, except for their ages, Dorothea was every bit Charles's equal, and she made up for her youth with a maturity beyond her years, a maturity she had clearly possessed for most of her life. It was obvious that she would only be satisfied with a man who could match her in maturity, cultural refinement, and the sort of native wisdom it takes most of us years to acquire.

Dorothea saw Charles as a man of princely dignity, yet utterly capable and strong. Charles was a man who had spent his life in the details of his work, and, over the course of a lifetime, he had been transformed by that work. The daily confrontations with the challenges, crises, and resolutions his work entailed had broken through his defenses, made him honest, and rebuilt him into a man who was careful with details, rigorous in his thinking, and faithful to his word. Life had sanded and polished him.

Charles clearly needed the love and redemption Dorothea could offer him. He needed to leave the confines of his Gender Myth and be drawn back to his Personal Myth, back to where the pain was still fresh. He had run away from so many important relationships in his life that he desperately needed someone with whom he could be more present and true. In some deep recess of his Personal Myth, he held out the hope that he would eventually love someone so much that he could shut out the distractions of his work and begin to feel again. When he met Dorothea, he realized that he had met the woman he could love in such a way. She was beautiful and wise, and she was strong enough to hold him and his pain. She could love him despite his flaws and the many mistakes he had made in his life, including his failures of empathy and love in the past.

And this is exactly what happened: a tape-recorded session in which Dorothea described their first lovemaking captures the tone of their relationship and also the tone of lovemaking in the Personal Myth.

"We were in Charles's apartment, unwinding in front of the fire after what had been a difficult day at work for both of us. Charles asked me what I was thinking and I said, 'I was thinking about my mother—how difficult life was for her because she made it so difficult.'

"Charles said, 'Your mother sounds like somebody right out of a Victorian novel, sexually frustrated and envious of her daughter's freedom.'

" 'She was torn apart by guilt,' I said. 'In a way her guilt and jealousy still frighten me.' And then Charles did something I will never forget. He took my hand in his big paws and whispered, 'I only want to make you feel safe.'

"At that moment I felt desire such as I had never known before. I yearned to be naked in front of him. Somehow he understood this and turned away, his eyes shut. I could see that he was weeping. I was, too. I drew him to me and started to undress him. He made as if to stop me. 'You're in pain.' he said. 'There's pleasure in this pain,' I said. I felt like a virgin, like Eve leading Adam to the fruit of love. I undress him and his body is sumptuous—the strength of youth, the softening by age and experience. We are both weeping as we make love—at the past sorrows, at the pleasure and the sense of redemption which permeates the space between us. Without a word spoken, we know our tears mean the same things. Our idea of love owes something to that evening. I felt safe beyond compare," Dorothea said.

We can see that Charles and Dorothea's love was rooted in the Personal Myth from its earliest beginnings, and that it was this myth which continued to nourish their feelings. At the very beginning of her description of the scene, Dorothea feels the sting and fear of her mother's betrayal. The wound is still fresh and she, the father's daughter, and brave as she is, still doesn't feel safe. At that moment she is moving into her Personal Myth and confronting its shadow. Charles, who had turned his back on women he loved when they had needed him exactly at moments like this, is driven to make amends. He responds that he only wants to make her feel safe. Dorothea responds by wanting to make love, but Charles balks. "You're in pain," he says. Why? She is open and vulnerable to being taken advantage of by him, perhaps. He is dubious of his own motives, and so self-critical that he wonders if he might be disingenuous in his apparent concern for her pain just so that he feels justified in making love with her. And, given his history, he is aware that he needs, for once, to be empathetic in a woman's time of need.

Dorothea, for her part, loves him and needs to make love with him. She presses on. The purity of the moment envelopes them both. The sense of safety that Dorothea refers to after the lovemaking reveals that she has been warmed by the glow of making love in the Personal Myth.

Being here means being close to the old wounds and betrayals, but this time the memory of the betrayal does not detract from the love experienced in the present. For while the memory of distant pain stirs a certain nostalgia, the safe, enveloping love of the Personal Myth hearkens even farther back in your past before the birth of time to that rhythmic beating darkness where you were swaddled in your mother's flesh. In adulthood, lovemaking in the Personal Myth is suffused with feelings of gratitude for the rewards of love we now hold.

At the outset of their marriage, Charles had told Dorothea that he had an incurable heart condition and could die suddenly and relatively young. Dorothea's love was both brave and enduring. No matter their fate, she wanted a child by him and eventually had a girl. In the course of this loving relationship, all the demons that had haunted Charles's past—his perceived failures with his mother, his former wife, and his children—surfaced as he knew they would. That's what brought the two of them to me. They pursued their inner worlds with an honesty and a fervor that are rare among couples having problems. Part of that dedication may have been due to their awareness that Charles might not have long to live. As it turned out, their fears were justified. After they had been together for five years, Charles's heart failed and he died.

Death is the ultimate betrayal that awaits us all. Love in the Personal Myth makes us aware of our shared suffering and our eventual death. It is important for us to be able to express love from this myth when we need to express our understanding that love must be expressed now since we cannot count on tomorrow.

Unshared Myths

Despite the cruel brevity of their time together, Charles and Dorothea were blessed in the way that life had brought them to the same point in their development and then put them into each other's lives, where they could make love in the way that each wanted and needed. Life is not always so neat or so kind, as we can see in the story of Rebecca and Carlton. Not only did these two access desire from very different domains—Rebecca, to effect a sort of fidelity to her husband, despite his total failure at sexual dialogue, made up the fantasy of being mounted by a bull, while Carlton thrust and pumped his priapism into her unreceptive body—but because they had yet to understand the power of the myths, the emotional energy of their lovemaking, as well as the physical excitement, was mismatched.

Rebecca and Carlton: His Lack of Familiarity with His Personal Myth Made True Lovemaking with Her Impossible

When Rebecca and Carlton first consulted me, they had lived through eight years of virtual abstinence. For a time Rebecca had tried to maintain sexual desire for her husband through her fantasies, but when she broke up with the tender lover she had on the side, the utter desolation of making love with Carlton drove her to shut down completely.

Rebecca cried a lot in our sessions. Her tears were important. They were the tears of many men and women, desperately disappointed lovers who have realized that the tender love stories they had hoped to find in their marriages had instead broken down and broken their hearts. Rebecca's tears were the most mournful, in part because of the pitiably ineffective response they got from Carlton. At the first whimper from Rebecca's choked throat, Carlton invariably produced an expensive silk handkerchief, which he offered in one unhalting sweep of his arm—"the cold hand," as we came to call it when, at last, Carlton was ready to face the familial origins of his total lack of emotional response.

Rebecca's tears were more of mourning than of nostalgia. Her childhood had taught her that husbands are betrayers. It was no secret in her family that her father, a successful businessman, had women in several outposts across the country. He acted as if this were the most natural thing in the world and in no way a betrayal of his wife, whose acquiescence to this robustly playful, loud aggressor was so complete that it seemed voluntary. As Rebecca was growing up, she always felt unaccountably uncomfortable in her relations with her father. Even the horsing-around games he played with her in childhood had a sexual edge to them. As she reached puberty he would often come into her room to kiss her goodnight if her light was on. Torn between her wish for a reassuring goodnight kiss from her Daddy and an inexplicable dread of him, she would quickly turn off her light in order to avoid his visit. While she maintained that his visits were nothing but innocent, I felt that there was some connection between this dread and her dread of sex with Carlton. I have called Carlton priapic since it is the word which best describes his sexuality. In Greek mythology Priapus was the god of male procreative power. The son of Dionysus and Aphrodite, he is the ultimate phallic symbol, his image that of unbridled sexuality. And there is no doubt that Rebecca experienced his sexuality as unbridled and threatening.

Had Rebecca wanted to make love solely in the excitement and attraction of the Gender Myth, these two would have had an easier time of it. Rebecca's Personal Myth was centered on a father who was probably inappropriately unbridled—that is to say, violating Rebecca's boundaries—and always ready to sail away to the next port and the next woman. What she needed in lovemaking was sexual healing which would allow her to reenter that Personal Myth. There she would reconnect with the pain of departures and betrayal, and realize that now she was in the arms of a man of her own who could make love with her as she needed to be loved—at least some of the time. Why couldn't Carlton choose to stay home with her and build the cozy country house of her dreams, and make love with her under the stars? Why did he always have to swipe some saliva onto the head of his penis to facilitate its entrance into her totally unprepared body, pump himself dry, and then show only the back of his head as he dressed for another important campus engagement so necessary for a young academic on the rise? Alas, her dreams were not to be very quickly realized, even after she and Carlton started talking with me. While Rebecca was able to access her Personal Myth without too much work, Carlton steadfastly denied his Personal Myth for years. Anticipation of the grievous disappointment of each sexual encounter with Carlton reinforced Rebecca's bodily resolve to eschew sex for as long as possible. This was her unconscious means of avoiding the painful consequences whenever her hope for tender love was rekindled and then extinguished, "quenched" as she came to say when she permitted her anger to speak directly, "by that gush of unconscionable sperm which had once flattered me so." But don't give up on Carlton and Rebecca yet. We will revisit them. Even couples whose mythology seems mismatched, whose sexual fantasies seem light years apart, who have totally lost intimacy, have a chance.

Natalie and Terence: Conversant in Their Personal and Gender Myths, Different in Their Desires

Terence is a gentle man who writes and illustrates children's books. His familiarity with his Personal Myth and his ability to reconnect with his childhood feelings have made him a professional success. This is of course rather rare. It is usually the contents of our Gender Myths which provide the energy for our professional lives, while the Personal Myth, when it is integrated, usually provides the surcease from childhood pain and the endless search for an escape from that buried pain necessary to feed lasting love. Terence, not surprisingly, is a Protector, one without a deep victim/accuser shadow. He simply desires the tender, caring quality of lovemaking in the Personal Myth. He wants to meld body and soul with his wife. Natalie is a powerhouse, a trial lawyer known for her eloquence and the lengthy oratory, ever on the tip of her tongue, with which she can transfix a courtroom or a dinner party or her adoring husband. In the Gender Myth, Natalie is a Fixer through and through, and she wants a Fixer hero in bed to ravish her. There is something about the Fixer in bed which wants to fix and be fixed. This same language is used by Franny, the heroine of Susanna Moore's book *In the Cut*:

> *"What are you doing?" I whispered. Even though I knew. It was as if I had to pretend that I did not know what he was about to do to me. Opening what was closed. Insisting. Fixing me. Unsealing me. At last. I who did not wish to belong to one man. I who did not wish to belong to anyone. I did not want to be fixed, to be held down, the closed opened, the heart broken.*

Natalie has a rage-filled Personal Myth. The daughter of a woman writer who never wanted to have children, Natalie is obsessed with hatred for her family, and ever ready to hurl vitriol at the merest mention of their names. She is perhaps slightly addicted to her hatred of her family and her past. She has absolutely no interest in the tenderness of the Personal Myth in her life except for her loving relationship with Terence and every member of his family. Every night, after a day of brilliant success in her Gender Myth, she and her Protector husband, whose adoration she returns, can talk comfortably in the language of the Personal Myth. Her ability with words is so great that she can talk brilliantly in any myth, and she loves Terence and is happy with their frequent intimate discourse. In bed, the relational and the sense of the generational hold no attraction for her. She is bored. Her interest in the tender love of the Personal Myth is less than zero, on the scale of pleasure somewhere just below a good professional shampooing. Fortunately, she and Terence have been able to come to an understanding that Bo, her lover down in Texas, is not a threat to their love. Terence, not tortured by his shadow, has always accepted this part of their marriage without the rancor one might expect of many Protectors, whose idea of intimacy would not likely include a third person.

Most couples whose Gender Myths work as these two do, and who can talk about their Personal Myths, have it made sexually. Natalie and Terence are an exception. Perhaps it's because her sexual healing requires an edge of violence to help her exorcise her anger at her family story. Terence was not yet able to expand his sexual repertoire to perform the kind of sex that Natalie craved; that might have healed her by allowing her to experience the heroic in herself in the most intimate setting, one almost as intimate as the parent-child relationship.

Life circumstances recently brought this particular situation to a crisis point. Natalie was offered a tenured post at a law school in Texas. She jumped at the opportunity. Not only was it an excellent job, but she could be near Bo, her lover, who was CEO of an oil drilling concern in Midland. On the other hand, Natalie recognized the friend she had in Terence, and she did not want a di-

vorce. In fact, what she asked was that if he didn't want to accompany her physically (he had already uprooted himself once for
her), he would wait for a year or two for her need for Fixer sex to
run its course. "Chances are, I'll want to come back, that I'll choose
you," she told him.

But this time Terence stood up to her. Although he wasn't yet
able to draw upon the Fixer hero in himself to summon the sexual
energy that she asked of him, he was strong enough to do some fixing of his own and to oppose her domination rather than just follow along. His first step was to say that he couldn't follow her
around, nor could he wait for her to make up her mind.
Interestingly, this was the beginning of the kind of energy that
Natalie needed from him, but for them it was too little too late, or
at least at the wrong time. In theory, given their copious resources
in the realms of the intimate discourse and Gender Myth suitabil-
ity, this couple had a good shot at staying together. In real life, they
went off amicably in opposite directions.

Sexual Healing: From Having Sex to Making Love

It is my belief that when a couple, through their work alone and
together or with a couples therapist, have come to know their own
mythology and that of their partner; the domains of their sexual
desire and the sexual energy of each myth, they possess the ultimate guide to making love. And making love—not just having
sex—is the highest achievement of two lovers over a lifetime.

Viewed in the context of the myths, sex is a healing and sacred rite between two people. Unlike the modern moralists who
have taught that sex is the surest road to hell, the earliest religious
traditions taught that sex was one of the paths to union with the
divine. Divinity is the state of wholeness in which opposites are

joined and become one. Men and women have the potential to experience the divine procreative forces of the universe during lovemaking.

Wholeness is still the highest goal of life. Understanding ourselves sexually is one of the essential requirements on the path to that goal. The sages knew that husband and wife could not explore the sexual realm without dealing also with their personal and spiritual issues, all the barriers to intimacy. We must learn to enjoy and develop our understanding of our sexual natures in order to develop intimacy with ourselves and others and to grow spiritually.

As we come to understand our own and our partner's mythology, we are able to access different kinds of desire—desire infused with the particular energies of each of the three myths. Long-time partners whose lovemaking is alive and well may make love in the Personal Myth one day when they both share a need to retreat to the sanctuary of Edenic sex, perhaps to escape from unhappy realities in the rest of their lives. That same couple might, after an unplanned period of abstinence, play out their wildest fantasies in some country inn to make up for the lapse. Or, in spontaneous appreciation of her man's Gender image, a woman might invite him to a "quickie" before she leaves for work as a way of explosively releasing the excitement their Gender Myths had built up in a particularly inspiring conversation the night before.

Chapter Eight

Broken Contracts

Falling in love is one of the headiest experiences offered us by the gods. When we finally recognize our true companion, we experience a deep sense of coming home to a place where we have always yearned to be. We connect first in the Gender Myth: here is the person who is making exactly the right statements about herself. A seamless blending of interests, lifestyles, and futures seems possible. Thus a conscious—we may even tell ourselves carefully considered—decision is made on the basis of the two Gender Myths. One man recently explained to me that he had decided to marry a woman he had recently met even though she would actually be Wife Number Three. When I expressed surprise that he had jumped so quickly—suspiciously quickly, I thought—he dismissed me. "No, this time I was very careful. This one meets all my criteria. The first one was the girl next door, and I just sort of fell into it. The second one was wild and exciting, completely the opposite of the first one, and I made the mistake of leaping into it for all the wrong reasons. This time I've found someone who's much more like me. We can talk about anything. We come from the same background. We have the same goals, the sex is good, and I want to take care of her." These two people were experiencing the sparks of the Gender Myth. But I was witnessing the beginning of a relationship between two people who did not understand their personal or shared mythology and would soon find that, over time, the natural evolution of events would introduce high-stakes situations in which more would be made clear, and they would swim or sink depending upon whether or not they wanted to do the work. At this moment in the relationship, each person was presenting only part of the picture. This is not an intentional deception. It occurs in just about every beginning, because each person's knowledge of his or her Personal Myth is not yet deep enough to permit the couple to see where each one has different needs and expectations that were implanted long ago. Each is giving the other what he himself needs in the Personal Myth and has no idea that this is entirely different from the partner's needs. The excitement of their matching Gender Myths has likely led them to jump into bed, where even more excitement is to be found initially. Part of the delight of a Gender Myth courtship is the element of surprise. Even those who have been searching for the perfect lover for some time feel pleasantly ambushed. The fact that they are caught off-guard seems to add to the evidence that fate has brought them together for the right reasons—as indeed it perhaps has. What the lovers don't realize at this point is that even if fate has handed them exactly the right person, the person who will make their childhood love story come out right, hard work lies ahead: the work of truly knowing and learning to love another person.

In courtship, the Sexual Fantasy Myth is particularly deceptive. There is a wonderful sexual tension engendered by the mystery of the other person. "Is this finally the person who will accommodate even my most unsavory, unspoken sexual needs?" each person wonders. The promise of courtship permits each of you to hold on to the belief that the impermissible is alive. In this phase, in fact, the impermissible, the unexpressed, is permanently alive. Even after an extended courtship, once you have committed to a long-term relationship, the sexual relationship inevitably changes. It is for this reason that what seems like a natural sexual dialogue during courtship will eventually evaporate unless there is exploration of both partners' mythologies.

But, alas, most of us do not dig so deeply until circumstances force us to. Lasting love rests precariously on the answers we get to a delicate set of questions in each of the three myths:

PERSONAL MYTH

- Do you love me?
- Do you really love me?
- Will you love me forever?
- Dare I trust you?
- Dare I trust myself?
- Can it be that I have finally found someone who understands my childhood pain?
- Will you dismiss my anxiety as foolish?
- Does rage chase you out the door?
- Must shame remain in hiding?
- Does sadness leave you cold?
- Do you have the qualities and specific capacities to heal my childhood wounds, and the strength of character to right the wrongs and injustices that were inflicted on me?
- Do you promise that I will not have to face again the disappointed child who never recovered from "their" broken promise to me, but who loves "them" still—or ought to?

GENDER MYTH

- Does my way of being in the world comfort and impress you?
- Do I make you feel secure?
- Does my sensitivity to all things that matter to you make you feel safe?

- Is sex as good for you as it is for me?
- Do you really enjoy making love that way?
- Is it true, as you seem to hint, that I can try what I have not asked any other lover to do with me?

These questions define and reflect the mythic basis of our quest for love. The answers we get, such as they are, persuade us to sign the contract. It would be one thing if this contract were outlined explicitly between two people as in a prenuptial agreement, with the texts and the terms of the myths spelled out and fully understood by each partner. But this is not the case in most liaisons. Even if the mythic contract is overt, the words you use, truly meant at the time, are not fully heard or understood by either party.

In the Personal Myth you promised to heal each other's childhood wounds and betrayals, which still cause pain and limitations for both of you. That healing would come about, you both unconsciously believed, through a love so complete that old wrongs and injustices would finally be compensated for and righted.

In the Gender Myth each of you promised to live up to your heroic ideals within the world while supporting one another to become your best selves.

In the Sexual Fantasy Myth each of you promised to explore the sexual realm with each other and to bring about the fulfillment of your respective sexual fantasies, longings, and desires.

No matter how earnestly and carefully you entered into your partnership, the breaking of these unstated, inchoate life contracts is inevitable in a real marriage. In my opinion, it is here—not at the altar—that marriage begins. The breaking of these contracts follows a predictable pattern. Rather than thinking of it as an ending, understand it as an opportunity. In Chinese, there is a pictogram called Fire in the Lake. This pictogram means Danger but also Opportunity.

Let us watch as Ginny and John play out this conflict. Ginny is a freelance portrait photographer with a flourishing business which brings in a surprising amount of money. John is an architectural school dropout, now a talented builder-carpenter with grand dreams. This is a second marriage for each, and each believed that he or she had thought long and hard about whether the marriage was right. Clearly, it worked well in the Gender Myth. Both had a similar aesthetic sensibility. Both were highly visual and enjoyed spending time together feasting their eyes on art exhibits, buildings, even people, and then discussing their opinions. John, an arch-Survivor, was delighted to find such a sensitive yet strong woman. Ginny was a Protector who had survived her parents' drawn-out divorce battle in childhood and then the lingering death of her mother from Alzheimer's disease. Sometimes she thought it curious that her mother had died so helpless, for when Ginny was a child her mother ruled the household, a vengeful, threatening queen, whose anger would suddenly strike for no reason. One of the worst things Ginny and her sisters remembered from their childhood was their mother becoming angry at them, often for reasons which were unclear, and "putting them in Coventry" which meant that she did not speak to them or even acknowledge them for days. During these times, she would only communicate with whichever girl was being punished through her husband. "Henry," she would say, "please ask your daughter if she would like some more meat." What Ginny never understood was her father's pained but silent complicity in this obvious cruelty. Why did he never speak up for her? Even as a nine-year-old, Ginny understood how damaging their mother's abandonment was for her and her sisters. Why did their loving Daddy ignore it, why did he always support Mother?

Perhaps he just gave up himself. After a year in which her parents' battles seemed to be becoming more and more vicious, and the fallout worse and worse, Ginny overheard a conversation which she would replay consciously or unconsciously for the rest of her life.

"You know the courts will give me custody, Henry, so there's no point fighting me on that one. I want the girls to stay in New York for the school year, so I think it would be rather difficult to share custody during the year. I can't have them flying down to Washington once a month. We can't afford it, and they'll never be able to do well in school if they're always moving around."

"But what about the summers? I can work my schedule so that I can rent a house nearer you all and see them for at least a month and some weekends."

Ginny was stunned. No one had even spoken to her about a divorce. Some of her friends' parents were divorcing and she felt very sorry for these friends as they shuttled back and forth from house to house or were hostages in their parents' ongoing battles. She walked through the living room where they were talking, but they stopped speaking and waited for her to leave again. So they were just going to do this. They weren't even going to tell her, ask her opinion, give her a choice. She climbed into her bed and held her stuffed monkey close, wondering what would become of her family.

When the girls finally were informed, all the arrangements had been made. There was no room for opinions or discussion. Daddy was moving to Washington. Mother and the girls were moving to a smaller apartment in New York.

On the day of the move, Ginny stood for a long time in the room she and her older sister had shared. She wondered whether she would ever be happy again. She hated the new apartment building which smelled of cooking, its hallways lit by guttering fluorescent lights. She hated the new apartment, and she hated her mother's boyfriends, but eventually the resilience of childhood came to her rescue, and one day she realized that she was going to survive. In retrospect she realized that it was probably many months after that day when she finally felt settled, but it seemed like the very next day that her sister came in to tell her that she had overheard their mother on the telephone. She and Mr. Simons were going to get married, and the whole family was going to make a new start—this time in Rochester, New York. Once again,

Ginny was seized with a visceral panic so deep that her stomach cramped and she thought she was going to throw up. "What's the matter?" her sister asked. "I think it'll be fun. Mr. Simons said it snows a lot up there, and it's right near Niagara Falls." Ginny couldn't even hear her over the words in her head: "I'm falling off the edge of the world and nobody even cares."

John, who had previously been married to a Fixer lawyer with a deep abusive shadow, connected right away to the gentle Protector in Ginny. He saw her compassion and sweetness, her gentle spirit which manifested itself as a love of animals and cooking and gardening. She was also deeply involved with a local group which ran a hotline for abused women. Clearly, this was the sweet yet strong woman he had always been searching for. Together they would build the happy home which had been stolen from him by his last wife, a woman who had never even cooked him a single meal in ten years.

In John, Ginny saw an accomplished man whose sense of beauty was augmented by what appeared to be a clearheadedness and a good business sense. She saw in him a deep loyalty and an ability to persevere. "If something is important for us as a couple," he seemed to be saying, "I won't rest until I have made things all right for us, and I will be there for you in a way no one else ever has." At last, she thought, here was a man who wanted to love her as she needed to be loved, who could carry some of the load, who wanted to talk to her. She was tired of always being out there fighting. Her first husband, a doctor, had never seemed to have time for her. They shared few interests, and somehow his compassion for his patients never seemed to extend to her. The strength and stability she had thought she had seen in him were illusions. They always seemed to be moving to a new residency, a new hospital, a new practice. She needed stillness and security to do her work. Over time, he had developed a drinking problem which had even threatened his career. Their sex life disappeared. When she found out that he had been involved with a succession of nurses at the hospital, she left him.

Like any couple newly in love, both John and Ginny ignored some of their partner's nuances, the darker sides where the rescuing heroes shaded into something quite different. Like all of us they had glimpses of things they didn't want to see and, during the bliss of early relationship, the excitement made this denial all too easy. Like many Survivors who enter into their martyr shadows, John could go over the line when he felt his loyalty had been violated by someone important, becoming exceedingly mean and virtually abandoning Ginny, his loyalty to her all but gone. And Ginny, the gentle healer, could go into rages when frightened or threatened, which terrified John.

For their first two years, Ginny and John lived happily in an old farmhouse they were restoring in Concord, not far from Walden Pond. Most weekends were spent painting and sanding and going to auctions to buy furniture and other objects with which to feather their nest. One thing they were clear on was that they wanted a home to grow old in together. John had lost his former home to his wife's Machiavellian schemes and when Ginny appeared on the scene he was still in mourning for it. Ginny understood his pain and knew that she could right this wrong. She, too, had lost too many homes. She had been robbed of too much safety by all the changes during her childhood, and as she struggled to make ends meet as an artist. She wanted to know that this was going to be her home forever. No more furniture being damaged during moving, no more packing up her possessions in boxes from the liquor store. Change, to Ginny, meant instability, unreliability, and loss of control—themes from her childhood to which she reacted now, as then, with both sadness and anger. Now there would be no more losses. She and John were going to build a life together and their home was their anchor. Ginny always believed in Archimedes' words: "Give me a place to stand and I can move the world." Even before they were married, John had touched her to tears by going to a lawyer and making out a will leaving her the house in case he died before they were married.

The first inkling that all was not right in their world came one

morning. Ginny was downstairs making instant coffee in the mi-
crowave. The house was still a shambles, but at least it was a quiet
one that day. She was tired of all the noise. The house seemed to
be filled with plumbers, electricians, and roofers, each of whom
seemed to be playing a different tape on his boombox, the volume
high enough to be heard over his particular power tool. But she
knew not to complain. They were nice boys and they were in the
process of building her home, the nicest house she had ever lived
in. John had made sure to finish first a small space in the attic
where she could conduct the business part of her profession and a
small area in the basement for her to use as a darkroom.

John came down, freshly showered, in an aura of soap—his
morning smell. Ginny wanted to melt into his arms and inhale
him. She was sensitive to his various scents which changed depending upon how much he sweated and his moods. There was a
spot at the center of his chest where she would often rest her nose
for minutes at a time. It was here that she could take a reading of
how he was feeling—whether he smelled worried or calm. John
fought a little against what seemed an almost intrusive understanding of him, but secretly also loved it.

He poured himself a cup of coffee, kicked a scrap of lumber
aside, and said with a cheery smile, "Oh, don't you love this?
There's something about a construction site that makes me want
to live this way forever!"

Ginny felt her stomach plunge. "What do you mean? I thought
you wanted a nest. I hate living this way, and I never want to
again."

"It's in my blood, Ginny. I'm a builder. I like to watch a project take shape and then when it's done I need another project to
bring to life."

"Project? This is our home. You can have as many projects as
you want, but home is home. You promised." She was truly fearful
now. Her hands trembled and she had to hold her coffee cup in
both hands.

"Don't worry," he said, coming over and enfolding her. "If we ever sell this place it'll be for a lot of money and we'll get an even better place. You've seen what I can do."

"John," she said, pulling away from him. "You're changing everything. I don't want a better place. This is our home. This is where we were married. This place is us." She began to cry.

John wished he hadn't broached the subject. Probably she had PMS, but it was true, he was beginning to get restless. This house was going to be his best yet. He knew he could get a lot of money for it, and one thing he knew about himself was that he could always create another house. Didn't Ginny understand that this need to create was part of who he was? Was she going to take away from him the very thing he needed to survive, his passion, the way he had always survived?

John knew that he had to keep on the move—not necessarily physically, although that had often been the easiest way to respond to the feelings inside him. He just knew that change was vital. He had watched as his father's steadfastness eroded the security of his childhood. "The Slacker" was how his mother had referred to her husband. "Bill, why can't you see that you're stuck in a dead-end job, and dare to move on? Jim Horne left that company five years ago for just that reason and now he's a VP. Don't you have any ambition at all? Even if not for yourself, what about for the children and me?" John loved his gentle father. It was from him that he had learned the value of loyalty: John's father had stayed on with his firm out of loyalty, even though he could have made more money elsewhere. Certainly he was not putting his family in serious financial jeopardy by doing so, but he failed in what he and John's mother had set out to create in life. John realized that his mother, whom he didn't particularly like because of her vanity and her assaults upon her husband, had a point. Hard work, ambition, and pressing on had a value, while staying in one place could be a sort of death.

Ginny went out to the garden, where the first of the bulbs she had planted in the fall were starting to show. It had given her such joy to overspend on her garden, knowing that, at last, she would be able to watch the plants for decades. Wasn't he doing to her exactly what he said Sandy had done to him? Threatened his home? He had promised. . . . Why had he left her the house so soon after they met if he hadn't truly understood? Was he just a liar? She was seized by an icy fear. Without realizing it, she was re-living the physical sensations she'd felt in childhood as her parents battled over their Martinis in the living room, times when she had huddled just out of sight, watching and listening to decisions being made about her life, in terror that she might just be discarded. Then, and now, she felt as though she were being abandoned at the edge of the earth and was about to fall off. She couldn't shut her thoughts off. They tumbled over and over in her mind. From time to time she felt dizzy and realized that she wasn't even breathing.

John had a double Martini at lunch that day. Ginny had withdrawn into her office and he supposed that peace had been restored. He certainly wasn't about to go check. Better just to be quiet and let it pass. It would take a year to finish the house and by then maybe he wouldn't want to sell it. The only thing was that he was worried about the money. They were spending a lot by doing everything properly. He knew he had told Ginny that they might as well, since it was to be their permanent home, but money was something that was never far from his mind. The worst fights he could remember in his childhood were scenes with his mother berating his father for mishandling money and his father's stubborn silence. One time when he asked his father why they were fighting his father had just looked ashamed. At that moment, his mother had walked into the room, obviously having overheard the question and explained that Dad was going to send them to the "poorhouse." John could remember that moment perfectly. To this day whenever someone mentioned the word "poorhouse," he could see the place with long plank tables and alms bowls that he had imagined that day. Throughout his childhood he was torn between his mother's legitimate desires for more for the family and his father's honorable fidelity. John, while never truly poor, never felt he had quite enough. He certainly wasn't going to allow Ginny's sentimentality to jeopardize their safety.

After that, both Ginny and John backed off the subject of selling the house. John still thought about it and thought from time to time of an even better house he could design, one which would work better for the lifestyle they were developing together. Ginny tried the best she could to quell her fears about falling off the edge of the earth, and spent time entertaining potential clients, hoping to find new projects for her husband. Clearly, that was the issue. He just needed to have projects, and as long as he did he'd leave their nest alone.

Ginny did manage to find him some projects. A cousin of hers in New York City asked him to help her renovate an apartment, and Ginny even contributed her divorce settlement to helping John buy an old schoolhouse which he planned to restore and resell. Ginny threw herself into building her own business. If only she could outrun him, she felt she could make enough for them to be financially secure without selling the house. But how could she do that if she had to live with insecurity and chaos? She was beginning to feel nervous and tired all the time.

For a year, the subject of selling the house didn't resurface, but there were other fights, and each had an eerily familiar feel. "You don't want me to feel secure," she shouted at him in frustration one day when he mentioned that he had just read that real estate prices were on the upswing again. "You seem to forget that there are two of us in this marriage and that one of us needs to feel grounded while the other only pretended that he did."

"I do need to feel grounded," John replied, his jaw clenched tight, refusing to meet her eye. "But you don't understand that sameness is death to me. My creative energies are drained when I'm asked to stand still."

One day Ginny came home to find a new shed going up next to their garden.

"What's this?" she asked, already feeling unaccountably upset.

"I'm building you a Greek Revival garden shed with columns

in front and fancy moldings around the windows and doors. You're
going to love it. You needed a better place for your tools."

Ginny reeled from the feeling of another decision being made about her life without her consent. She was momentarily speech-less, but only momentarily. "I don't believe this!" she cried, fling-ing to the ground the bag of groceries she was carrying. "First of all, thanks a lot for discussing it with me. Thanks for blocking all the afternoon sunlight from the garden and thanks for spending money we don't have!"

"It's only going to add value to the house," John said.

"*Value?* I don't want to add value to the house so that we are forced to sell it!" She ran into the house and got into bed, sobbing with an all too familiar sense of betrayal and outright terror. John was sweet to her that night and apologized for his "overenthusi-asm." After that, each of them tried to stay off topics that could upset the other. For John it was not difficult to keep his thoughts to himself to avoid upsetting Ginny, but Ginny saw with increas-ing unease that he was more and more inside himself. Where once he had seemed so proud of her around other people, he now kept silent. More frightening still was that he rarely looked at her any-more with his eyes dancing with affection. John seemed to be in retreat.

Then, as they were on an airplane headed to London for a va-cation, John suddenly turned to her over his drink and said, "Oh come on, Ginny, wouldn't you like to sell the house for a lot of money, bank a lot and build something smaller? I mean the place is a cash cow and several people have asked me if I'd sell it. It would give us more money to do the things we like to do. We could travel more, you could have a better studio."

Ginny looked at him and burst into tears. "How can you talk about selling our home, and especially how can you do it now when we're supposed to be going off to have fun?" For the next two days she could barely bring herself to speak to him. London went by in a blur. She could hardly sleep as she thought of packing and mov-ing yet again, and the chaos of building or restoring another house.

The loss would be too much. She kept thinking of driving out of her driveway for the last time, saying goodbye to her garden. Worst of all, she felt powerless to change John's mind.

John did not appreciate Ginny's reaction. Now he felt truly stymied. Hadn't he made a living as a builder for years? Ginny was making a lot of money, but he wanted to have something more in the bank so that they could have more fun together. Couldn't she damn well see that he was doing this to bring them *more* security? He was trying to make their life better the best way he knew, and he knew how better than she did.

"Ginny, you're just too pie-in-the-sky about all this," he exploded one night.

"And you're a liar," she retorted, bursting into tears. "You told me that you wanted a home, that Sandy had stolen your home and that what you most needed was a nest and you wanted that nest with me, but you sold me a bucket of suds!" She burst into tears and ran upstairs, slamming the bedroom door hard behind her. Enraged as she was, a deep sadness came over her as if someone had died. She wasn't going to let this happen. She was going to be heard! She flung open the bedroom door and ran downstairs. John was watching television as if nothing was going on. She snapped it off and stood in front of the set. "You listen to me, goddamn it! I married you because I loved you and I thought you loved me. Now you're trying to kill me and you're not going to get to." She was red-faced, shrieking. John had seen this demon side of her emerge only once before, when she was very angry—and justifiably so, he'd thought at the time—with one of her sisters. "You've done nothing but lie to me about who you are and about this house. You let me put my money and my time and my love into this place on false pretenses. You were happy to take my cash and tell me that we wouldn't have to sell the house, and now you're telling me I can have my cash back and more when we sell the house. Well, guess what, buddy, I was trying to buy my home, my security. If it was the money I'd cared about I would have put it in the stock market. But

you lied to me, you made assumptions and robbed me of choice. I
could kill you!"

John sat horrified and immobilized. A brief recollection of one night when his mother had yelled at his father flittered through his mind, but he couldn't take his eyes off his wife. Couldn't she stop screaming at him? All she was now was a voice, a Fury. "I didn't marry this *voice*," he thought. "I don't even recognize this woman." A sense of recognition, and even of inevitability, overcame him. He had been here too many times before. His Ginny had been transformed into a Wife, generic and vicious. He moved to pick up the remote control. What was there to say? All he wanted to do was escape this harangue, which he was feeling as a tight band around his chest. Maybe he was going to have a heart attack.

Seeing him go to turn the television back on was the final straw for Ginny, whose pulse was pounding so hard she could barely see. She leapt at him, prised open his fist, and threw the remote across the floor, watching with satisfaction as it spilled its delicate circuitry. As an afterthought she went over and stomped on it. He'd never use that TV again to shut her out!

That night John slept in the guest room. He could hear Ginny sobbing next door, but this time he wasn't going to cross the hall to comfort her as he had always done in the past. She was a witch, she was possessed. He tossed around most of the night, voices crying out in his head. He wanted to cry, he wanted to go across the hall and shake her senseless. Maybe he'd just burn the house down, get the dogs out and burn it. The house was all she cared about anyway. To hell with her! There were other women around. He'd show her. Talk about buying a bucket of suds. He'd thought he'd married a sweet, compassionate woman and instead she had lied to him about who she was. She wasn't a strong, balanced woman who could heal him. She was selfish and evil. She was a killer inside—no better than his last wife, just different.

The next morning he left the house early and went to a coffee shop for breakfast. When he came home that night, Ginny had made his favorite meal of lamb shanks and white beans and opened two good bottles of red wine. She hoped that John didn't remember her words too clearly and that he, too, would want to make up. With luck, some good lovemaking by the fireplace—one of their most romantic spots—would dispel the bad feelings. Even so, she was sad inside as she worked in her kitchen in her dream house, waiting for her dream husband to come home to her. Was it really all going to disappear?

As John came up the driveway, he was comforted by the lights of the big old farmhouse and the smoke rising from both chimneys. Of course he wanted a cozy nest, it was just that he was getting the urge to sell and move on. What did Ginny want? He had promised that he would put the next one in her name, and that they would never sell it unless she wanted to. Couldn't she understand that he had their best interests at heart? He was beginning to feel angry with her. Safety and security were something you carried inside. Last night was exceptionally horrible, but he was prepared to attribute it to hormones. The trouble was that Ginny was changing. She was beginning to act like a weepy child, not the strong woman he had married. Well, he couldn't let her get at him. He'd just go into his shell and try to avoid conflict from now on. He'd try to do it her way and let her pay the price that went with his no longer having his heart in it.

After dinner Ginny suggested they go sit by the fire, but John said he was tired and wanted to go to bed. Disappointed, Ginny followed him. She still wanted to make love. But, for the first time in their life together, she was unable to arouse him sufficiently. "I'm sorry," he said, "I've just had a long day. Maybe we can try again tomorrow." He knew he wanted nothing more than to hold her and feel her body, but he wasn't about to make that move.

In truth, Ginny herself wasn't feeling much in the mood for lovemaking, but she felt she ought to try. Lovemaking had always been good for them, and it had always brought them back together when some situation had caused them to drift apart. Now she just felt sad and empty. Where had their love gone?

Things didn't improve very much over the next months. John was having difficulty becoming erect. "Maybe it's just approaching middle age," he joked one day. "I'm just not as interested in sex as I used to be. It's like that part of my life isn't so important anymore."

But his lack of desire wasn't a joke to either of them. By now the shadows were deepening around the marriage. Both of them wondered whether they should just give up.

John and Ginny chose therapy over divorce. With some couples who seek therapy, one partner or the other, or both, have drifted—or been driven—into a wasteland of deep despair. They are weary from their struggles, and lack any sexual desire whatsoever. Hope of recovery is all but abandoned.

John and Ginny were in terrible straits. Entrenched in anger, hurt, and melancholic disappointment, they seemed bewildered about "how their differences had come to this." They feared they would not make it. I knew within the first hour that they would. When all the fancy criteria are set aside, there is one question that matters: Do they want to? Ginny did. John did. Underneath the question—asked and answered more indirectly than directly—is a more crucial inquiry: is love's fire completely extinguished? Embattled partners do not want to be rushed to answer. It is bad politics and, even worse, bad strategy. It gives the enemy a military edge. Teasing the territory gently, what one discovers in those that will make it back is not that they do not love, but that they feel unloved. Helping them recognize the distinction, at the right moment, breathes hope into the embers and speeds the pace of change.

The turning point, when the couple *knows* they will make it, occurs at different times and along different routes. It was a good ten or twelve sessions into the therapy before John and Ginny knew. This is not the place to chart them. However, I will lightly skim the ground I covered with Ginny and John, a couple typical of those who choose their partners well, find themselves off course, and use Myth and Shadow Work to get back on track, more soundly committed than they were at the blissful outset.

Ginny and John had made fortuitous matches in two of the three mythic realms. Ginny, the adult woman, admired and was sexually drawn to John, the adult man, no less than he was attracted to her. What each did in the world; the artistic contribution each made, their high professional standards—their gender identities—enriched their lives and their love. Ginny's Protector Hero and John's Survivor waltzed with a grace neither had known in their short-lived first marriages, until their shadows took over the floor, bumping, tripping, and bruising each other. Although the sound of the music changed from Waltz to Danse Macabre, the demons' dance, in the privacy of their hearts they continued to hear the original music and rhythms of a gender choice that spiced their love.

That they had also chosen wisely and well in the sexual realm, never doubting each other's wish to give and readiness to receive their most precious treasures of body and imagination, became clear soon into the therapy. Why they stopped making love made no sense to either of them when I pressed them on the subject. Some couples, like Ginny and John, just slip into withdrawal without meaning to; some martyrs like John withhold desire in stubborn refusal to concede. When I knew that Ginny could follow my lead, and that John would allow her to, I said, "Ask him if in this long drought he ever seriously considered an affair. Ask him if he prefers another sexual partner. Ask him if he no longer loves your body. Ask him if he's forgotten the best sex you had together." Nodding more vigorously with each question, Ginny gasped with the last one, letting out a screech, part scream, part explosive release. John leaped to her side and threw his arms around her, jerking his head this way and that in search of whatever it was that threatened her, ready to smash it. Satisfied of her safety, he exploded as a parent does at a child who has stepped off a curb on a busy street. "You damned asshole. There is no one but you. There is no one like you." Then he cried, released Ginny, and slumped into this chair, as one does in defeat.

It wasn't until later that Ginny revealed that her screech had not been a scream but something resembling an orgasm. She told this to John after a night of lovemaking, not, as some romantics would have it, on the night of the just-described "Event," but on the night of another session and another event, which came weeks later, their abstinence sustained in the interim.

John and Ginny were abstinent, but not for lack of desire, as we have just seen. Their resolute choking off of any appetite for love was willed by nothing less than two broken hearts. Their cravings, alive and well but buried within them, were smothered under the weight of revisited childhood disappointment. From the first "Event" (our playful name for Ginny's "involuntary orgasm" and John's declaration of love), they knew that I knew they would be lovers again soon. But they were not ready yet. No words were needed; more work had to be done.

In this work, every incident even remotely related to "house as nest versus house as opportunity for bigger nest" took on a High-Stakes status. The heroes were ever ready to take up arms, and did, on every occasion. Their shadows, revolting and fearful, dominated their lives. Their first respite came when I put the Heroic Modes Chart (see page 77) into their hands. Each felt explained, understood, and validated. When a couple comfortably embraces the idea of the heroes' shadows and quickly welcomes the mirror, as this couple did, it is a good sign. This work went well. I think they sensed that a breakthrough was imminent, and that they were eager to become lovers again.

It has happened often in my work. When both partners trust enough to revisit their childhood vulnerability, and tell the stories behind their Personal Myths, and can listen compassionately to each other, it is an occasion for a "peak experience" of stupendous relief, learning, reconnection, and the release of sexual hungers. Ginny and John did not disappoint this book's prediction. After their second honeymoon—better than the first, they insisted— they settled in for about six months of work and consolidated their gains, which were especially noticeable when they developed the capacity to repair themselves after retrenching in some of the old ways.

John and Ginny are like many couples who start out believing that the contracts they have made will be long-lasting. Their first contract, the Gender Myth, was made on the basis of strong, mutual attraction. They shared a dream for living in the country. They had high aesthetic interests and each admired the other's career choices. John was deeply moved by Ginny's artistic photographs, the ones she did for art's sake. And he thought her commercial photography, at which she was extremely successful, was clever. When he discovered her talents, he sighed with pleasure. He made a point of noticing these talents, for they enhanced what he already loved about her physical attributes. Ginny believed that John had left architecture school for good reasons. He was as much interested in building what he designed as the designs themselves. He was a craftsman par excellence. When his clients praised his work, she felt it throughout her mind and body, "a full-body experience," as she put it. "This is a man who meets my intellectual and artistic expectations."

Like many couples, though not all, they sailed through the steps in courtship that lead up to the making of the gender contract.

1. The initial archetypal encounter
2. Making the heroic presence known
3. The desire to know the other's gender ideal
4. Displaying one's own personal gender ideal
5. The seduction poem: "Come live with me and be my love"
6. The first sexual encounter
7. Agreeing to the gender contract

Theirs, like most marital contracts, were less clear than they thought. We have not invented the expression "blinded by love" for nothing. They were more "certain" than they should have been. The pleasures of sex and each other's companionship left them in confused innocence. They engaged in a blind confederacy, an agreement to ignore certain undertones and nuances. Ginny knew that John was capable of a stubbornness on some things that left those he cared about helpless and at times enraged at his immovability. John had seen hints of what was to come when Ginny's customary sweet temper was transformed into frightening rage.

Although they had no basis in courtship to discover each other's childhood stories, each sensed that the other truly understood what had gone wrong in their own families, and was sympathetic to the needs for love that each brought with him or her from those family experiences. The contract they made between their Personal Myths was more or less propitious, but as with most couples, it was not terribly well-informed.

In the first months of marriage, they saw only the light side of each other's heroes and adored what they saw. However, one seemingly trivial disagreement raised the specter of what was to come— the dark side of the hero. John had trusted a client to pay for his time to design and build some cabinets. The client reneged, denying that he had made the agreement John thought he had. For days, John sulked. He sank deeper and deeper into thought, rejecting Ginny's solutions to the problem, which he knew made sense. This client was an old friend. John walked away from the project refusing to be paid for the work he had done. John and Ginny fought about this decision. "We need the money," she insisted. "Why must I pay for Peter's dishonesty and your martyrdom?" This fight, which ended in a stalemate, was the occasion of the onset of mythic turbulence.

Mythic turbulence usually begins with censorship: "Not that, *this*!" Each player says, in effect, "Be the hero that I would be in this crisis." Such censorship is tantamount to saying "I do not value the hero you are showing yourself to be." Now the partners feel betrayed. "I believed that you married the hero I am," each says. John and Ginny got through this difficulty as they usually did. "Let's stop this nonsense. Let me take you to bed." After lovemaking, Ginny's anger would subside and John's spirits would rise.

The Mythic Struggle Is Inevitable and Necessary

I am convinced that struggle of the kind John and Ginny had begun goes with the territory. We commit to love, every last one of us needing to grow, whether or not we want to. We enter the adult love relationship as incomplete human beings. In the language of this book, we each have shadows that have to be faced. The function of a committed love relationship, then, is to provide an arena within which this growth takes place. Necessary as it is, most of us enter this arena kicking and screaming, ready to do battle, insisting on holding on to who we are. For those who get through the ritualized struggle, love grows. It is as if the love-battle itself "grows us up." Thus, it is inevitable and necessary that the initial love contract, binding for life, as we pledged in the marriage ceremony, is threatened or broken as we get to know who our partners really are, and as we discover that the lover's promise that we would be allowed and encouraged to express who we really are is not so easy to fulfill.

Three Arenas for Struggle

Although we may think the fights lovers have are about money, or how to spend their vacations, or about raising children, the fights that count in the making or breaking of the initial mythic love contracts are about something else, something deeper. The fights that count are about identity, the nature of love, and how to make love as we define these crucial matters in our three myths.

Why is love such a riddle? Why does it seem to get so damned messy? Why does conversation that starts out so simple turn to babble, or anger, or utter despair? Why do our fights seem to happen the same way when, as we see one coming, we want so much to stop it, and not to go the way of the Vicious Cycle?

The Vicious Cycle

If there is or ever has been a couple, serious about growing their love relationship and about expressing the self fully in that relationship, who did not develop a version of their own vicious cycle, I haven't met them. The Vicious Cycle is the battleground in which our three mythic heroes state and fight over their claims about and demands for love.

Elsewhere in this book, I have called the vicious cycle the couple's ritual impasse. Its features are familiar to all couples. An event takes place or a subject is raised that strikes a chord. The partners engage, disagree, have a spat, and set it aside. But it happens again. And again. Spats become disagreements, become arguments, become fights, become pitched battles. If some couples never bring it to the level of pitched battle, the features of the impasse are the same as for those who do: a darkly disturbing conversation which is carried along by hauntingly familiar themes around which the partners take stubborn positions that go nowhere except into escalating runaway. The circularity, the failure ever to reach any resolution, is wearying. Later it becomes ominous, disturbing.

Broken contracts occur over struggles and disappointments that take place in all three mythic arenas. The most profound disappointment is the one that takes place in the realm of the Personal Myth.

The Battle of Personal Myths

The battle of Personal Myths is a struggle over whose definition of reality will prevail. The problem is that in these struggles, there are always two equally valid definitions of reality. It all begins with each of the two adult lovers experiencing something in their environment that invokes the childhood experience of betrayal and disappointment, only neither sees it this way. What they do know is that they see some aspect of reality which they define as a threat. Reality, therefore, is the way "I" see it. Every adult carries within himself a set of betrayal themes, the very themes that prompted him to create and tell the childhood story. They are the same themes that led her to choose a particular partner to heal the betrayal. Thus, these themes have a special and tragic power.

We would have no problem if every time something in current reality invoked our childhood story of betrayal our partner was the completely mature and perfect lover who would be there to support us. Intimate discourse breaks down and escalates into vicious cycles when each partner is asking such maturity and perfection of the other at the same time. This is impossible, of course. Broken discourse follows. Each partner thinks he or she is communicating clearly with the other when, in fact, they are not at all. Their *text*, their communication of what they believe to be rational thoughts, feelings, and representations, is driven by an unformulated *subtext*. Until we tell our stories in a context that supports dialogue, this all-important subtext remains unknown, out of reach, and not part of the conversation.

The Scene: A couple has been at a dinner party. Driving home, and later in the living room, and finally in the bedroom, they carry on a conversation that begins in innocence and ends in disaster.

"Mabel has a way of ignoring John, who seems crushed when he's dismissed," the woman says.

The man says, "I see her completely differently. She busts her ass trying to please everybody in the room, her husband included."

The stage is now set for an argument they have had many times before. It isn't about Mabel and John, necessarily, but about the themes embedded in the situation—different themes for each, as we already see. They will argue over whose take on reality is the real one. They will escalate; perhaps have a rip-roaring fight. They will end up not speaking, occupying the far reaches of their bed or indeed separate rooms. Here is a fragment from one of these familiar battles.

WOMAN:
You're not listening to me. Damn it! I need to be heard.
Subtext: Mother never listened. She thought only of herself. She never saw me. In me she saw her own image.

MAN:
What is it you expect of me? I've given my all just now as always.
Subtext: Can I ever do enough?

WOMAN:
Your "all"? "Always"? You don't know how to give. Not what I need.
Subtext: What I need is my older sister, who showed me how to fight for my right to be heard. When she died, I lost the only ally I ever had in that family.

MAN:
You don't know the first thing about receiving, that's your problem.
Subtext: Mother . . . you're drunk again. I'm scared. I don't know what to do.

These themes, the spoken text and the unspoken subtext, confound the couple's attempts to communicate and converse about what might have seemed a trivial event. The stances they take when they negotiate their definitions of reality are heavily invested with their own experiences in disturbingly similar realities in childhood. In their subtexts, the child in each is crying out for his or her childhood story to be known and screaming for rescue, but finding only the errant, truant hero. As their cries and laments get louder, they escalate into the runaway known as the vicious cycle.

Recognizable Themes and Actions

Our stories are plots that often, though not always, begin with the commonplace. Whether commonplace or horrendous, they are always sensationalized by the child's imagination and sense of powerlessness. The stories are built around familiar themes: abandonment, not being listened to, humiliation, neglect, selfishness, possessiveness, seduction, indifference, and failure, among many others, and the characters in the stories are guilty of equally familiar actions, taken too strongly, or too weakly, or not taken at all: criticism, attack, blame, and contrariness; silence, disengagement, judgment, placation, and indecisiveness; impatience, terrorism, and perfectionism.

The conversations which the unnamed couple above, and John and Ginny, have when an event or theme invokes their childhood stories are doomed until the stories are finally brought to light, understood, and told to the partner.

The apparent rejection of our love stories, our partner's failure to come forth as our "inner child's" rescuer, and the rebuffing of our own adult heroic offering, take place within the context of these doomed conversations. Wanting better words, the couple concludes: "We simply cannot communicate. We are not on the same screen. Our differences are irreconcilable."

I would put it differently. I would say that their myths are not speaking to one another. They have not told their stories in an environment of mutual understanding, empathy, and curiosity. They are unaware that in high-stakes situations they begin speaking in tongues, in the language of their own myths, and that if their partner is in a similar place, they are not speaking the same language;

that when our best offerings of heroic love are rejected, our demons
enter the room to cast their shadows on all that is taking place
there, and that when two demons are in the room at the same time,
doing the Dance of Shadows, productive communication is simply
not possible. I would further say that if the couple does not find a
way to correct the course they are on, they could enter dangerous
waters, or crash the relationship on unseen shoals. Couples who
fail to correct the course of these doomed conversations come to
the most despairing proclamations of the love story: "It has happened again. I am not loved!" The melancholic disappointment
that gripped the child in the original love story now visits the
adult, with perhaps even greater consequence. For where there is
little hope, rage or other extremes of behavior take root and grow,
and lead to new betrayals.

The Battle of Gender Myths

The vicious cycle of the wars of the Gender Myth heroes looks no
different on its face from the ritualized turbulence stirred by the
wounded children skirmishing in the domain of the Personal
Myth. Conversation between the sparring adult Gender Heroes is
doomed in the same way, because the partners are steeped in their
own mythologies and speaking different languages without being
aware of it. Once again, their frustration at being unable to communicate what they mean to say, or of having their proud heroic
voices censored, silenced, dismissed, or cruelly criticized, sends
them into a screaming spiral.

The difference between the couple's battles in the realms of
the Personal and Gender Myths lies in the shadows associated with
each of these myths. The shadows of the Personal Myth derive
from a curious contradiction: beneath the sadness and disappointment at having been betrayed by one's partner is an accompanying sense of responsibility. It is the same internal voice which piped

up in childhood and said, "If they don't love me, it must be my fault, not theirs. I must be unlovable."

As you may recall, the hurt child reacted to betrayal along a continuum from less to more serious: from anger to rage, sadness to grief, anxiety to fear, and guilt to shame. The stronger the childhood reaction, the more accusatory and self-accusing the adult shadow. However, the disappointed child which holds forth from deep within the adult psyche because her or his partner has failed to keep a promise can be quite vicious if rage was the childhood reaction. If the child's reaction tended instead toward sadness, the adulthood reaction is more likely to be similarly grieving rather than enraged.

The wars of the Gender Myths tend to be more explosive, involving as they do the rejected adult hero with all his or her resources. The shadows of the adult heroes may not be deeper than the child's, but they are able to scream louder through their adult voices and actions. The storms the shadows of these adult heroes create can be taken to volcanic levels. At times the heroes cry out for love so frantically they do their partners physical harm. These shadow dances can become even more frightening when they combine the forces of the Personal and the Gender Myths; when the grieving, fearful, enraged, or shamed shadow from the child's myth joins the abandoner shadow, the abuser shadow or the victim/accuser shadow of the adult gender hero. In situations which invoke both shadows, we often see a level of mythic turbulence that threatens the very meaning of the relationship.

Most partners' shadow dances never reach this level. Nevertheless, when the turbulence comes to rest after yet another ritualized escalation, the dance of warring myths creates a theater of difference, a sense of alienation, a degree of despair and disappointment, all of which disastrously reduces desire or destroys it entirely. However, this is not always the case.

Some years ago, I saw a woman, Clare, who came to me with a problem which seems to answer some questions people ask about the loss or preservation of passion in long-term relationships.

Clare had been divorced for ten years. She was in a new relationship which she felt compelled to take seriously. Her pledge,
made after her divorce, that she would never remarry, had been
kept. She'd had several relationships over the years, none serious.
George was different. Unlike the others—Clare was so straight-
forward about her attractiveness to men that one simply accepted
it as fact—George's proposal shook up her convictions.

Clare was a top-notch executive secretary. She had always
done well and fully expected she'd continue to be rewarded for her
instantly recognizable intelligence, her unflappable reliability, and
her management skills. Nowadays she would be in the executive
office herself, I'm sure. For the first time in years, she felt antsy
about her life, which, she said gratefully, always ran smoothly. She
was a still-youthful forty-three. Her eldest child was in her first year
of college and her son, a high school senior, was thinking of col-
leges away from home. Maybe this was a good time to make a
change herself.

Clare had always taken care of herself. When she divorced
Roger, her former husband, and, yes, it was on her initiative, she
asked very little of him financially. "Help out with the kids," she'd
told Roger. "As for me? I'd rather not be beholden. The very idea
of it sticks in my craw." But now this sweet guy, George, had come
into her life. George has some family money. "He doesn't flash it;
actually, it doesn't mean much to him," Clare says. He uses it only
to balance losses from his small publishing company—a haven he
has provided for talented poets and undiscovered fiction writers.
"He is mother, father, mentor, and guide to these artists. They love
him. I think I do, too," she told me. George, she said, worshipped
her. He'd never married because he had never gotten around to it.
He had had relationships, but Clare was different from all the rest,
he insisted. "You think it's all physical," he'd said. "Well, it isn't. I
find you the most accessible and still the most infinitely un-
plumbable person I've ever met. You've made me come alive. I'm
grateful. I'd like to spend the rest of my life with you." How could
she not be seduced?

"My problem," she said, "is whether to share a secret with George." She enjoys her sex with George, but not this nor any sexual relationship she'd ever had, "comes close to what it was . . . and still *is* with Roger."

"Is?"

"Yes, we're still lovers. Ten years divorced and we are still lovers."

Here is the story she told. Roger was ruthlessly ambitious. Success, power, achievement at any cost, at whomever's expense, fascinated him. Every triumph was a lark, a source of pleasure. He made no apologies for this or for his total disinterest in the caretaking of his children, of Clare, or of anybody else. He enjoyed his children's achievements but the rest was a bore. All this came to light in the first five years of her marriage. She wrote him off as a real co-parent and as a partner, but not as a lover. I was sure I could punch holes in this story, but I would have been doing it for my own reasons. Clare was not asking me to. So I inquired about her lovemaking with Roger before helping her decide what to do with George and her secret.

It became clear to me that Clare was a Survivor with a relatively benign shadow. Roger was a Fixer who strongly denied the relevance of his childhood story. The force and drive of his shadow to conquer and abuse, to destroy altogether if necessary, any obstacles in his path to glory was one reason Clare wanted a divorce. Feeling the depth and darkness of his shadow, she decided to walk away from it. However, I suspect, that same force and drive was what turned her on sexually. Survivor that she was, she needed to contain the experience, to set a boundary—in this case, the *Same Time Next Year* schedule. But because her shadow wasn't deep, and didn't lead her into martyrdom or self-abandonment, she was able to allow herself the enjoyment of this exciting sex.

From what she said, it was clear that their Sexual Fantasy Myths spoke to one another in a dialogue that built excitement as it went through unpredictable dips and turns, each more surprising and sexually evocative than the last. At every new twist in the story they told, Clare felt even more in control, although Roger was the mastermind behind it all. She couldn't say how he accomplished this. That was part of the mystery that—anticipated in the days leading up to their next tryst, and then more fully realized "when my flesh met his"—was the centerpiece of their sex.

This was not the first time I'd faced a dilemma of the kind Clare unapologetically put on the edge of my table, where it teetered for the three sessions she had allotted. No, she did not want a longer course of therapy. Yes, she felt she could manage what guilt there might be, should she decide to continue her trysts with Roger. No, she was not concerned that sex with George would be compromised. Had she not already mastered the art of playing out in her mind the more exciting scenes with Roger as a way of warming up to lovemaking with other men she'd let have a serious place in her life? "But one you'd be married to? Look closely at that one, Clare," I told her. "Yes, the deception and betrayal would be a problem for me," she admitted. "Despise me, if you wish. But I could argue that the trade-off would work for George, sexually and in my growing love for him." At the close of the third consult Clare agreed that the "moral face-off" we'd had had helped. Her final decision, she said, would come later. Perhaps she would resolve things by not marrying George after all. This was unfair to me, she said, because she knew that from her depictions of his character I had come to like this man George, whom I'd never met. "I must say," I told her at the door, "I seem more conflicted on your behalf than you do." Her last words remain with me as a reminder of the arrogance of the power therapists too often assume. "Therapists are mere mortals," she said smiling. "Only God knows everything."

In the end, Clare did marry George. Asked to bet on the outcome, I would say this: At least one more time Clare did rendezvous with Roger in their own version of *Same Time Next Year*. Her intent was to wean him, rather than drop him abruptly. She came to see that George's love and a different kind of lovemaking were what she'd wanted after all. I know none of this, of course. Perhaps I'm still playing God.

These two factors, good sexual dialogue of matching Sexual Fantasy Myths and the ability to preserve the mystery of sex, is what fulfills the contracts made in this mythic realm. It is rare, but I believe altogether possible, for people in long-term relationships in which the contracts in the other two myths are under siege, though not fatally, to hold their relationships together on the strength of the match of their Sexual Fantasy Myths. For most couples, this is not the way it goes. For most, the erosions in the other two realms, under pressures wrought by disappointment and despair, sweep away the lust and passion of sex.

To return to Ginny and John: here is a couple who have broken their unstated contracts in all three myths. Let us review each one.

In the Personal Myth, both John and Ginny needed safety, but each had a different definition of safety. For Ginny, safety meant a nest where she would be able to hunker down and stay forever. This had not been granted her in childhood, and she had understood this to be part of her deal with John. In fact, she believed that they had agreed on it in advance. A home together seemed to be the centerpiece of their future. John too needed safety, and a home was important to him, but for him safety was also freedom from financial worry. When Ginny opposed him, two things happened: first, he re-experienced the childhood insecurities he had spent a lifetime trying to cope with by making himself into an accomplished Survivor. However, he felt doubly thwarted without really understanding why, because not only was Ginny not making things right for him in the Personal Myth, as he had unconsciously assumed she would, but she was not accepting him for the adult hero that he felt he was. It was clear to him that the best way to fix their situation was to sell the house, make some money, and move on. He was good at that. Why couldn't Ginny see it his way?

Ginny, for her part, slid straight into the shadow of her Personal Myth, which was telling her that she wasn't lovable enough to deserve the home and the security she needed. At the same time, she fell down the rabbit hole into the deepest shadows of her Gender Myth, where she became the victim, accusing John of deprecating her Gender Myth hero, the woman who could surround him with the comforts of home and heal the pain of his last marriage. At this point Ginny and John ceased to be two adults trying to make decisions about their future together. They became like most of the couples on the verge of beginning a marriage— five, ten, or more years after the ceremony. I see it so often. Only the details are unique.

As the situation continues to escalate they become further estranged, and instead of any longer even trying to be the partner's rescuing hero, each partner begins to try to cut his or her losses. They become two disappointed children blaming and trying to change one another. To add to the terror and dread, each is recalling, if only unconsciously, all the other times they have been here before, gripped by the shadow of the Personal Myth. As each adult hero screams louder, still hoping to be heard by the partner, the banshee voice of the Personal Myth shadow, the mother of all shadows, is screaming back, "You're right! You're unloved and unlovable!" Although neither partner realizes it, each is re-experiencing the original childhood disappointment.

Even as each of them tries to reach out to the other to heal the pain, to make the situation come out right for both of them, they are only doing so in a manner guaranteed to repel the other and worsen the conflict. This permits each to blame the other for not seeing that his or her perspective on reality is the ultimate truth. Each is asking for the same thing—healing in the Personal Myth—but because the shadows are doing the asking, neither advances toward the other.

During the conflicts that arise in this situation, it is common for partners to hear themselves saying things that are especially wounding and destructive to the last shreds of love they share. Often each partner senses he or she is trying to destroy the other, or at least wound the other so deeply that the person will wake up and ask for love or give love, or at least drop the wall that he or she has built up. It is an agonizing merry-go-round in which each partner is trying to reach out to the other while at the same time tearing that other partner apart.

At the time I met Ginny and John, the degradation of trust arising from their repeated struggles over their ritual impasse made it impossible for them to speak of anything of importance until each of them began to understand their myths and shadows and the nature of the heroes they were searching for, and trying to be, in relation to one another. They had not made love for over a year, although they continued to engage in occasional halfhearted, usually scheduled, attempts at having sex. Ginny would arrange a rendezvous, but each time, the emptiness of the experience—if indeed John could perform at all—sent her into the bathroom, where she cried quietly in the shower so as not to put even more pressure on the husband she sensed she was losing.

At this point in a relationship, a period of mourning sets in. Each grieves for him or herself and, in a less obvious but still significant way, for the other. The feelings of failure on both sides has a deadening effect on the relationship and on desire until, as Rebecca once said of Carlton, "I woke up one morning and realized there was a stranger in my bed."

Remarkably, love is still so important to most couples that they may persist in this condition for years, even after all desire is gone. They stop making love to one another. Affairs may begin. The partners treat each other as foreigners, each feeling betrayed by the other. Their natural instinct is to rekindle the relationship and somehow resurrect their love. Yet even though each secretly wishes to get the relationship going again, they still blame each other for its conflicts. Why? Because they are still in the grip of the shadow.

No one is to blame for entering into marriage or long-term relationship with all the wrong expectations. The knowledge and understanding needed to succeed in relationship can only come from being in a long-term committed relationship with someone you love. You can only succeed by learning as you go, which means that mistakes, misdeeds, and failures—broken contracts, in other words—are a fundamental part of the process.

There is profound disappointment when the contract breaks down. Neither of you has lived up to the expectations that the other had of you or of your life together, because both of you—like nearly all couples starting out—had unrealistic (and largely misunderstood and unstated) expectations that could not possibly be fulfilled by the other. The realization that the original contract was impossible does not have to be the end of the relationship. It can actually be the beginning. It is a moment of both danger and opportunity—Fire in the Lake.

The danger of course is that one or both partners will refuse to stay in the relationship and do the work needed to create a contract truly based on their heroic aspirations and founded on personal responsibility. One or both partners may depart, rationalizing yet another mistake by blaming the partner, or by giving up prematurely and saying that the choice was wrong, or by running to another relationship. What is needed is an exploration of your own and each other's mythology and the creation of a new mythic contract. Go back to the mythic questions on page 127. Ask yourself these questions and ask them of your lover. Find out what the real expectations are and see which are most important to each of you. Make a list of those you can agree to meet for your partner. Make the mythic contract conscious and write it down; it will bind your marriage and allow you and your love to grow beyond anything you could have imagined.

When you create your new mythic contract, it must be done with the understanding that you are very different people and that those differences actually serve each of you in your respective self-development. Respect and even admiration for your differences as people make each of you more exciting to the other. Your relationship becomes less governed by expectations each has for the other—a sure setup for disappointment—and more by the recognition that each of you needs to communicate with and understand the other. It is at this point that the magic can begin.

Chapter Nine

The Dark Side of Love

She withdrew, shrinking from beneath his arm
That rested on the banister and slid downstairs;
And turned on him with such a daunting look,
He said twice over before he knew himself:
"Can't a man speak of his own child he's lost?"

"Not you!—oh where's my hat? Oh, I don't need it!
I must get out of here. I must get air.—
I don't rightly know whether any man can."

"Amy! Don't go to someone else this time.
Listen to me. I won't come down the stairs."
He sat and fixed his chin between his fists.
"There's something I should like to ask you, dear."

"You don't know how to ask it."
                              "Help me, then."
                    ROBERT FROST,
                    "Home Burial"

To me these lines from Frost's poem are among the greatest illustrations in literature of the dark side of love. The darkness in this marriage engulfs the reader with its unfiltered anxiety. Its tones of dramatic uncertainty and ambivalence threaten to swallow the reader. The couple's intensity is dramatic in the sense that their interplay is almost theatrical; this couple has used these words before, and will again, under the direction of a story line that keeps them obediently and inescapably in their roles. Their terrifying despair is so dense it almost chokes you. The ghostly echoes of betrayal are haunting these people, whose shadows are bringing the tortured Eros to his knees.

I suspect that many of the couples I treat have households as dark and bleak as this one, although when they discuss their dark nights with me they can only understate them. When the shadows dance, as both partners' do in this dark love poem, we are plunged into the tragedy of broken contracts and lost communication. At these moments the couple may well be convinced of their profound incompatibility. In the darkest nights of their souls each may find the other's mere presence unbearable. Their wild flights from the field of lost hope, those frantic boltings into the night, are fed by some desperate desire to escape not so much their oppressor-partner, though it is that in part, but also the grim constriction of the psychological space they've created with that partner. Though they may try to stop those wild flights, all too often they cannot. In fact, many couples are better off not trying, because flight precludes violence. They recover with the light of day, even bewildered by the lengths to which they have taken grief, unreason, and broken discourse. The dark forces seem to dominate for so many days on end that the partners fear they'll never see the light of day again. They are so driven by their untold stories that it seems they will never discover or express the source of the dark forces which engulf them. After each hair-raising scream for acknowledgment by the other, they are convinced that communication between them is impossible. But when they settle into their Myth Work (belatedly at this point), most of them are proven wrong. Even those who report a mental anguish so debilitating that they think they'll never recover, can and do recover. Through Myth Work, when they learn—and truly grasp—that each is crying out for love, they can begin to listen—and hear.

We are all dying to be known, but we do not get our wish until we discover what it is we really need to tell about ourselves to make our partners listen and hear. In our dread of being wrongly explained we remain impenetrable. Until we learn that being truly seen and understood is both what we want most but also fear most, and that what our partner "sees" is only the part of ourselves that we cannot see, we will continue to be imprisoned by our limitations, whose existence we shrilly deny. Once couples begin to tell their stories in the safety of the therapy room, even the fiercest among them become like innocents. When they are able to hand over to their partners their demons, rather than just the best faces they allow to be known, the "I am not known" plea loses its power.

I do not wish to imply that this process is easy or light. Each of us plays our darkest truths close to the breast, because we are afraid of losing psychological advantage. But it is precisely the loss of advantage, the willingness to set it aside, that begins the peace process. Each partner must come to realize, in his or her own time and own way, that calling forth the heroes to show love by fighting to the death will never be accepted as the courageous and loving act he or she honestly believes it to be. To prove your love you must surrender.

Three Couples

When couples have reached the stage of recognizing and addressing their broken contracts, nothing is easy—especially if they have been entrenched in their ritual impasse for many years. Some, of course, will traverse the stages from bliss to lost innocence to the dark side and ascend fairly easily, more whole and better able to love. A larger number of couples aren't so fortunate. For them, the work is harder, but even those who believe themselves to be the worst case should take heart. The dark side of love is not as Stygian as so many couples groping their way through it may believe. You can come back through the magic of Myth and Shadow Work. Of course there are also those who decide, after doing their work, that their lives have changed and that they no longer have the same goals or needs, and who part amicably.

Lucy and Burr: We Are Newborn

Lucy and Burr certainly knew the dark side of love. "I don't think we ever made it through two weeks in our entire marriage when we both thought we'd 'make it,' " Lucy once said to me in a private session. When they began therapy, Lucy was "at the back door," threatening to leave. On two other occasions she had actually done so. The last time, she had secretly joined the couple's son, who had, three years earlier at age seventeen, fled his father's hard ways to "do it my way." This time Burr's entreaties worked. "I love this woman," he said at that first session. "She claims I don't know how to show it. That's bullshit. I'm here. She's the one who's been out the door—for twenty-seven fucking years."

Still, from courtship to this day, each has been the other's gender ideal. Burr is so entranced by Lucy's ability to magically transform aspiring actors into Denzel Washingtons and Meryl Streeps in the plays she directs at the local high school that he has never missed a performance. Lucy, for her part, loved and respected the man Burr was and what he had done with his gifts. "If Burr decided he wanted to fly, he probably would," Lucy once said. "He can learn anything. And we've all benefited by his Midas touch. He no longer has to work hard. Yet he's a joy to watch. Every day a new challenge, every week a new triumph. He's tireless."

But there was more to Burr's Gender ways, and Lucy's too, for all that: their heroes' shadows. "What a goddamned fucking stupid thing to do! What person with even half a brain would think to do it that way?" he would shout. The kids, his son more than his daughter, shuddered at the sound of this voice, the revolting voice of loathing; the voice, curiously, of his own father, whom he loved with gratitude and unyielding loyalty. This son, Peter, grew mute, took his rage out on his stomach, and fled on the day following his sixteenth birthday. Lucy left, came back, left again, and returned again, pointing to the back door each time Burr failed to bring his voice of loathing under control.

Though she fled, Lucy never cringed. "You may not find me here in the morning, Burr," she'd rant, her finger leaving punctuation marks in his chest as she repeated her words until she felt heard. Her threats usually stopped him cold, which freed her to launch her own sizzling tirades. An on-the-attack, fired-up victim/accuser, like Lucy in her shadow, can be as abusive as a Fixer's darkest shadow. Burr's irritating martyred Survivor and Lucy's enraged victim were an uneven match. Though Burr had his moments, and could wrestle his wife to the mat, she was somehow always ahead at the end of each round, if necessary not merely hitting but kicking where it really hurt, below the belt. The first time she left, she'd had an affair. "That was wrong, but never ask me to apologize," she insisted. Yet there was that way she looked at him when she feared he was ahead on points, her head tilted to express pity, her eyes and mouth in an expression of utter disdain, which he read as she intended: "Do you think I'm incapable of doing it again?"

At each bout's end, while bandaging their own and each other's wounds, Lucy would "turn therapist," which greatly irritated Burr and threatened a new escalation. Her "tedious theme," as he put it, was Burr's father, whose foul myth and rigid standards made him famous in a business community in which he commanded fear and great respect. Burr, as a boy and man, claimed to feel not only respect but veneration, reverence, and loyalty—all of which amounted in Burr's mind to love. Examining this man's character was tantamount to a betrayal, something Burr adamantly refused to do. His mother, the co-conspirator in our model, was a dutiful workhorse of a wife who pulled her load in support of her husband's efforts to free the family from immigrant poverty. As I've said before, Survivors in family situations like this are fully prepared to sacrifice their own needs, to forget their pains, and to deny their vulnerabilities. Typically, they marry Protectors who are equipped to make up for these deficits, and then reject their partners' offerings at every turn. Survivors are loath to whine.

To shield their children from her husband's unattainable or unsustainable standards, from his coldly demanding manner when helping them with homework and other tasks, and from the voice of his shadow, which surfaced whenever he detected the faintest sounds of whining, Lucy answered his pleas for yet another chance, and always came home to try again. But try as she might, she could never get him to tell his childhood stories as they needed to be told.

Burr finally did tell his story. It took some doing, but what made it easy finally was my matching with him tactic for tactic, defense for defense, justification for justification, all familiar to Survivors who are formed to sacrifice the self in the name of love for a parent who could not express love directly. Burr hated the very idea of therapy, "the victim's haven," as he called it. Some (Protector) therapists who have not fully faced their own shadows do encourage their patients' shadows by egging the patient on in feeling his victimhood, I agreed. "But you, Burr, you'll be cured the day you come in here of your own volition, ready to share your pain, revealing your vulnerability for once."

One of my goals was to reconcile Burr with his estranged son. Burr did not believe it was possible. Peter, who had not set foot in the household for three years, hung up the phone when he heard his father's voice. In two very willing phone conversations, arranged by a skeptical Lucy (who eventually learned that some of Peter's stubborn silence was to please her), I discovered that the boy loved but did not feel loved by his father. "He's given me so much, but he has no way of knowing what I value, who I am. He needs to be taught a lesson in how to love." Peter agreed to one two-hour session in which he would help me help his father learn something about love.

In the session, Burr, Peter, and Lucy learned something. Burr's performance, the key that opened the doors to discovery, was as much a surprise to him as it was to his wife and son. As he and I talked about the crucial years of his childhood, he allowed me to take him beyond his mantra. Yes, he was afraid of his father, at times; no, he could not express anxiety about an exam for which he hadn't prepared; yes, yes, yes, his father was loving, but he hardly knew him because he worked seven days a week; okay, so volunteering to work in his father's factory on weekends was an attempt to get close, but instead what he got was praise for being near-perfect in what he did; and no, he doesn't remember ever being held by him. Bit by bit, as Burr let me guide him into his most compelling story of childhood, his voice lowered, slowed, and changed from that of the man to that of the child. At his story's climax, he admitted to himself for the first time that he, not his father, had made the rule that asking to rest was an ungrateful act, a betrayal of the hardworking immigrant who sacrificed everything for his children's right to happiness. He had needed to construct this rule in order to define for himself such terms of love as he could meet. Struggling to sort his insight, he lost control of his feelings, spilling out the ocean of tears he had sandbagged since boyhood. Then silence, broken finally by Peter. "Don't you see, Dad? It is possible to love yourself without betraying your love for Grandpa."

Peter's heart had opened with his father's. "I'd like to come back; there's a girl I want you both to meet. But she and I have a lot of sorting out to do. I've learned a lot about myself from what took place here. When I clean up my act, I'll get back to you."

Burr and Lucy are one of the couples who descended into the dark side—and stayed there for many years—but who came fairly naturally to the work, once they found their way to the right kind of therapy for them.

This pair had broken contracts in the Personal Myth, but their Sexual Fantasy Myth had held firm. Desire was bounced around with the tides of their struggle but never disappeared into the depths of their despair. Even though communication in the languages of their other myths was hopelessly bottomed out in their babble, their sexual dialogue refused to join in the confusion of tongues. So it was not their communication in their Gender Myths nor in their Sexual Fantasy Myths that set this pair back; it was the Shadows of their Personal Myths and their heroes. Furthermore, they had more natural flexibility in the choreography of their communication than many couples have. Neither got as stuck in one role, and each had a greater ability to bystand, than is natural for many couples.

Lucy, it must be said, was eager to tell her stories—and did to all who would listen. She told them to friends, to her students, to family—all of which drove Burr crazy. But most unfortunately, she told stories of her life and marriage to their son who, in listening too well and too sympathetically, became bonded to her in a conspiracy of shared love-hatred of Burr.

Lucy's breakthrough came from a revelation in a dream, which led to some of the most profound journal work I have yet seen. Her medium of discovery was not recollection of her past stories but rather the writing of the playwrights she loved most. Using her uncanny ability to recall lines from Shakespeare, Marlowe, Ibsen, Synge, and other great playwrights, she was carried with dreamlike ease on sojourns into her own dark recesses, there to discover a sadness deeper than she had ever known. (Its source is unique, and the meaning she made of it would be trivialized if I were to toy with disguise in the name of anonymity.) When Lucy surfaced from the dark destinations her writers had led her to, she no longer needed to rely on flight and threats to make her point with Burr. "I've locked the back door and thrown away the key," she announced when she was ready. "I'm here for the duration." Burr's determination to stay together was a big factor—he had the grit of the arch-Survivor.

The couple went on to do serious Myth and Shadow Work in less than a year. Both felt the work was successful. They had tried therapy three times before without success. "My fault," Burr had said in our wrap-up session. Lucy snorted. "Still the martyr. Thought you were cured." Even when we'd all three decided it was safe to stop therapy, Lucy hadn't felt quite finished. Her husband laughed. "Survivors don't get hooked on therapy the way Protectors do." But Burr's agreeing to come back if needed and to come in for "checkups" eased Lucy's mind.

LUCY:

"I came home late last night after a team meeting."

BURR:

"She was waving a document, very excited. I'd been working at my computer and I was tired."

LUCY:

"The document I was waving was about women's relationships with their adult daughters, a pretty important subject to me and Burr, and I was fired up to read it to him."

BURR:

"It was nearly midnight. I'd been up working since five in the morning. I was exhausted but pleased with myself. I just wanted us to crawl into bed together. For company—not sex."

LUCY:

"That cod-liver oil look on his face was a dead giveaway. But I'd written most of the report and wanted to share my stuff as we'd been doing lately."

BURR:

"My mistake was not to beg off right away or else to really get into it. I did neither."

LUCY:

"Instead, he listened impatiently. Every second twisted my gut tighter."

BURR:

"I realized that my mind was rejecting every sentence that she read. My ugly dismissal voice—I thought I had it under control— spewed from my mouth like a geyser."

LUCY:

" 'That fucking voice,' I thought. I wanted to hit him."

BURR:

"I knew how pissed she was. As I skulked off to bed, I regretted my stupidity. My love for Lucy was like a bungee cord pulling me back. I thought, 'Christ, my shadow's here again. It's winning out the way it always used to.' In our bed I listened for a half-hour, hoping she wouldn't be too mad, that she'd undress in the dark and slip in beside me, her backside cupped into my frontside."

LUCY:

"Let me tell the rest, Burr. This morning—after that glitch last night—Burr put down his paper when I joined him at the breakfast table. He looked straight into my eyes and said, 'I'm so sorry, Lulu. (That's his love call.) I really don't want to hurt you, ever.' He never took his eyes from mine. He just looked into me. I felt somehow 'opened,' I guess. His voice was so steady and so sincere. I felt this . . . this passion stirring inside me. Not the wild lust of adolescence. Something rarefied."

BURR:

"Let me finish the story. Through all the messy years, somehow the sex has held up. You've said we were lucky, David. Lucy took my hand and led me back up to our bedroom. Since I've gotten older and Lucy had her 'changes' our sex has been good but not the wild hormonal sex we once knew. But what happened this time came from a place we'd never been before."

This couple, who had been deeply ensconced in their shadows and on the brink of desertion and divorce so many times, had benefited from their Myth and Shadow Work. Not only had they learned how to bridge the different languages of their myths, but they had also learned to Talk. This excerpt from a conversation with me at their "six-month checkup" shows what talk can be like when two people have come to understand their own and their partner's mythology and have made peace with their shadows. The morning after they had experienced a not-unusual kind of marital turmoil, they were able to overcome the ill feelings with good moves on each part and far more flexibility in the choreography of their communication than would have been possible at the beginning of their therapy.

Harold and Amy: The Deepest of Shadows Can Be Penetrated

Harold, a surgeon who was famous as the most compassionate physician at the hospital on whose staff he served, was also known for his obsession with the theme of safety and justice—an obsession the origins of which he discovered in therapy with me. The craziness and irrationality of his mother, from whom he had distanced himself forever in anger and fear when he was a teenager, led him to define his wife, Amy, as a menace to his sense of safety. Harold saw himself as a victim of his wife's disorganized ways. He complained incessantly about the chaos surrounding her. Amy, a Surrealist painter, was trapped in his world of tightly bound definitions of right and wrong, of good and evil, and—worst of all—of who she was as a person and as a woman. Her guarded plea— "Please, Harold. Just once. Come to the edge of my world, my space, and see *me*. Hear what *I* think. Even if you don't agree. Please"—would plunge him into a fit of rage.

It took years of therapy for Harold to relax his One World/One Truth perspective and for Amy to gain the confidence to hold out for it. When he did, his and Amy's efforts to repair their broken contract began to be rewarded. Until then, all the good therapy work they had done had, in my opinion, served merely to hold their marriage together. Now, for the first time since the first phase of their fifteen-year marriage, Harold was able to express gratitude for Amy's gifts of love. On a winter vacation following the couple's breakthrough, lovemaking was taken out of cold storage where it had been kept for well over ten years. I am not counting their very rare "desperate attempts at sex in the name of sanity," which were "abysmal failures."

If, as in this case, the dark sides of any couple's three love stories house unassuageable shadows which make their grim presence known early on, the couple would do well to start therapy right away, or not marry in the first place. But couples like this do marry, and I am not prepared to say that their choice is wrong. Had a therapist made that judgment in the case of Harold and Amy, the couple would have proved the therapist wrong.

Throughout his years of therapy, Harold had tried several of the best men and women in the Cambridge therapy community. In the end he wore them all down. He knew he wasn't getting what he needed and left to continue his search. I, as an unyielding Survivor, share with men like Burr, and others in this book, a natural distaste for people like Harold who overplay the victim. But I held on to my compassion for this sweet-and-sour soul like a dog with a bone, determined to win his heart. Eventually, the fruits of their Myth and Shadow Work became apparent. If I brought anything to the table it was my refusal to be put off by his scathing temper and other defensive maneuvers that obscured the size of his heart and his need to be loved. Though for a long time it infuriated him when, instead of cringing when his shadow raged at Amy or me, I threatened to embrace him if he couldn't quiet his menacing demons, I eventually broke through. My own heart melted one evening when, after putting out yet another firestorm, I heard him say as he and Amy were walking out the door, "You know, David really loves me."

Why did these two make it look so hard for so long? The short answer to this question is that Harold was possessed by the dark suspicions, destructive beliefs, painful memories, and fears in his shadows. As a Protector with a deep shadow, an almost unbelievably self-centered victim/accuser, Harold believed that he was the helpless, hapless victim of external evil and injustice. And as long as he remained possessed by his shadow, he perceived only one truth: his own. The very thought that Amy might have had her own version of reality was beyond his comprehension. Yet Harold's rage never fully satisfied him, because the real evil eluded him. It escaped like water through his fingers. His tirades left him exhausted, unrewarded, even shamed—though he couldn't admit it. Until he had done enough of the work, and worked very hard indeed, he was unable to reach the darkness in his external world. He refused to believe he was looking in the wrong place.

When he was ready, Harold came into my office and told me the contents of his Personal Myth in one sitting. Here is an excerpt of a session which took place some time after his breakthrough.

AMY:

"The other day Harold came home from the hospital and I was still in my studio painting. For a moment I was afraid of what was going to happen when he found out that I hadn't started dinner, but then something new inside me, some shred of trust and courage, made me relax. A few minutes later, I heard him walking up the steps that divide the studio from the rest of the house. 'Amy, what do you have planned for dinner?' he asked. Again, I braced myself for an outburst of sarcasm at the very least, but nothing happened. He repeated my name, but again he didn't sound mad—just curious."

HAROLD:

"Actually, I was just hungry at that point. [He was speaking as if this were the most natural way in the world for him to react to such a scene.] I realized that if she hadn't started dinner, it would be hours. I'd been in surgery most of the day and then seeing patients all afternoon."

AMY:

"The next thing I knew, he had put his head in the door of my studio—which in itself was rare. Harold almost never came into my world, either physically or emotionally. 'How soon before you're finished?' he asked me. Again, I was shocked. In the past, my finishing my work would not have been an issue. I was still shaking, expecting to get in trouble for his hunger."

HAROLD:

"So I told her I'd go pick something up at Bread and Circus and be back in half an hour, but that I expected her to set the table while I was gone and be ready to sit down with me."

AMY:

"He was scowling a bit, and I decided not to push the envelope by telling him that I'd really like a few more minutes to take a shower before we ate."

This small scene represents a giant leap forward for a couple who not many weeks before seemed like the most hopeless of all my cases. For several years I saw Harold alone and the two of them together, just trying to keep them from sinking so far into the depths of Hades that they could never return. Each week was a crisis almost always initiated by some small, unintentional lapse on Amy's part; something which would never even have rippled the surface of most disturbed marriages. Now, here was Harold letting pass things which usually would have made him boil with rage and torment at being victimized once again by Amy's lack of respect or caring. And Amy herself, although she still was somewhat cowed by her husband, was speaking in a new voice. This voice grew stronger over the next several sessions. She had gone from apologia to confidence. She was delivering insights without asking permission to speak, while Harold actually listened and appeared to be hearing. They even began to feel safe about changing and canceling appointments. One day, a few weeks into this new version of Harold and Amy, I realized that only the three of us were in the room. Their shadows were absent. Some months down the line, while on vacation, Harold and Amy truly made love for the first time in many years.

Alex and Barbara:
When Is Enough Enough?

Sometimes love, willingness to work, and discovery of the three myths are not enough to keep two people together. This happens often, though not always, when the one or both partners have deep shadows which they have not yet been able to control.

ALEX:

"Today, Barbara, I'm going to ask you a question. How much is enough?"

BARBARA (SPEECHLESS AND STUNNED):
"What do you mean?"

ALEX:

"Just what I said, but today I'll also give you the answer since I've asked the question before. Enough is enough. I've had it. I can't do anymore. Today is the last day. I've worked and I've worked, and it has never been enough." (Barbara bursts into tears.)

ALEX:

"Don't cry. I know the worst of this is the shock. You'll be okay. I promise I'll take care of you financially. I've thought it through. Obviously we won't be going ahead and getting married, but I'm going to give you the house in Ayer, and I'll give you a settlement which you'll be able to invest and live off."

BARBARA:
"But why? I don't understand."

ALEX:

"I asked you several months ago in this room when you'd be content that I'd done enough, but you only asked for more. And I came to realize that no matter how much work I do our shadows aren't going to go away enough to make this work."

This indeed was Alex's and Barbara's last session. We had worked for nearly two years, and although I was as stunned as Barbara, I had to admit that Alex had probably come to a wise decision. Once Barbara discovered her Survivor's mask and got in touch with her real heroic mode and its shadow, she became a classic Protector with a deep victim/accuser shadow. Once she fell into the depths of this rabbit hole she was unable to see her way back out. Ever the victim, she refused to do her own work, and insisted that Alex work harder before she would engage. "Don't even try to get me to do that work until he does, David," she once said to me. "He's got to go first. He's got more of a problem." She would question Alex from a distance almost as if she were playing therapist. By doing so, she drove her fiancé crazy.

Although Barbara was willing to tell some of her story, she did so as a bystander, never really getting under her own skin. Eventually Barbara's deep shadow, which manifested itself in other arenas as well, wore Alex down. He no longer felt he was in partnership with her; he never felt that he could hold the mirror for Barbara or that he could make any requests of her without losing her love.

Lucy and Burr and Harold and Amy were able to make it back by learning about their mythologies and learning how to keep their shadows from running the show. Barbara was so deeply entrenched in her shadows that she was unable to look into the mirror and do the work she needed to do on herself in order to make her partnership with Alex work.

As partners begin to listen to and truly hear their partner's myths, they begin to understand the other's vulnerability and desire for love. Once that vulnerability is exposed, compassion begins to give birth to a much gentler and richer love. The ability to access the Personal Myth can strengthen or retrieve desire. There is no greater aphrodisiac than a dialogue from the heart.

Chapter Ten

Bringing Love Back into the Light

Even if you are buried in your shadows and unable to communicate in any of the three myths, there is a way to escape from this maelstrom of miscommunication and to learn to speak, once again, in the language of love, just as you thought you were doing in your archetypal encounter and in the months and years before your shadows insisted on being heard. I call this process Myth and Shadow Work. Like the biblical Tower of Babel, marriages based on the unconscious language of unexplored myths run the risk of crumbling into devastation, bitterness, betrayal, separation, and divorce. Myth Work transforms partners into people who speak not one language but three and then six—their own three and, eventually, those of their partner. Shadow Work is consciousness-seeking. It is a continuing self-dialogue whereby we take responsibility for learning about our own shadows and set out to bring them into the light.

Myth Work

As we have seen, even when we believe that we are communicating clearly, we are each interpreting the other's words and actions from a reality filtered through the lens of our conscious and unconscious needs rather than from an accurate reading of what the other is trying to convey.

Ironically, the more important the communication and the greater each person's needs and desire to be understood, the less likely the two will understand, or even hear, each other. The higher the stakes, the more confusing the picture becomes. High-stakes situations are those in which we experience a threat to our well-being and also to our heroic status in our partner's eyes and, at the same time, care deeply about the outcome. In these situations, we feel threatened, unsure if we are loved, and desperate to control the outcome and to be loved by our partner. The tension is already high because of these unexpressed needs and desires. The more each of you fails to communicate, the more frustrated and disappointed each of you becomes. The lack of communication crescendos into open conflict.

When you face such situations, your adult gender hero is called forth to protect you from danger or from an unacceptable outcome, and you assume your role as Survivor, Fixer, or Protector hero. Once you begin to operate from your heroic stance, your language changes, depending upon which mythic domain you are operating from. For example, a Fixer will speak differently from her Personal Myth than she does from her Gender or Sexual Fantasy Myth.

If a partner weren't involved, none of this would necessarily be a problem, but there are six mythic languages potentially being spoken. Communication between the two of you who care so deeply about each other is often reduced to a multilingual mess where neither can hear the other over the screams of each one's shadows. Myth Work helps you to identify these basic language differences and the different images they invoke, so that the meanings, thoughts, and feelings that arise are no longer misinterpreted or rejected. You will learn to Talk rather than just talk. This Talk is communication conducted with an awareness of your own three mythic languages and a sensitivity to your partner's language propensities and requirements.

When you do become cognizant of the different mythic languages you and your partner are speaking, your languages will become purer and cleaner, allowing the two of you to deal better with one another. For example, the husband may be speaking in the language of his Personal Myth while his wife is speaking from her Gender Myth. While he is re-experiencing many of the feelings of the betrayed, angry, or frightened child, she is speaking in the language of her heroic mode, which is informed by her vision of where they must go and what they must do in order to solve a problem. He may be saying, "Show me that you love me!" while she may be saying, "I'm strong. I need you to be equally strong right now." This is obviously a discordant conversation in which neither person's needs are heard or met. The feelings and needs implicit in their words are very different, because they are expressing themselves from different places within their beings. Without being aware of it, they are failing to communicate. Accordingly, neither can truly know how better to understand the sources of the other's needs and then shift the conversation accordingly.

Besides permitting better communication between the two of you, Myth Work clarifies your own identity. Knowing your own Personal, Gender, and Sexual Myths lets you choose new ideals for yourself. Deepening and expanding the range of your composite identity permits the rewriting of contracts. It is even possible to construct a new Sexual Fantasy Myth—not as many people try to do from sex videos or instruction manuals—but from the core places of Self which have been opened, and from liberated desire.

If it has succeeded in doing what it can do, Myth Work will release you from the terrible predicament of false or inaccurate description by yourself and your partner. Now it is you who supplies the accurate description of yourself. If your partner has done the work as you have, each of you has restated your mythic identity in your own language.

The end results of this work are a deep knowing of your partner and self-healing. By reconciling each of your Edenic myths of perfect love with the actuality of your personal myth into one real shared love story, you can re-experience intimacy and connection, and rekindle desire.

Myth Work in the Personal and Gender Myths

The healing tasks which must be undertaken in the Personal and Gender Myths are listed below. The basic ways of healing yourself and your intimate relationship involve:

- storytelling
- loving listening

The following are essential aspects of storytelling and loving listening. Let them serve as guideposts for you in your work.

- rebuilding curiosity
- flexing and expanding the choreography of your communication
- recognizing thematic triggers
- reframing the story
- releasing and escaping from language traps

Storytelling

The kind of storytelling that I am talking about, the kind with the power to heal, involves diving into cold, deep waters to retrieve the Big Story from your childhood. As we have seen in the first part of this book, no matter how loving your parents or how happy your childhood, your Personal Myth is filled with stories of failed love and betrayal. These betrayals may not have been earthshaking on their face—indeed, the adults around you probably didn't even register the event or notice the depth of your reaction to it. But in these moments when you felt misunderstood—no longer part of a perfect symbiotic parent-child unit in which all your needs were understood and met—are the seeds of growth. This is the inevitable beginning of growing into a separate being and leading your own life. It is also in this glimpse of imperfect love that desire is born.

The central meaning that you derive from this childhood betrayal becomes the centerpiece of the shadow of the Personal Myth. This shadow develops because it is impossible for a child to believe that the parents upon whom she depends for life itself are imperfect. To entertain such a thought would threaten her world, which is founded upon the belief that her parents are omnipotent and all-loving. As a way to cope with the paradox of imperfect parental love, the child creates a confusing construction: "I am unworthy of love from people such as my parents," she concludes sorrowfully. "Therefore, any failings they may have are because of their disappointment in who I am." The shadow from the Personal Myth is the most powerful of all our shadows, because it is the oldest and the first to have formed. It is the memory of our fall from paradise. It is the original pain of separation, and even though it is a necessary separation we will always feel it most deeply. Its mantra remains with us until we rediscover our story of imperfect love.

This childhood scar, large or small, remains half-remembered within us, both helping and hindering us as we proceed through life. It helps by spurring us on to seek union and healing with another, but at the same time it hinders such a union by never letting us completely forget our unworthiness. Depending on the child's original reaction to these feelings, which may be at least partially biologically determined, the result is some degree of anger, sadness, fear, guilt, or all four. And these are the responses which surface in adulthood every time the themes of the childhood betrayal arise. As adults we handle these feelings of powerlessness by assuming the voice of our adult gender hero.

The stories which must be told are all very close to the surface. We must simply decide when we are ready and let them out. When people do, it is often a peak experience when they realize that the shameful secrets they have been guarding so long aren't perceived as shameful by the rest of the world's people, all of whom are guarding and nourishing their own shame, fear, and pain.

The way to access the important childhood story when you feel gripped by your shadow and are feeling your darkest and most distant from your partner is to go through all the experiences of your life and find those which are telling you how to behave in the moment. Does something seem familiar? Are memories coming back to you? Take a look at the questions for discovering your Personal Myth. It is guaranteed that you will find a familiar structure, because the themes of the Personal Myth have been triggered and are operating in the room.

You disclose your important stories both face to face and by writing them in a journal. An important part of this storytelling involves sitting down with your partner and discussing your respective mythologies, particularly as they relate to a specific recent conflict. You tell your partner what you felt during the event and why you acted as you did, not based so much upon what he or she did to you in the present but upon what you felt and what these events made you remember and feel from your past. By telling your stories, each of you has the opportunity to apologize, because the more you see what you are doing and why you are doing it, the more you can come to recognize that both you and your partner were trying to cope with the same questions: "Am I loved?" and "Am I lovable?" Both of you are saying in your own ways "I need your love. I want you to love me."

Loving Listening

To listen another's soul into a condition of disclosure and
discovery may be almost the greatest service that any
human being can ever perform for another.
DOUGLASS STEERE, Quaker

Loving listening is a different kind of listening from just keeping quiet while another speaks. The kind of listening that must occur between two partners who are trying to deepen or retrieve their love for one another is more attentive to both the spoken and the unspoken. It is a listening with the heart. It is prepared for surprise. This kind of listening is possible only between two committed partners. It is an act of safekeeping, of sheltering what the speaker has gathered and told. Without a loving listener, there is no bringing under shelter, no safety for the necessary storytelling.

The listening of Myth Work is difficult when those who must tell and those who must hear have lost faith, trust, or desire. But without loving listening, there is no way to bridge the chasm between them. Thus if they wish to be true lovers they are without choice in the matter. Proceed at your own risk if the two of you do not share the wish to help one another cultivate loving listening. The need to be listened to properly is tightly bound to desire.

Rebuilding Curiosity

When we have fallen into the shadows of love, everything is tinted by a dark light, yet paradoxically the mystery of the Other is also lost in the darkness. The Other is known—too known. We have no more of the unquenchable curiosity which magnetizes our earliest encounters, the desire to learn the Other's deepest secrets, to know this person as deeply as we can. When we lose this vital curiosity, our partners lose their heroic status in our eyes. A terrible black magic takes over. Our lovers are no longer special. They become commonplace—mere objects in our houses, or worse. Suddenly little things irritate us. This is when differences over toothpaste tubes and toilet seats become important arenas for battle. We can no longer bear the way she cuts her meat, the way he hums as he works, her perfume, his neckties. We have shifted into a different way of perceiving.

Another way in which we can lose the curiosity needed to sustain love and desire is by trying to explain our partners to ourselves. When we put up the lens of our own analysis and explanation, not only do we rob our partner of the right to define his or her own identity, but we naturally lose curiosity about who that person really is. Losing curiosity, believing that we know everything about a partner, can also leave us open to looking for that mystery elsewhere. A loss of curiosity is often an accelerant to infidelities.

It is dangerous to lose that curiosity, and it takes difficult work to regain it. You have to say to each other, "I've forgotten what it's like to want to know you." And then you must each make a conscious effort to let the light shine on each other again. One of the remarkable things that can occur when you try consciously to rebuild curiosity in each other is that it spurs each of you on to know and understand yourself better. Your curiosity ennobles your partner. It restores his or her dignity. The message becomes, "What you have to say is valuable and surprising to me. I need your point of view to expand my own."

Flexing and Expanding Your Action Profile

As important as the content of our mythic languages is the structure of our communication. Structure is invisible, but it exerts powerful effects nonetheless. It's what is meant when people say to one another, "It's not *what* you said but *how* you said it." When structure takes over, we are no longer responding to the *what* but to the *how*.

In all face-to-face communication, four, and only four, "behaviors" are available, *independent of content:* we can move, follow, oppose, or bystand. Each of us tends to have one or two favorites (our strong actions), one we perform least skillfully (our weak action), and one we overuse or use inappropriately (our stuck action). (You will find a longer discussion of the choreography of communication in Appendix A.)

A couple's ritual impasse is always an example of a limited behavioral repertoire characterized by stuck and limited moves. The problem with such an ineffectual, unsuccessful pattern is that it impedes communication. If one or both partners is incapable of following, deeper understanding and clarification will be impossible. If there is no ability to bystand, listening and hearing accurately is virtually impossible.

I believe that part of Harold and Amy's breakthrough came as the result of two new maneuvers on Amy's part. She had long been unable to express her needs. Every session in my office and, seemingly, every interaction between them at home, turned into a crisis fed by another of Harold's shadow's victim/accuser attacks on something Amy had done. There was no way Amy could do anything but disappear into the foxhole of her Survivor shadow while the firestorms blew over. She couldn't express her need for closeness and intimacy. She was too afraid. She rarely made strong, clear moves and hardly ever openly opposed.

But one day something in Amy changed. She became more assertive, moving away from her abandoner shadow and daring to stand up for herself. During the middle of one of Harold's attacks, she suddenly stood up. He sputtered to a stop, surprised by this turn in her behavior. "Harold," she said, visibly trembling, "I don't have to take this. If you act like this one more time I'm going to get up and walk out. I won't be abused anymore." Harold did not continue his tirade. In fact, he was noticeably quieter for the rest of the session.

During the period leading up to their breakthrough, Amy had an interesting opportunity to revisit her childhood. She had grown up in a Boston Brahmin household with well-meaning but distant parents. The touch she most remembers are those of her mother's white kid gloves held at arm's length. During a visit to her sister's home on Nantucket she had suffered a deep gash on the sole of her foot which had become infected. To Harold, famous for his compassion for his patients' pain, this was no reason to change his plans. He raged when Amy asked him to turn down the television because of her headache. He sulked when she asked if he could go out for dinner because she felt too ill to cook. Perhaps her standing up to him in my office gave her the strength to make a new type of move. Or perhaps she just felt ill enough. Instead of staying around and letting Harold continue to complain and accuse, she got on a plane and went to her parents' summer house in Rhode Island. She went home again and allowed herself to become a child, and the parents who had perhaps failed her needs for security and closeness in childhood took her in and cared for her. Finally Amy was able to drop the Survivor mask she had been wearing to protect herself in her marriage, and her parents were able to nurture her as never before. Because of Amy's several unaccustomedly bold moves, Harold had been forced to open up to Amy. As time went on, each also developed a better grasp of the essential ability to bystand and watch from outside themselves.

Recognizing Thematic Triggers

When you come to better understand the themes of your Personal Myth, you have the tools to recognize themes that will trigger behaviors which will escalate in high-stakes situations. Awareness of both your own and your partner's triggering themes, and the understanding of what constitutes high-stakes situations for each of you, helps you control automatic actions which feed your ritual impasse. For John and Ginny, those themes were John's belief that change was crucial to his strength and Ginny's need to feel a rootedness which had been denied her in childhood. When these themes arose in their most casual conversations, it was enough to fuel the vicious cycle from which they couldn't extricate themselves until they had learned the contents of their personal stories and how these stories and their shadows continued to influence them.

Once we become aware of these themes, we can do our own editing and censoring of the shadow voices which would otherwise incite our partners' shadows to riot. Once again, even if it is only you who are willing to play the censor's role at the moment, half the work is done. You gain the capability to stop the automatic reaction. Once you understand these thematic triggers, you must be willing to let them go and you must allow your partner the freedom to do or not do the same.

One of my patients, a strong Survivor who, by his heroic nature, has a hard time when people anticipate problems, is married to a Protector who, by her nature, is protective of herself and others. The wife, Claudine, is due to have surgery on her sinuses sometime in the late summer. She and her husband, Gil, have a trip planned for the autumn. "Well, we won't be able to go before October at the earliest," she announced to him at dinner. "I may need two months or even more after the surgery before I can fly."

"Is that what your doctor said?"

"No, I haven't asked her yet, but I do know that flying can be dangerous and painful when you have an active sinus infection. I'd be even more cautious after surgery."

Gil felt his shadows starting to gather. Claudine was speaking in the language of a Protector who was starting to fall into her victim shadow. All he would have to do to start a fight would be to abandon Claudine when she needed to feel safe by scoffing at what any Survivor would deem overly self-protective behavior. But having done a good job coming to know his abandoner shadow and how it could get him into trouble, he resisted and didn't let himself say what he was certainly thinking. Instead, he was able to take responsibility for controlling his own shadow.

He replied, "I want you to enjoy the trip and be comfortable. Let's see what your doctor has to say before we buy our tickets."

Instead of countering with a putdown, which would rob his wife of a legitimate need to feel control over her body, Gil allowed her to be herself with her own views, her own anxieties, and her own wisdom. This gave Claudine the opportunity to find a middle ground. By not allowing the shadows to escalate the situation, Gil had also put the responsibility back onto Claudine to do some Shadow Work of her own which might help her to see that her victim side causes her to over-empower forces outside her body. The more Shadow Work a couple has done, the more control they have over such situations where their shadows might otherwise take control.

Reframing the Story

The frames we use to understand events are, themselves, forces. Reframing our stories is a way of offering a plausible new explanation for behavior which may have been colored by emotions. Although therapy itself is a reframing of our entire life experience, reframing can be done on a smaller level. We can take specific stories and the behaviors which arise from them and limit our repertoires and look at them through a new lens. Gaining this ability also helps to defuse future escalations.

John and Ginny, the couple presented in the previous chapter, learned to do this. As you may recall, John was anxious to sell their house and move on. Ginny interpreted his behavior by telling herself that he wanted to sell the house just because he wanted to take the profits from it and speculate in real estate, thus doubly jeopardizing their security. Although John was perhaps inadequate in his ability to explain why he wanted to sell the house in a way that Ginny could understand it, Ginny was also unable to hear what John was saying because he had triggered one of her important childhood themes. In a sense, they became a one-truth household in which Ginny's version of reality prevailed. But one of the things that John was trying to tell Ginny, albeit in too small a voice, was that he had another reason for wanting to move. The house John had been restoring when he met Ginny had shadows of its own for him. Although in the divorce from his first wife he had given up the large apartment they had shared, the house in Concord had once been theirs. They had bought it to restore and John had received it in the divorce. Before he met Ginny, John had planned to restore it and then move on, and make a truly fresh start in another town, perhaps even another area. For a while he thought that they might be able to make a fresh start in it together. At the same time, he realized he had overspent on details which would make the house more salable. When Ginny began to resist his plans to sell he felt threatened as a man, but he also felt himself the victim of someone who was refusing to listen to him because of her own agenda. He felt trapped in his past, and as if his life were on hold. During some of her darkest hours, Ginny began to think back to the earliest origins of the couple's troubles. In her mind's eye she kept revisiting that scene on the airplane when John had turned to her and announced his plan to sell the house. She had received, with tears and sulking that went on intermittently for months, what John believed to be a heroic offering with benefits for each of them. As she cast about in her mind, she retrieved one fact which, at the time, she had passed over as insignificant. John had told her that the house came with baggage from his first marriage and that some part of him still felt that, as long as he lived there, he was under the wicked spell of his first wife. Ginny had ignored that issue and heard only that he wanted to sell the house because he was restless for new projects and wanted more money to play with—something he also said. His wife now lived on the West Coast and never contacted him. There was nothing left between them, Ginny reasoned.

But John saw it from a different angle. It was true that his wife was no longer in his life, but he had never felt their divorce settlement was fair. Rather than staying to fight her, he had chosen to take what he could get and leave the rest. The house was his escape hatch. He would sell it, recoup his losses, and get on with his life. When he met Ginny, a part of him did want to give her the territorial security she longed for, but part of him expected to be able to convince her that by selling, pocketing some money, and finding a new place of their own, they'd both be better off. When Ginny didn't buy in, he felt trapped. Suddenly he saw himself as a fifty-year-old man, stuck in a house full of ghosts, with a woman he no longer felt he knew or even cared about and his life passing him by. There were things he wanted, things he wouldn't be able to have if he didn't get some of his money out of that house.

It was after they began their work with me that Ginny was able to reframe their story and see John's truth from behind his eyes rather than from the pressure of her own needs. John had to learn to stop abandoning his feelings and the relationship with Ginny. He had to learn how to talk about his feelings.

Releasing and Escaping from Language Traps

Language traps are ways of using words that hook another person's shadows. You can get into these traps when you create them through your own use of language, or if you are oversensitive to another's use of language. In the first case, consider the Survivor hero, Gil, whom we met above with his Protector wife, Claudine. Although Gil neatly avoided a fight by keeping his impatience under control when Claudine was being, in his opinion, overprotective of herself, at a later date he lost control of his shadow and did start a fight over a similar issue.

"Remember that cataract operation I had?" he asked Claudine one day as they were driving to a cocktail party. "I just found out from my doctor that he wrote my case up because he'd never had a patient who had absolutely no blurring right after his operation. I'm going down in medical history!"

To be sure, Gil was in a mood to pick a fight that day, and his allowing his Survivor hero to boast in this way was perhaps uncon-sciously calculated to hook Claudine's shadow, because Claudine had worried about him as she would have about herself on the day of the operation. She had insisted on accompanying him to the doc-tor's office, although this made him feel uncomfortable. Claudine, remembering her concern for him that day and perceiving now that he was devaluing her heroic offering, responded defensively. "You're lucky I got you to go to the doctor at all. You would have gone on buying drugstore eyeglasses and gone blind."

They arrived at the cocktail party with grim faces.

In the second case, lack of understanding of another person's sensitivities to words or language can cause a different sort of trou-ble. The wife in a couple I see in therapy uses boisterous bad lan-guage that dismays her husband. To her, four-letter words are fun to use—colorful and descriptive. These same words plunge him right back into his Catholic boyhood which was dominated by stern nuns and an even sterner mother. He is unable to convey to her in words the degree of his distaste for this language. She's hav-ing difficulty controlling her automatic four-letter barrages and she has no idea how angry it makes him.

Work in the Gender Myth

Whereas most of the riots and escalations that originate in the Personal Myth are the work of demon voices that are, for the most part, below the level of awareness, most which occur in the Gender Myth start out in conversations that fail because of language differences, different resolution styles, and stuck be-haviors. You can overcome many of these problems by becoming more aware of your communications style. The important tasks include:

- utilizing the heroic modes chart (see page 77)
- acknowledging and understanding communication differences
- not allowing two shadows in the room at the same time
- agreeing to practice changing the nature of the discourse when stuck

Using the Heroic Modes Chart

Use the heroic modes chart on page 77 as a framework for understanding your heroic mode, its shadows, and its possibilities. Besides identifying your primary heroic mode or modes on the "east-west" axis of the chart, try also to see where you lie in the "north-south" axis—in other words, how deep your shadows are. If you are a Fixer, do you tend to descend only as far as the gray zone (conqueror), or do you slip all the way into the shadow and become an abuser? Circle the areas of the chart on which you reside.

Visualizing yourself on this chart helps you see your possibilities. It also gives you and your partner a pragmatic new tool for understanding what your differences are about. It can help you to defuse the impasses, struggles, and monologues by reframing and explaining what has kept you in the dark. You will also gain a better understanding of the heroic aspects of your partner. Rather than being a bad person, he or she is more easily seen as a hero gone wrong.

Understanding and Acknowledging Communication Differences

In communication between two people, meaning is conveyed by more than words alone. Worlds of meaning are conveyed by the structure of communication. Each heroic type communicates in a particular way. Couples have varying abilities to notice these differences in communication styles and to identify and make use of them when talking to each other. Even if you don't come by this ability naturally, once you and your partner become sensitive to these nonverbal communications, you can start to make use of them. Your ear will become sensitized to the different heroic voices, how these voices change depending upon which myth is operative, and how the choreography of the communication is affecting your ability to listen and hear.

Not Allowing Two Shadows in the Room at the Same Time

If only one shadow is present in the room during a conversation, the chances are good that it won't ruin the communication, but if two shadows are present, the communication will go nowhere until one of them leaves.

Both of your shadows are present if, during a conversation, neither of you is listening or hearing. You're interrupting each other, each rehearsing your next verbal bullet. Not only do you feel desperate that you are losing the argument, but your feelings for your partner are usually grotesquely negative.

At this point, if you have control over your shadow in that moment, the smart move is to silence it and bystand. This will allow your partner's shadow to retreat. If you succeed but your partner's behavior doesn't change, you have two choices. You can stay and listen in the name of love, so long as you're not being a victim or a martyr—in other words, motivated by your own shadow. Or, in the name of love (both of yourself and your partner) you can leave the room—not angrily, not slamming the door. Simply leave the field.

Changing the Nature of the Discourse When Stuck

If a conversation isn't working, it is crazy, suicidal even, to remain in the field. It is at this point that you must change the nature of the discourse. You must find a third way. There are a number of ways to do this. The least sophisticated, and least apt to resolve anything, is to change the subject.

The best move is to leave the field together; to separate from your shadows simultaneously and together look down on yourselves from above. This is the most difficult yet most effective move for healing and resolution of differences. It allows you to be together in a complicated place where you can feel both understanding and compassion for the two people who have been trying to ruin their love.

Myth Work in the Sexual Fantasy Myth

When two partners have fallen into the true Stygian depths, there is a good chance that their broken contracts in two or more myths will have led to the loss of desire. For many couples, regaining lost desire seems like the most difficult and daunting of all tasks. Part of this may be because of the way in which so many people begin their relationships—by going straight to bed rather than by gaining a deep understanding of each other first. Thus we assume that rabid desire is the easiest and most natural part of a relationship and that if we no longer feel our partner's sexuality, we have lost all. Nothing could be further from the truth since, as I have said, sex is the most sensitive barometer of the health of a relationship and one of the first to register problems in the relationship as a whole. Sexual desire can be one of the slowest parts of the relationship to return even after the couple's Myth and Shadow Work is well underway and starting to be successful.

When a couple has gone through the terrible pain of broken contracts and perhaps not made love in months or even years, they may no longer view each other as sexual. And while much of this can be reclaimed through Myth and Shadow Work, there are other tools that can be used to help reclaim lost desire. They are:

- eroticizing the familiar
- eroticizing imperfections

Eroticizing the Familiar

That familiarity breeds contempt is a depressing bit of folk wisdom, but one which is often true in the realm of sexual relations, even between partners who are not experiencing difficulties. Once again, I must underscore that the mind is our most important sexual organ and I must remind the reader of that all-important construct upon which lasting love and desire is based: Deep Knowing, Mystery, and Gratitude. Through deep knowing of our partners we are able to appreciate the differences, the depths and the nuances of that uncharted terrain which is our partner. Paradoxically, the more we know of that person, the greater the mystery. Our partner, the depths of his or her soul, continue to elude us the closer we get. If we remain open to the mystery, we have a chance to maintain desire, because it is the mystery of the Other which fuels our initial desire. We must find our way back through the pain, the contempt, and our own truth to the mystery of that other person— so familiar, so loved, and yet so uncharted.

Eroticizing Imperfection

We are all imperfect in some way, and even if we are not now, we will become so as we age. If visual perfection is our only stimulus for desire, we are in trouble. We have all seen middle-aged men and women who involve themselves in series of inappropriate relationships fueled only by visual fantasies. From the outside, it is clear that no one can run fast enough to outdistance time and aging. Eventually, these men and women will be unable to attract the visually perfect lovers they desire. It is for this reason that those who can use their minds to eroticize imperfections in their partners—and to accept their own imperfections—have another essential tool for the maintenance of desire over a lifetime.

One of my clients once said to me, "My wife is upset about the weight she has put on. She is becoming embarrassed to show me her naked body, but what she doesn't understand or believe yet is that I see her body as beautiful. I really do. It will never lose its attraction. What a deal for *me!*" Indeed, this man and his lover are both lucky, for he is clear that the locus of desire is in his mind, and he feels blessed that this is so.

Shadow Work

In Book 7 of his *Republic*, Plato describes the allegory of the cave. He tells of human beings living in an underground den which has only a mouth open to the light. They have been there since childhood. Their legs and necks are chained so that they cannot move and can see only in front of them. Above and behind them a fire is blazing at a distance. Like us, the prisoners see only their own shadows which the fire throws on the opposite wall of the cave. To the prisoners the truth is literally nothing but the shadows of the images. When we are in the shadow, we are those prisoners.

Shadow Work is consciousness-seeking. It is a descent into the underworld in search of the dark side of the soul for the purpose of bringing our shadows back up into the light of day where we may come to know them and reconnect with them. Our shadows are a projection of reality rather than reality itself.

The problem with our shadows is not that we have them, but that we deny their presence. When we continue to suppress our shadows, they overwhelm our sense of reality so that we come to believe that their voices are the ultimate truth. When a person says she cannot receive the kind of sexual love she desires, she truly believes that there are no other options. Harold's denial that there could be any perspective but his made it impossible for him to glimpse his shadow. Instead he could only view his behavior as appropriate and just. To deny that there is any other perspective prevents true communication between lovers.

Once we become aware of our shadows we start to understand how subjective our view of reality really is. Even more important, we begin to experience a new degree of freedom to view life differently and to behave in new ways. In other words, we begin to grow.

We have shadows in all three myths. The shadow of the Personal Myth is the mother of all shadows. It is so powerful because it is the universal disappointment, the universal experience of longing for something we don't get—perfect love. It is the voice of the wounded inner child seeking desperately to explain to himself the incomprehensible actions of the adults around him. It is the child's way of taking responsibility for not being loved. As we have seen, the failure of the parents to provide perfect love (an impossibility) is translated into a deep inner feeling of unworthiness which we carry with us until we begin to learn about it and deconstruct it. When we finally do the Myth Work with a partner who is capable of communicating in the Personal Myth, this yearning, longing part of us is redeemed and cared for at last.

The shadows of the Gender Myth are the voices of thwarted heroes who are failing to be recognized for their heroism in high-stakes situations. These shadows are less devastating to a couple's communication than the shadow of the Personal Myth, because they run less deep in our emotional life. Our heroic modes and their shadows develop at a less vulnerable time in our life and are therefore less plangent. It is in the shadow of the Gender Myth that the Survivor hero shades off into the abandoner, the Fixer into the abuser, and the Protector into the victim/accuser. The shadows of the heroes can act as a sort of malevolent stage director forcing us to speak and behave in ways which are guaranteed to push our partners away just when we most want to pull them close.

The shadows of the Sexual Fantasy Myth are the unspoken desires, the shameful secrets that block our sexual and sensual energy with those we love. Successful Shadow Work enables us to achieve a greater degree of self-acceptance by learning how our demons define us. It helps us recognize and defuse the dark voices which spoil our bids for love and intimacy. The paradox of Shadow Work is that you begin the process hating yourself and end up feeling compassion and love for yourself. By bringing back into consciousness the parts of you that have long been separated, denied, or ignored, you are able to love the person that is really you. You will learn that your shadows in all three myths are not the voices of The Truth, but a subjective view of reality that was born in the past and still continues to haunt you. Through Shadow Work, you will come to see that it is, at best, only a partial view and is highly influenced by past events.

In the Personal Myth

When either or both of you are feeling unloved, you are first plunged into your Personal Myth, where you re-experience disappointment and betrayal and, if you sink deeply enough into the shadow of this myth, vulnerability and self-criticism. The Shadow Work which must be done in the Personal Myth is the discussion of the undiscussable—that is, you must bring the demon voices to the surface.

Harold, the rage-filled surgeon with the painter wife, had one of the deepest victim/accuser shadows I have ever witnessed. The following is a typical scene which occurred before Harold released, first to me, and later to Amy, the childhood rage which fed this deep shadow.

Harold stands in the foyer of his house looking through the mail, having just returned from a long day of surgery at the hospital. His briefcase is on the floor next to him. Momentarily distracted by the mail and a meeting coming up later that evening, he inadvertently leaves his briefcase in the foyer while he goes upstairs to change his clothes. Amy, his wife, is in the kitchen cooking. When she goes out into the hallway to greet him she notices the briefcase lying where someone could trip on it. Dinner is on the boil, so she calls upstairs.

"Harold, could you move your briefcase when you come down? And also I'm running a little behind, so don't hurry."

Harold cannot believe what he has heard. He dresses for the meeting. He is nervous. He will be presenting his clinical findings on a procedure he's developed which reduces his patients' postoperative pain. But he can't get Amy's words out of his mind. He's rehearsing his reply as he makes his way to the kitchen. Running late? She has clearly forgotten his meeting and how much doing a good job means to him. He will have to go off hungry or arrive late. He begins to feel crazed, the way he did as a child. Amy catches that familiar pained look, the look of an injured boy, on his face. She sighs. Her heart sinks. She knows that one of their scenes is about to begin.

"Amy, come here. I'm very upset."

Amy knows that Harold will go on and on. If she doesn't drop her spoon and join him he'll be even more upset. If she does, she'll probably burn the soup. She sits down. The scene begins.

"What do you mean by telling me to pick up my briefcase? I'm the only one who keeps order in this house—in our entire lives for that matter. If it weren't for me, our lives would be a stinking mess. I left my briefcase there because I'm off to a meeting at the hospital when I finish dinner—if you manage to get it cooked on time. But you probably don't remember that, do you? That's because you never pay attention to what's important to me! 'And by the way, don't hurry because I'm running late!' Great. Well, now *I'll* be late for the meeting."

As Harold rants on about the injustice of the perceived reprimand over the briefcase and her thoughtlessness about his meeting, Amy's mind slows down the way it used to when she was being chastised by her parents. Now, as then, she thinks up answers to the questions being put to her, but she can't get them out of her mouth. So she stops trying, sighs her secret, silent sigh, and attempts to make herself invisible. Three minutes later she is brought back by Harold's shouting. "God damn it, you've disappeared again! You're crazy and you drive me crazy!"

Such scenes were frequent and typical in this couple's life and in my office. In fact, on one occasion the screams of Harold's deep victim/accuser shadow were so loud and so outraged that they penetrated the double doors of my office to the waiting room beyond, so upsetting an eight-year-old who had come in with her parents for a family consult that she cowered when Amy and Harold left my office.

Not long after the day Harold left telling his wife, "David loves me," he decided to tell me his Personal Myth in a private session. "I have a story to tell you," he said. "It's something I've never discussed with anyone." And he proceeded to tell me of the shame and rage of his childhood. His mother, Esther, figured prominently. Esther was a powerful and articulate woman. She had an intuitive understanding of everyone's weaknesses and how to exploit them. She could reduce Harold to tears in an instant and her husband didn't fare much better. Harold was a slow-moving target who was therefore battered all the harder. Much to his mother's dismay, he was not a star at school. He was one of those boys who teachers kept describing as "not living up to his potential." Esther, who came from a family of scholars on one side and successful businessmen on the other, was appalled at his subpar performance. For Harold it was the only way he could fight back. Even without its being completely conscious, Harold realized that doing badly in school was his most effective weapon, the only way he could control his own life. He began to fail everything. Soon he was put into special classes. Summer school kept him away from the home he hated. So wild was his rage at his mother that even the injustice of being ostracized as a dunce was preferable to acquiescing and performing as she wanted.

In the briefcase scene, Harold's shadow is brought forth because it confirms his unconscious inner belief that he is the problem. Who will step in and stop his wife's (and before that his mother's) craziness? His father couldn't. His therapist doesn't.

In his brutal way Harold is doing what we're all doing. He is asking his wife to right the injustices of his childhood. He's not really angry that Amy has asked him to move his briefcase, although he'd never admit it. Her request is merely a trigger for the fury deep within his shadow. He flew into a rage because the conditions were right. He was plunged into the injustice of his childhood with the same sense of powerlessness that he had felt under similar situations in childhood. As a grown man, he is capable of handling the situation differently, but he has defended against so many past injustices that he can no longer discern what it is that he is angry about—the pain from the past, or the present situation which, to an outsider, would seem harmless.

Harold's telling me the "shameful" story of his humiliating academic failures and his rage at his mother was the beginning of a major breakthrough, which was perhaps partially fueled by Amy's standing up for herself during one of his rages in the office and her subsequent flight to her parents' house. His realization of the role he played in his feelings of unlovability were a sort of peak experience for this unhappy man. His taking responsibility for his shadows also allowed him to feel compassion for himself, for his wife, and even for his mother.

In the Sexual Fantasy Myth

The shadow of the Sexual Fantasy Myth is the holding back of sharing so that love does not infuse lovemaking. To enter adulthood without a sexual shadow is very rare. Every one of us has something which holds us back, something which prevents us from exploring sensual pleasure. By acknowledging these sexual shadows, we have the opportunity to transform them into more creative sexuality. While the intimate relationship is the best setting in which to transform one's sexual shadows, the sexual dialogue that you develop with your partner need never be discussed verbally, and your sexual shadows need not be brought into the light of day.

One of my clients, Molly, a medical doctor, found a way to heal her sexual shadow in a remarkable way. Molly was a Protector who denied her shadow, which meant that she was constantly in the victim role. She suffered with her patients to the point at which she sank into despair with each new disease, injury, or tale of woe. Her only outlet was to unload her burdens by complaining to others. She complained so vehemently about every irritation large and small that she drove away everyone who came into contact with her. People couldn't wait to get away because she infected them to the point of sickness with her litany of complaints. Without understanding how, she was also driving away men who might have loved her, and so she grew increasingly desperate about her chances for ever having sexual pleasure and love in her life.

Through an odd series of events, Molly found her way into one of the local dominant and submissive communities. She had just entered this community when she started therapy with me. I expressed serious concerns about the safety of this activity and the self-destructive attitudes that her involvement might suggest. However, she resisted all my efforts to get her to temper her behavior. As it turned out, Molly's participation within the "Scene," as it is called, was remarkably healing. Participating with an experienced "mentor," she experienced—for the first time in her life—enough trust to explore her inner world and her sexual identity. She began serving as the submissive partner, which put her directly in touch with her victim shadow. In fact, her shadow was honored within the Scene. Molly soon became known as a great submissive partner. As she put it, "I am willingly giving over my power to the dominant, but I am not shamed by this act. I am honored for it. I do it in trust, and I experience ecstatic sex in the process."

Molly was, in effect, rescuing her shadow by bringing it into consciousness and actively acknowledging that she was giving over her power willingly. Such a person is not a victim. A victim gives up her power against her own will. Molly was learning the difference, and her understanding was carrying over into the rest of her life. For Molly, the Scene was more than sex. It was an exploration of her Sexual Fantasy Myth and its shadow. That exploration was a confrontation of parts of herself she had long denied. While I do not recommend participation in the dominant-submissive community, I realized once again that exploration of the Sexual Fantasy Myth and confrontation with the shadows are ultimately healing—as long as they are done within the context of love. The saving grace for Molly was that she was involved in the Scene only a short while before she fell in love with a man who was also involved. The love she experienced with her partner strengthened the trust she needed to explore her inner world and to embrace her shadow.

The story of Blane and Tess, on the other hand, illustrates ways that deep and denied sexual shadows from the past can haunt a relationship years later.

Blane was pure WASP in the best sense of the term, and Tess was his female equal. Both were good-looking, well-mannered, and educated. Blane had much to offer a wife: a good family, financial security, a place in the community—and still more, because he was a kind and genuinely caring man. Blane's dilemma was that although he found his bride attractive, he could summon no sexual desire for her. He tortured himself for disappointing the woman he had chosen to marry. Unlike his mother, who had suffered his father's endless stream of mistresses in silence, Tess spoke up. She had been sexually frightened by the ardor of an earlier suitor and so she had welcomed Blane's sexual reticence during courtship. But, as their marriage went on, her sense of self-worth was undermined by their infrequent and decidedly cool sexual encounters.

At last Blane found a way to make love to his wife. One night, he called to mind a favorite memory of his mother framed in an open window of their summer house, drenched in afternoon sunlight, her serious eyes squinting from the breeze blowing off the ocean. Next he summoned from some strangely inspired place an image of his prep school roommate, Todd, Adonis-like in his beauty, unselfconsciously toweling himself in front of an open window after his morning shower. To his confused relief—Blane would not say delight—he soon became erect, a state he could maintain if he let his mind play back and forth between these two sensuously pleasurable portraits.

One might have hoped that through the power of his imagination Blane had found a way out of his dilemma, but his "decency" held him hostage. It was, for him, a violation of some unwritten law regarding a woman's right to be desired honestly for herself, by virtue of her womanly qualities. On the other hand, he believed that Tess had a right to be sexually satisfied by whatever means necessary so that she could at least conceive the children she so wanted. He would "bring up" the portraits for her, but on the condition that he do it for the purpose of having children and not for his own pleasure, which meant very infrequently. As a way of reconciling his dilemma, Blane would, at these times, put himself into a sort of fugue state so that he later had no memory of lovemaking. This provided a cover for what he deemed a self-indulgent use of fantasy to get him through the necessary sexual performance. Thus he fathered two children, seven years apart. For the rest of the couple's sexual life he preferred to struggle and to pay for his nameless offenses under a cloud of shame. Eventually he and Tess, in unspoken agreement, eliminated sex from their lives until they came to me for help with their marriage.

After struggling for a year to bring about some feelings of desire in their marriage Tess asked me to work alone with Blane. She probably knew of his problem, on some level just beneath awareness. When he revealed his dilemma to me and then, painfully, to Tess, he was relieved of a burden he'd carried for fifteen years. Did he want to consider coming out as a homosexual or at least exploring that as an option? He said he had explored the option in men's groups. I believed him. Could he continue to utilize his dual portraits as a means for bringing up sexual desire?

"I believe I could," he told me. "But I want to tell Tess the whole truth, and I'm certain it won't sit well with her. Besides I think it's too late for me."

Blane's position saddened me. Yet he was right. He did reveal all. Tess, initially shocked, was less upset by his confession than Blane had feared. After weeks of debate, they separated. After months of dating others, they got together again. Sex was to be forgotten. So far as I know, they are still together.

As this story illustrates, one of the great mistakes any of us can make is to deny the presence of the sexual shadow. To do so can only wreak havoc in our lives and in those of our lovers.

The Tools of Shadow Work

There are two important tools for doing Shadow Work. They are:

- using the mirror
- journal work

Shadow Work is not about the pursuit of some great revelation or powerful new insight, although this does happen at times. It is really about something else. It is about migration—moving away from the unloved self toward the loved self. Most often, the discovery that we have been mistaken about our unlovability comes softly. "My, oh my," one of my patients said over and over, first to himself and then to his wife and to me. "It's been there all along out of sight and then out of focus for so long. And then, my, oh my, I saw it clearly for the first time." Redemption through Shadow Work is not an award given by others. It begins with for-

giving oneself. The migration from the unloved self through dialogue is the means by which self-healing is accomplished.

Using the Mirror

The mirror—a metaphor for looking at parts of the self we cannot
see without our partner's help— is used when one of you is engulfed
by the shadow and accuses the other of being unloving. The partner who is not in the shadow must hold up an imaginary mirror to
her partner and tell him what she sees. She must explain in detail
all of what she sees him doing. At the same time, she must say, "I
realize that ninety-nine percent of what I am saying is my own projection and therefore is false, but one percent may be true. I am
asking you to go, reflect honestly, and take a hard look at that one
percent." At that point, the partner must go to his journal and
write, or go reflect on all that he feels and has observed about himself in that high-stakes encounter.

It is key that the partner who is offering the mirror is not in
the grip of his own shadow. Offering the mirror when you are in
the shadow is bound to be destructive. Also, remember that if you
do offer your partner the mirror, you must also be willing to accept
it back. You have the right to decline the mirror when your partner offers it, but you must remember that by declining to look in
the mirror or by rejecting your spouse's observations, you are also
rejecting your own healing and ensuring that your shadows will
continue to rule your life and your relationships. The only way to
grow is by accepting the mirror and finding that one percent which
is true. Your partner is helping you see a part of yourself which you
could not see without her or him. Agreeing to look into the mirror means taking responsibility for your shadows.

We begin to grow when our mate holds up the mirror and says,
"Look at this!" The first time we truly accept the mirror proffered
by our partner and use it to overcome our dialogic barriers, we are
shocked. We are all prone to rejecting what stretches us. But by

accepting that at least one percent of what that mirror is showing us is true, we can break through those barriers and discover ourselves in a way we never could without that feedback from a partner. Now, armed with that one-percent truth, we may begin to rewrite our narratives. But because our myths are not easily altered, and because our shadows know the art of deception and fight to maintain their dominion, we continue to need the mirror and a partner who is able to hold it up to us in a truly loving spirit.

Journal Work

Strictly speaking, journal work is not about writing or keeping a diary. Journal work is an attitude of openness—an opening of the self to the unexpected, a willingness to plough through one's shame, grief, rage, or anxiety in order to get to the other side. Writing is certainly the most disciplined way of manifesting this attitude, but it is not the only way. Some people find it easy to do this sort of self-examination in a journal on an almost daily basis. Others do so only intermittently, and others not at all, but they still do courageous journal work. We can also do journal work while walking in the woods. We can do it in our minds if we so choose. What I have learned, however, is that by writing in a journal we have a special tool for luring out into the open the voices locked into our family archives.

When you write in your journal and make your discoveries, especially about yourself, you will come to realize that you are healing those parts of yourself that have been cast into the darkness and have been unloved for so long. One of my clients once said to me, "Journal Work is an act of forgiving." We can consciously use Journal Work to minimize and, optimally, eliminate the vengeful and wasteful monologues that circle round and round in our minds after we've been hurt, bested, or wronged by our partner. Certainly these monologues are exceedingly hard to resist. This is because our shadows continue to try to trip us up so that we miscommunicate again and again rather than speak and act in ways which will show our partners that we are really asking to love and be loved. Our shadows would return us to that childhood anxiety where we "know" that we are unloved, unworthy of love, and incapable of giving meaningful love. In this way our shadows whisper self-fulfilling prophecies which keep us in the darkness of our caves just when we most want to reach out. Consider how utterly limited, restrictive, and narrow is the narrative landscape you put yourself into when you flee to the darkest reaches of your mind after a particularly pernicious conversation with, of all people, someone you more than likely still love. Among all else that it does, Journal Work expands your narrative universe. In shifting from monologues of blame projection and revenge to truthful dialogues with the self, it not only takes away the power of our demons to hurt us; it changes our conversation with others.

Bonnie, eager to "make this marriage work or get out before I, my sense of self, and my children are destroyed," grabbed at every tool that therapy, books, and friends offered up. Having kept a diary since childhood, Bonnie produced copious text on a daily basis. It was a nightly outpouring of anger. To release her tortured mind from its vengeful monologues, she merely transferred them to her journal, which was not a journal at all. Nor was the writing a transformative dialogue with herself. In other words, Bonnie did not use her journal work to explore herself, nor did she use her partner as a mirror. Rather than use the journal to capture and talk with her own shadows, she merely made it a catalogue of all her husband's shortcomings and her rage at him. She was never able to get through her rage. In effect, she was still a victim of her shadows, who were misleading her and blinding her to their malign influence.

When you write in your journal, there is a trick to capturing the shadows. Don't pursue them directly, but rather allow them to reveal themselves to you. Write about the details of your disagreement with your partner or whomever has made you feel unworthy of love and unlovable. Get all your anger out. Then allow yourself to rest. Forget about Journal Work and enjoy the relief the writing has provided you. The next day, while you're walking down the street or showering, you may have an insight which will permit you to see yourself from an entirely new perspective. You will see your-self demanding love in a way that ensures that you will not receive it. Or you will realize how powerful the effect of your mother's anger was on you, or how little you believe in your own self-worth. Sometimes it will all seem so simple and obvious that you will won-der why you didn't see it years ago. The most profound truths often come to us on little feet.

When you have an insight into your shadows, you may want to return to your journal and write it down. If you do so, don't place any pressure on yourself to change. Make no judgment or criticism of yourself. To do so would only frighten the shadow back into its lair. Instead, explore your shadow as if you have no intention of changing it. Making something fully conscious is actually a far more powerful way to change behavior than trying to change it overtly without fully admitting its presence to yourself.

The Rules of Shadow Work

In order for your Shadow Work to be successful, both personally and as a way of healing your relationship and restoring lost desire, you must take the following rules seriously and adhere to them strictly. It is part of the shadows' trickery to make it difficult for you to do so and to tempt you away from them at every turn. Be aware!

- Do not expect reciprocity.
- You do not have to share.

Non-Reciprocity

When you decide to explore your shadows, you must be clear that this is your own decision. It is completely independent of what the other person does. Your Shadow Work is about you. Calling upon your partner to reciprocate is natural. It is the voice of the shadow telling you, "Don't do it unless he does." This, as we have seen, was a serious problem for Alex and Barbara. By remaining unable to identify these thoughts as being part of her shadow, Barbara chose to put the entire weight of the work on Alex's shoulders while steadfastly refusing to do her own work. The end result was broken dreams and Alex finally saying, "Enough is enough!"

Sharing or Not

I differ from many therapists in that I do not believe that all secrets must be aired. In doing Shadow Work, it's important that both you and your partner understand that there is no obligation to share what you learn in your depths. By feeling that you can keep your own secrets, you are arming yourself to really go into that darkness. This understanding throws the shadow off guard, since the shadow does not want to be caught. Your message to the shadow is, "Shadow, if I can really get to know you—the shame, the pain—I don't have to expose you. Trust me."

Paradoxically, the understanding that you don't have to tell your partner about your shadows makes you more willing to share them. But even if you never do, Shadow Work can do its magic. We have seen this in the case of Harold, who was able to participate fully in the couple's breakthrough after he told me the shameful secrets of his Personal Myth shadow. To my knowledge, he still hasn't shared this story with Amy, but even so they are continuing to progress.

Many people find that the discoveries made in Shadow Work are so exciting and liberating that they want to share them with each other because they feel so freed and clear. They have captured something which has eluded them for most of their lives. It's important work and often worth celebrating.

Tools and Principles for Keeping You on Track

Sometimes couples find it useful to have a checklist to help them stay on track with the work. Here is a short list to help you keep focused on the important points of Myth and Shadow Work:

- In relationships, the pursuit of being right usually results in being alone. Learn that you don't always have to be right. Instead, learn to learn, so that you can be together. Do not assume that only one of you can be right.
- Shift the strategy from attacking to evoking, from changing your lover to being curious again.
- Avoid blaming your partner. Instead, take responsibility for exploring your myths.
- Don't look for the original cause. Often arguments come down to: "You started it all when . . ." The original cause can't be found. If it can, it's usually betrayal in the Personal Myth.

Chapter Eleven

The Journey Back:
Reclaiming Lost Desire

The journey back to love and desire varies in length and difficulty, depending upon how long each partner has insisted that his or hers is the only truth and whether there have been betrayals such as affairs or other destructive acting-out along the way. For those who can disabuse themselves of the illusion of one truth, the healing of the relationship and the journey back to love and desire can be shorter than one would think. On the other hand, those who hold on to their old opinions as if they are absolutes will make slower progress, if any at all. This is not to say that the journey back is easy no matter how well intentioned, open, and honest you both may be. Ultimately, being in relationship is the path and the solution to the problems of the relationship, which means that much of the time we must learn from our own mistakes.

What I have tried to do is give you ways of looking at relationship problems, and helping you frame them so that you can better deal with the issues before you. I have seen couples who have been so buried in destructive patterns and emotions that all seemed lost when they started therapy. And yet, these same people made it all the way back to the renewal of love and desire. Such things happen every day. They can happen to you and your partner.

I don't offer pat answers. Rather, my way is simply to help people see themselves, perhaps for the first time, without judgment or condemnation. The more you do the work described in this book, the more you will come to realize that being human is a paradoxical condition of both light and dark, enormous strengths and hidden shadows. None of us is different in this regard. It is only in the details that we differ.

There are no techniques that can solve the problems of relationships, but there are steps that should be kept in mind on the journey back to love and wholeness.

Simply Take the First Step

The first step on the journey back is a simple pledge:
I want to learn how to love, not win the war of being right.
I want to recover desire and take it to its true limits.
I acknowledge my dark side and the harm it does to me, to us, and to our love.
I turn to my light side for the courage I will need to face my shadows.
I turn to you for help in harnessing my shadows in the service of love.

Maintain a Positive Dialogue with Yourself

Commit to maintaining an ongoing dialogue with yourself that is both positive and nurturing. The best and most practical way I know to do this is by writing in a journal, either daily or several times per week. By placing your thoughts, anger, or disappoint-

ments on the page, you externalize them and see them from a distance. The fact is that journal writing by itself can improve your
emotional condition and your outlook on life.

A positive dialogue is not "happy talk." Rather, you must go
into the darkness of your soul, where your fears, doubts, shame, bad
memories, disappointments, and remorse still reign. In short, you
must enter your shadows and you must do so without judging or
criticizing yourself. Enter your shadows with love even as you feel
the pain.

Talk Lovingly to Your Shadows

Your biggest and toughest task on the way back to love and desire will be to confront your shadows. This means that you must
allow back into consciousness those parts of you that are in pain
and feel unloved and unworthy of love. These are the very parts
of you that are blocking you from nurturing yourself and getting
what you need in your relationship. To deny these aspects of your
being is disastrous. Everyone has shadows in all three myths although the depth of these shadows can vary widely. We all feel
unloved and unworthy of love much of the time. When we experience these feelings we are often overtaken by a kind of madness
which forces us to demand love in ways that guarantee we'll be rejected. Some people do this by shouting, some by physically attacking, and some by more subtle attacks such as infidelity or
other psychological abuse of their partners. If that isn't madness,
I don't know what is. Yet all of us suffer the pain of our shadows
and all of us behave in crazy ways in our search for love and acceptance. In order to heal the shadows, therefore, we must use a
paradoxical approach. Rather than condemning or repressing
them, we must welcome them back into the light of love and
acceptance.

It's a big mistake to believe that you can use will-power or positive imaging or some other technique to deny your shadows or make them go away. Such attempts would be analogous to denying the existence of one of your arms. You must honor the contents of your shadows by acknowledging their need to be reintegrated into your awareness. You do that by accepting the fact that you have dark, unwelcome feelings, by looking honestly at the behaviors that they inspire and examining these feelings so that you understand their roots. By bringing these parts of yourself back into consciousness, you can love yourself in the places where you have long felt unloved and unlovable. This is the path of self-forgiveness, healing, and self-love. Only you can do this for yourself. No one else's love can heal you in this way.

If you want to know whether or not you are doing your Shadow Work and therefore healing yourself, ask yourself if you are accepting the accuracy of at least one percent of your partner's criticisms of you. If you are listening to your mate when he or she holds up the mirror, and then going to your journal to examine your shadow in privacy, you are growing and healing your old wounds. When you both do this work, there is no hurdle that you cannot overcome. Two people who acknowledge their shadows to themselves and to one another are taking responsibility for themselves. This is the basis for trust in a marriage.

Practice Non-Judgment

I see myself in virtually everyone I meet and, frankly, it's a humbling experience. There are very few things that people do that I cannot envision myself doing under certain circumstances. In the pages of this book I have introduced many couples who have experienced what you might think are very individual problems. It would be natural for you to identify with one or two of these couples and see the others as completely different from yourself. I'd like you to think of these people as like you in many ways. The more we see our similarities to others, the more we are able to unify parts of ourselves that we have banished or rejected because they do not seem to fit into one or another of our myths.

This work of self-acceptance and acceptance of others is especially important in long-term relationships, where a self-righteous insistence on our own perception of the situation is often the club with which we bludgeon each other. Insisting on being right means that you must de facto blame your partner, which is one of the behaviors destined to lead to the loss of love and desire.

Love and Sex Are a Path to Growth

After reading this book, you should have a new definition of what it means to be in relationship and what it means to be in a sexual relationship. I have tried to illuminate the meaning of sex—not the easy sex people have at the beginning of relationships which quickly ends in disappointment and frustration, but sex as the threshold to self-discovery and the knowing of your partner. Love and desire rest upon a balance between this deep knowing, continuing curiosity, and the maintenance of the mystery of the Other.

When we set out on the sexual journey it is with a very limited understanding of ourselves, our lovers, and the meaning of love. In the course of that journey, we necessarily encounter many obstacles and trials. To use these trials for self-reflection and growth requires a certain individual heroism. It is heroic to honestly investigate our myths and shadows, and doing so makes us exciting in our spouse's eyes and inevitably leads to a better sexual relationship.

Talk Is the Ultimate Aphrodisiac

Many couples today rely on various types of pornography to revive flagging desire. But I believe that talk is the ultimate tool of love—

not sex talk necessarily, but talking about one's personal stories, one's heroic aspirations, and one's shadows. Take turns sharing these with your mate. In the course of this sharing, learn to apologize. This is the language of love and it cannot help but bring you closer together. Nothing nurtures intimacy more surely than sharing the tender secrets of your souls.

As one of my patients said, "We've done a lot of work, and we've been through a lot. We know we won't be done until we're dead, but now we're able to talk about anything that comes up without getting too deeply into trouble. We know how to talk to each other, and this is a tool we'll have for the rest of our lives."

Earlier I recounted that Rebecca, Carlton's wife, had said that at one point in their marriage they had grown so far apart she felt as if she had a stranger in her bed. Your lover becomes a stranger when you do not communicate with one another from your souls. Intimate discourse—talking about real feelings from both the past and the present—puts an end to the foreignness between people and restores trust and intimacy. Like many couples, you and your partner may be very busy. It's important, therefore, to schedule time to talk; to share what you each have learned in your journals or the insights you had in the shower or on the way to work.

Recovering from Infidelities

Often when love or desire is lost for an extended time, one or both partners will have an affair. Coming back can be frightening and mined with anxiety. After a betrayal has come out into the open, the partners must ask themselves some questions.

1. Does the defector want to remain in the relationship? How much?
2. Does the other partner want out?
3. How does the defector explain the betrayal? In systemic

terms: was he or she lonely in the relationship, angry, was the affair in retaliation for something? Or was the affair due to an addiction?

4. Does the defector blame the partner for the affair?

If the answers to these questions come out all right, then the couple has a chance to rebuild the trust and repair what was broken.

This subject is too vast and too important to treat lightly, which, regrettably, we must do. However, it is so common among struggling couples that I would be remiss to ignore it completely. I will confine my remarks to one segment of the population, as represented by one young couple, childless, still forming their careers, the pressures of which are partly responsible for the affair. Such couples offer a fair test of the book's theses. On the one hand, a still-young relationship can in general be presumed to have produced less damage to the partners as individuals, which might boost the method's influence. On the other, since there are fewer ramifications when young marriages dissolve, a method designed to reconcile them has less power of persuasion. Although what I did with the Lincolns, Jill and Cameron, does not necessarily apply to others, enough is generalizable to make the effort worthwhile.

Jill had an affair with a visiting professor at the university where she was working on a research project. The affair was facilitated by the fact that she and her husband worked in separate cities and commuted several hours by plane to see one another. When Jill's affair was revealed, Cameron was crushed and enraged.

The Lincolns did moderately well in the answers to the above questions. Neither wanted out of the marriage, but Cameron did not know whether he could contain his rage and need for revenge, and Jill, who would not abruptly break off the relationship with her former lover (though sex would no longer be part of it), importuned Cameron to "Please hang in there." She wanted to end any reason to further deceive her husband, felt aggrieved over what she'd done to Cameron, but also felt responsible for exiting the infelicitous relationship with her head high. Change always occurs in phases. I will describe only how I set the stage for the first phase, not even what I did.

In Phase One

I supported Jill's position, a calculated risk on her part, because it defined her as wanting to be honest and honorable, and open to new learning about herself. My message to Cameron and to anyone in this situation is, "Yes, you have a right to be morally outraged and upset with your wife. But know that you can only carry those feelings on for so long before she rebels at carrying all the shame and guilt. Do not fail to use this unhappy situation to learn. Keep your choices open." And to Jill, "The point of encouraging Cameron's moral outrage is not for you to wallow and relent and submit to abuse, but to equate his rage not only to the depth of his pain, but to a passion that will serve both of you if the marriage survives."

"My job," I said, "is to provide a container for the fullest expression of feelings, and for an exploration into the darkest corners of your souls. If you choose to learn instead of blame, you will accomplish in six months what other couples do in six years.

"Expect to be confused about sex, and whether and how to make love. If you find yourself wanting to hurt her sexually, tell her that but don't do it. If you are sick with shame but feel obliged to make love to him, tell him that but don't do it. If you do make love, keep in mind that four psyches will be vying for control: two innocent children who are confused and hurt, and two adults trying to make strong heroic statements. Take care of the children."

I sought to help the couple reframe the experience so that it was no longer viewed just as an injury perpetrated by one partner on the victimized other:

"Perhaps you can't recover from this. But instead of letting your righteous anger, your punitive guilt, and your shadows create a situation in which forgiveness and healing will be impossible, why not use the opportunity, unpleasant as it is, to find out about yourself, your partner, and your relationship? Time puts every marriage to a test of survival. When one partner has an affair, time is condensed, and this can be a good thing. In situations such as yours, the test takes on the character of a trial. That, too, can be a good thing, because trials call for the most careful consideration of evidence. No one is the same after a trial. But judgments are rendered, and God willing, justice is truly served."

Cameron and Jill are just now entering phase three. They have come through the trial, each a clear winner. I will go out on a limb: had Jill not had the affair, this couple would not have made it. In their third year of marriage, after one year of therapy work, this couple is as solidly committed as any young couple I have seen who were not playing pretend. They went deep into Myth Work, from which they have built a foundation of trust and deep knowledge about themselves and each other. How they handle family matters, some very difficult; how they help each other make decisions about career, friendships, and life; how they talk and manage difference; how they walk all these paths reflects the fact that they bought into the frame we built at the outset, and more than made due.

Reviving Sensuality and Sexuality

Reviving the sensual is an essential component of the trip back. Survivors who have stubbornly martyred themselves in the name of love will often have martyred their ability to feel deeply or to appreciate their own needs for sensuality. Protectors who have felt victimized in the situation may believe they will never experience sensual satisfaction with their partners again. Fixers who try to conquer may feel guilty when they awaken to their shadows. No matter what your heroic mode, it's important to confess your feelings to your partner. Open up to your vulnerability, which is the wellspring of feeling, tenderness, and sensuality within you. Sensuality begins with talking to each other more gently than you have been doing, putting aside the anger, the blame, the pain. From there, you should allow yourself to touch and be touched without necessarily proceeding to sex. Reopening to vulnerability can be testing for many couples. Do it only for as long as you can, but do it regularly.

Enormous anxieties arise when we lose touch with our sensuality, because we fear that we may no longer be in full possession of our sexual power. These fears must be confessed. Allow them to bring you closer, not to maintain the distance between you. Show your wounds and understand that your partner did not cause them.

Keep your expectations where they belong. Many couples expect too much of this stage of the journey back and therefore become anxious and disappointed. It is unlikely that this stage will feel like a second honeymoon. Many couples who plan romantic holidays at this point find themselves feeling strained and anxious. It is better to have distractions sufficient to assure that not all the attention need be placed on sex. At this stage, intimacy, not raw sex, is your goal. Holding and touching are more than good enough.

Practice gratitude. Allow yourself to nurture and to feel grateful for being nurtured and touched back. Sex will take care of itself.

Masturbation on the Return Journey

Many of the couples who stop making love turn to masturbation rather than affairs as a way to relieve sexual tension. While there can be good reasons for this practice within the context of a committed relationship—for example, when one member of the couple is sick—it can also become a problem. Masturbation can make the return to sex more difficult for some people, because of insecurities they may feel about each other and about sexual performance. The danger, of course, is that the fantasy life may eclipse the desire for lovemaking with one's partner. Men and women who have started on the road back to love have often told me of the difficulties they have had in giving up the substitute for the real thing.

For couples who are committed to restoring desire to their re- lationships, the best approach to the question of masturbation is for partners to confess to each other their habit, agree to suspend it in support of increasing desire and making the journey back to lovemaking, and share their ongoing anxieties as part of their intimate conversations.

A Few Words About Drinking

Be careful that drinking on the journey back doesn't hook your shadows. If, over a bottle of wine, you find yourselves escalating into a shadow dance, try to stand back. Then, when the dust has settled, make the issue part of sober conversation. But navigate carefully. The shadows may be present in disguised form in the sober conversation. The one whose shadow is most hooked by drinking will be less willing to talk about what happened or could happen again. The other partner may want to use the situation to moralize, a position guaranteed to hook the other's shadow. Instead of trying to make rules, the couple must agree that if the shadows are invoked while drinking, they do not engage in any discussion about the relationship at the same time. As your Shadows are more and more under control, this is less apt to cause escalations—or you will have better tools for dealing with them if they do arise.

Be Mindful of the Original Purity Within You Both

Ask yourself again and again: what is the essence of the child in me and in my partner? Remember yourself as a child. Look at pictures from your childhood. Give one to your partner and ask for one in return. Feel the purity of that child and his or her love. That purity existed before your awareness, your ambitions, and your concept of self and others. It is still greater than your judgments of yourself, and far more powerful. It can redeem you and your love entirely if you only let it. Spend time with yourself alone in the purest part of your psyche. It is there that you will find all the compassion, understanding, and unconditional love that you sought from others and still need to heal yourself. Release all your fears and judgments into that pure love. If you can, let your tears wash away pain and remorse.

Gratitude Is Essential

Feel grateful for life and for the mystery of love. No matter what has happened, it is good to be alive. No long meditations are needed. There is no need for any great spiritual revelations. Just consider the little boy or girl within you and how pure of heart he or she was and still is, and how much love you have for that child even now. Let the healing waters of the river of life flow. Love of self, joy, and gratitude arise naturally from this work. They are always available to you.

Remember Your Gender Myth and the Hero's Journey

You possess a vision for your life which was born in the Personal Myth and manifested in the Gender Myth. This vision describes the hero you want to be in your life, the person you love and admire within yourself. Meditate on that vision and do as much as you can to restore its ascendant presence. In the course of such meditation, examine yourself and do another brave thing: apologize to your partner and to yourself for your mistakes and for the actions you have taken that were triggered by your shadows. Your ascendant hero understands and forgives you, just as it forgives your partner.

Appendix A

The Communication Primer

What if, after reading about the couples in this book, you don't recognize yourselves in them, but nonetheless fear that your partnership could darken over time? Broken contracts and the onset of mythic turbulence are inevitable in any long-term committed relationship.

This section is written for people contemplating marriage or a long-term relationship, those who are recently married and want to get off to a good start, and long-term partners who have been on a fairly calm journey so far. I hope hereby to give guidelines to help these readers avoid some of the inevitable pitfalls that plague even the best relationships without exception. These pitfalls are:

Difference of Expression
Difference is, of course, inevitable and necessary for maintaining the vitality of a relationship. Until this is recognized, however, most important discussions are likely to end at a ritual impasse where true communication is nearly impossible.

Disappointment

Mutual disappointment follows on the heels of this ritual impasse, and when it occurs over a prolonged period, it results in melancholic despair. I believe that disappointment is an adult developmental phenomenon no more avoidable in the evolution of the intimate relationship than adolescence is in the evolution from child to adult. What is controllable is its depth, its duration, and the extent to which it damages the relationship.

Loss of Desire

The final pitfall is the loss or withdrawal of desire and, eventually, of all sexual intimacy. Melancholy, like all forms of depression, has a deadening effect on passion. Where hope seems lost, the libido fails to respond to stimuli which formerly aroused it.

In the first part of *My Lover, Myself*, I have shown how our childhood experiences and the mythology which arises from our stories make us vulnerable to experiencing these inevitable pitfalls in our adult love relationships. In the second part I showed how we can repair relationships that have fallen into a deep pit using Myth and Shadow Work. This primer is meant to be used as a preventive for couples willing to try to do the necessary work on their own without the help of a therapist or with very little professional help.

In a career devoted to research, teaching clinical practitioners, organizational consulting, and writing, nothing has commanded more of my serious attention and study than the couple in intimate relationship. Nothing is more enigmatic. No institution created by humans comes close to this one for the effort it requires to assure its survival. It is no secret that the entire therapy enterprise thrives on this difficulty, yet therapy does not seem to be able to reduce the swell of failures, testimony to the fact that solutions come hard.

Relationships that make it through the inevitable pitfalls go through three phases:

- The shocking discovery of difference
- The frightening crisis of trust
- The healing reconciliation of opposites

The cycle begins with an event around which you disagree; a fight that goes further than either of you intends; a breakdown of trust, love, and goodwill that leaves you feeling alienated; a decision to "let it go," move on, reconcile. You may kiss and make up, but you will "go there" again. In the map of desire that I am charting in this book, these cycles are an inevitable part of the journey. Their existence is not the issue. What you do with them is.

Let me caution that these phases are not traversed overnight. Time is needed both to discover the forces that will block the process along the way and to establish the habits of love you will need to counter them. Each of you needs time both to learn how your shadows have the power to undercut your true selves and to learn how to help each other tame your own demons.

This primer comprises "Three Frameworks for Keeping Love and Desire Alive," with guidelines, and "Ten Rules of the Road" for how to use them. If they work for you they will bolster your resistance to the insidious forces of decay and deconstruction which plague most couples who venture forth on the journey of love. If you are asking, "Is he trying to scare us?" my answer is an outright *yes*. Just look around you. If you do not see the wreckage in relationships of a fifty-percent divorce rate, we are in different worlds. Being prepared for the obstacles you will encounter can only help you to avoid them.

Also included are exercises of a kind many therapists recommend to their clients as homework assignments between sessions. Do them whenever you can, and when you do not do them after agreeing to, try to determine why you chose not to complete them. Your shadow may be doing its own work. In any case, be sure to discuss your reasons with your partner in a spirit of learning. This learning may be as valuable as the exercise itself. Also, when you have experience with the exercises, expect that you will come to understand how they are constructed. You may decide that they do not apply to your unique situation; that they are too generic. If so, you may want to design some of your own.

The Practice of Love: Three Frameworks for Keeping Desire Alive

I cannot state strongly enough how vital I believe it is to master these practices. *They are the lifeblood of desire!* These practices, Deep Knowing, Holding the Mystery of Love, and Expressing Gratitude, take personal discipline, unflagging commitment, and the uncompromising collaboration of both partners if love is to breathe, thrive, and endure.

It begins with Knowing, with wanting to know oneself and one's partner in the deepest sense possible. But knowing is not enough. Knowing must be balanced by Mystery, by a not-knowing, by a belief that the magic of sex is preserved not so much in the "having" and "knowable" as in the "unknowable" and "unattainable," in the delight found in appetite, in creative tension, in the eroticism of the question that is never completely answered. And finally, desire is most richly sustained by Gratitude, in an opening of the self to an appreciation of the incredible gifts love brings.

Deep Knowing

Deep Knowing relies on Talk, and Talk is the fruit of Deep Knowing. They reciprocate and feed each other. I define Talk as a highly developed form of exchange between two people in a love relationship. It is a composite language which is mastered only when two lovers have a deep knowledge of their own and their partner's most compelling stories—each person's three myths and

as many of their other stories as they can tell in a lifetime. Deep
Knowing, then, comes from narratives of self-definition that transform us in personal discourse, gender conversation, and sexual dialogue—the three languages of love and desire.

Talk is a work of art. To learn the art of Talk, we must travel the distance between hearing and *loving listening*. Listening is more than hearing and loving listening is more than listening. With loving listening, we discover the diction and the register of our lover's voice, like a poem which must be heard many times and only then perhaps studied. If you listen lovingly to every nuance as she tells her tales, you will hear her from within.

Lucy, a woman who had just passed an important milestone on the "journey back" from the dark side of love, said, "I want to tell you, David, about this strange thing which happened when Burr and I were with my family in California. Burr left the family gathering, and I followed him outside where he had gone to smoke his cigar so as not to blow secondary smoke at us. We sat in what seemed like timeless silence. Then, I began to speak from this deep place within, something I've not dared try in fifteen years—I'd feared being rebuffed or swallowed whole. Burr listened in a way I don't ever remember his doing. Ever. I got up and planted the sweetest kiss on his lips. 'This is for me, not you,' I said. It struck me then that through all our years together we heard each other's words, but never listened."

Lucy and Burr were discovering loving listening. This kind of listening calls for an attentiveness that leads much further and goes much deeper than other forms of listening. This listening is more creative. It is prepared for surprise. It is expectant. It is a listening with the heart. The heart may perceive what the eye has not seen nor the ear heard. Learning to listen in this way adds an extra dimension to relationships. Do not think it is easy; that it is a

technique one can master through some exercise—mine or anyone else's. This kind of listening must be cultivated through the
three disciplines of love.

Deep Knowing entails more than storytelling and loving listening. It involves gathering your life's materials and experiences
as text for new stories that you and your partner create together.
Relish and memorialize these experiences, for the forces which
work against good memories are powerful and insidious. One
must take them on with a kind of conscious will. Create a library of good memories and store them on shelves in your mind
where you can find them whenever you need to offset the bad
memories wrought of failed communication in the battles between myths, or the wounds inflicted by your and your partner's
shadows.

A good place to begin is with your archetypal encounter.
Remember the rush, your delight in your discovery of the perfect
Other. Remember the sexual urge this individual ignited in you.
Store this memory and the "story" of it in a special cubicle of your
mind's library. It will come in handy later in your journey.

I am going to remind you of how that wondrous episode unfolded, but don't be alarmed if you cannot fully recognize yourself,
or if my admittedly idealized rendition doesn't match your experience. Trust that all the elements were there, even though you may
have been too bewitched to recognize them.

Steps in Courtship Leading to the Mythic Contract

You may think it odd to be asked to get to know a process that
seems so natural and automatic. Not so. Does knowing how it
works take the pleasure out of it? I don't think so. Knowing of
which I speak is imbued with freshness, curiosity, inquiry, and discovery. Not knowing the steps you have taken which led you to
make your Mythic Contract will be paid for later.

1. The initial archetypal encounter

The Knowing, vital to the maintenance of desire, begins here with our certainty that we've found the lover whose part we have reserved in our Gender Hero story. But the Mystery also begins here. Not merely in the magic of inaugural sex, but in our curiosity. In setting out to know this creature who has magnetized you, what you feel most is curiosity.

2. Making the heroic presence known

If your heroic identity has "scored," you will know it. In courtship, some of us wear masks which will later come down, revealing our true heroic essence. The deception will lead to the making of false contracts. You are doing yourself and your lover no favor. The better course is to discover your own hero and present it with integrity.

3. The desire to know the other's gender ideal

Young or beginning lovers who are drawn to the sexual opportunity may skip an important step in the courtship process. If you get lost in sexual paradise, you will delay getting to know your lover's gender ideal. Note the doubt-casting nuances.

4. Displaying your own personal gender ideal

Lovers tend to commit two common errors during courtship. They "see" too much, or they "fail to see." *I told him so,* Eric's friend says when he learns of Eric's imminent divorce; *he was blinded by the sex.* Or, Mary to her mother, *Let's face it, Mom. My sister will never marry. Beautiful as she is, she sees only the warts on the men who pursue her.*

Remember, nobody but a fool is likely to show all of his colors during courtship. But don't forget that all of us enter into courtship with scars and warts and blemishes, physical and emotional, visible and hidden. We bank on love to take us as we are and to glorify our value to the world. And although we fight with tooth and nail, we only become whole when we heed feedback from our partners, who see our shadows better than we. In courtship these show up as nuances which leave us in doubt. In making our contracts we collaborate in "blind confederacy," ignoring the undertones and nuances of which I speak. Counteract this danger by creating an atmosphere of full-sighted confederacy. Ask for feedback:

- What do you see that I do not see?
- What do you see that worries you about me?

Asking for such feedback makes you responsible to yourself and your intended partner, and it relieves him or her of the burden of initiating what would otherwise seem critical.

5. The seduction poem: "Come Live with Me and Be My Love"

6. The first sexual encounter
In my experience, few modern couples agree to the gender contract before they make love. Whatever you think of the morality or the wisdom of this cultural practice, that's the way our world seems to work. Rick and Ruth waited as long as they could before they had sex. They covered the five previous steps as carefully and thoroughly as any couple in this book before giving in to their chafing libidos. Their marriage has thrived and they have been able to negotiate its few rough spots with ease—not because they proceeded with restraint, however, but rather because each "needed to know." Only then, after their gender ideals and heroes became known, was each ready to sign on with sex.

The first sexual encounter probably doesn't tell you what you need to know about your partner's Sexual Fantasy Myth. Nor does it reveal with any hope of accuracy what the sexual dialogue will really be like. But shelter the peerless wonderment of this first sexual encounter and keep it in your library of memories.

7. Agreeing to the gender contract
Even if you begin this course after you have been married for

a while, go back to the beginning as if you are just starting and *write*
your vows. Your vows represent your willingness to go on record, but not with a promise to love, honor, and obey but rather:

- Here is who I know myself to be.
- Given who I am (to the extent that I know), this is what I bring to the relationship. This is my unique value.
- Given that, this is my dream for the best that I can imagine happening.
- Everything I have vowed is a reflection of what I know and love about you, what I think you need in a love relationship, and the depth of my desire to bring it to you.

Guarding the Mystery of Love

The Deep Knowing necessary to sustain love and desire begins in the archetypal encounter, but so does the Mystery. Like desire itself, the mystery of love is charged by the high hopes of closing the gap between the wanting and the having, and between the knowing of and not-knowing of the other. But in the research and exploration of Myth Work, you may tend to forget the mysteriousness and the charisma that originally captured your interest.

Lovemaking combines both the Deep Knowing and the Mystery. From the first encounter onwards, we are drawn to the secret of the Other in which there is not only beauty but mystery, that most powerful magic of the unknown. Some secrets are not lies. They are the mind's way of playing out the mysteries of love and desire. Think of your partner as a traveler from another land whom you are endlessly curious to know, but never will completely.

To preserve the mystery of love we must safeguard desire, for the two are most happily entwined. Of all that it is, one characteristic of desire stands out—it has a futuristic vigor. Notice how much of the intensity of desire is in anticipation, in the "looking forward" to what we want to have or possess. Each time desire is fulfilled, enough mystery must remain to restore its vigor.

Yet somehow we seem to get it all wrong. When we are rendered dumb by love's contradictions, ambiguities, and paradoxes, we shun our lovers for leading us blind into this maze. Better we should remind ourselves that the immense mystery in which we are immersed should be savored, not shunned. The root meaning of the word "mystery" is to shut one's eyes and ears. Mystery is silence and darkness. We must come to believe in the great energy in the darkness of not-knowing. Trust in it despite the fear it engenders. Learn to trust in "other," and in the surprise and ambiguity of "opposite."

Expressing Gratitude

Our affluent society stays affluent by making the containers of joy and happiness bigger just when they are about to overflow. The economics of affluence demands that things which were special for us last year must now be taken for granted. This same principle can spill over into our love relationships. Instead we must wake up to the fact that the partner we have chosen is a gift and that the only appropriate response is Gratitude. Yet during Myth Work—natural or designed—feelings of separation, obstruction, distance, alienation, and loneliness are inevitable. They arise from our morbid thoughts about love and lovability. There is a loss of tenderness toward our partners and a withholding of our natural tendency to comfort them. We forget all too easily that they are experiencing distress and are in as much pain as we are ourselves. The estranged, inhibited, and cold attitude which arises acts as an impenetrable wall. Touching our partner feels like a betrayal of self. Yet being touched and cuddled is essential for the health of the relationship. The failure to touch for prolonged periods can be like a death sentence. "Coming to our senses" is an urgent remedy when we are "out of touch." Mentally will yourself to "get in touch." Apologize, show gratitude, and touch. The ultimate function of this kind of loving gratitude is to prepare the memory for forgiveness of the second disappointment—that which inevitably occurs in a committed relationship and hearkens back to the original childhood disappointment. With that forgiveness comes forgiveness of the self and the partner. The myth of perfect love is, if not restored, positioned for a second chance.

Touch is a component of this Personal Myth Work. If as infants and children we were comforted and touched, we know how much we need it. If we were not, we need it all the more. In one couple I work with, the wife remembers never being touched by either parent. Her husband was embarrassed by touch. Their sexual dialogue reflected that. They abstained for years. Their Personal Myth Work did a job against outstanding odds.

Explore with your partner how each of you wants to be touched. When your partner satisfies your need for touch or for sex, notice it, experience it, and express gratitude. Gratitude gives an added depth to sex. It centers you, and allows you to commune with the truth in each of you.

Not only is Gratitude one of the cornerstones of a love relationship, it may be essential for the well-being of our entire body. In his landmark book *The Stress of Life,* which laid out the theory upon which all later stress research was based, Dr. Hans Selye stated that the two most significant attitudes for determining the quality of one's life were gratitude and revenge. "It seems to me," he writes, "that among all the emotions, there is one which, more than any other, accounts for the absence or presence of stress in human relations: that is the feeling of gratitude—with its negative counterpart, the need for revenge . . . I think in the final analysis that gratitude and revenge are the most important factors governing our actions in everyday life."

Make the air thick with yearning. Write your obituary. Put your-self on your deathbed. Write of your appreciation of days past, without maudlin sentimentality—just a profound and genuine gratitude for a life shared.

Ten Rules of the Road

1. Sanctify the value of difference.
2. Protect sex from the politics of difference.
3. Tell your stories in a safe environment.
4. Face your shadows with courage.
5. Keep a journal of personal responsibility.
6. Know your behavioral profile.
7. Outwit the tyranny of time.
8. Pursue well-being as a serious investment.
9. Keep your body and all of its senses alive.
10. Maintain a positive balance in your emotional ledger.

During courtship, couples make their own vows which bear some resemblance to these ten rules. Against their will and judg-ment, however, many lovers let these heartfelt pledges slip away. The powers of deconstruction are relentless. They can bend our wills even when we think we're prepared for trickery. Be prepared for love to lose ground unless you and your partner band together against these powers. Unless your alliance prevails, you run the risk of joining the ranks of so many promising lovers whose broken contracts result in a needless failure of communication and the loss of sexual desire.

Write these ten rules as a frontispiece to both your journals, and highlight them. Refer to them alone or together every time your alliance is seriously threatened.

1. Sanctify the value of difference.

The mismanagement of difference is love's greatest enemy. I am not referring to general descriptions, so popular in the culture today, of differences between men and women, who are said to come from different planets. I am talking about the differences which emerge in actual face to face exchanges in any close relationship, in particular when the discoursing parties are regularly discussing matters vital to one or both. The key word here is *vital*. People who believe they are in high-stakes situations behave very differently than when they are in low-stakes situations. (High-stakes situations are those in which the heroes are called forth to defend one against dangers which appear to be life-threatening, such as where one will live, who defines reality, whether to have children, even how to spend money. Low-stakes situations, on the other hand, are more likely to involve the dreary day-to-day arguments over toilet seats, doing the dishes, and other small irritations.) Political parties, special-interest groups, religious sects, and even nations are governed by these same rules. The differences which inevitably surface in these social arrangements frustrate, anger, and alienate the players, sometimes catastrophically, as evidenced by the rash of wars, "ethnic cleansings," and suicide bombings which divide the adversaries and plague the sensibilities of the world's helpless onlookers.

The principles behind lovers' quarrels are virtually identical to conflicts that play out on larger canvases. We might even argue that in love relationships, the consequence of mismanaged differences are more devastating. The numbers of people who are seriously harmed—directly and indirectly, sometimes for generations on end—by marital and family conflict defies accurate accounting.

There's no better place for lovers to begin than by asking, "How are we to understand difference? What do we do to resolve differences?" Clearly, this entire book is a multi-pronged attempt to answer these two questions. This Primer takes the book's explanations down a notch. It asks, "What is the most basic issue underlying difference in close relationships?"

In brief, difference is the struggle to control definitions of identity: who has the power to define self, other, and reality. We express our identity to ourselves through our myths. If our partner doesn't acknowledge our identity, or identifies us falsely, we feel invisible. Not holding out for our own sense of identity sends us reeling into a black hole where we disappear. Accordingly, a prerequisite for the healthy life of any close relationship is the appropriate description of ourselves by our partners. They validate us through their accurate description of us. This is what I mean by acknowledgment. Difference, at this most basic level, then, is a response to inaccurate description. Your partner does not describe you as you describe yourself. This leads you to question whether he truly loves you. How could he if he doesn't know you, you ask. Such are the dreary expostulations of lovers who are forced into competition over who is and will be empowered to describe self and other. You must donate every quantum of energy in your collective will to limit this competition in honor of the love you seek to preserve. Let each voice be heard. Focus your loving listening on how your partner's voice differs from yours and value that difference. Before competing over whose definition of reality gains momentum, defeat the enemy we call difference by making a consummate effort to welcome it.

EXERCISE: I SPEAK IN YOUR VOICE, NOT MINE

Follow these rules strictly:

1. Go to your journal, unasked.
2. Pick a time when you are overflowing with gratitude for your partner (not when you're wondering how on earth you could have picked this wretch).

3. Make your best effort to say: Here is how I hear and understand your "I." I speak in your words, not mine, I speak from behind your eyes.
4. Hold your creation in storage for use at a crucial moment—when, indeed, you *are* wondering why you chose such a miserable creature.
5. Be aware that in choosing a doubting moment rather than a moment of certainty to reread your entry, you are tricking the contradictions of love.
6. Do this exercise as many times as it takes to get it right.

This exercise was designed to preempt definitional competition and its poisonous effects on the structure of identity in close relationships. When it succeeds, it makes a point which seems so obvious that you may wonder why it needs to be mentioned: *There is no truth, there are only truths.* You may be thinking, "Everybody knows that when any two parties disagree there are two truths, not one." This may be clear to you when the two parties are "them"—those other people out there someplace. How many times have you heard someone say about a partner, "She sees the world in one way: hers. If I don't see eye-to-eye with her, I'm defined as an unloving bully." Or, "He insists that he believes in valuing difference, but if something's important to him, there's no room whatsoever for my opinion." I'd be surprised if any one of you hasn't heard or made such statements. If you haven't, you probably will in time. And, if you are not prepared, it will cause trouble.

The myth of No Difference or the Rule of One is common among people who endorse the rules of hierarchy—that those who are at the top know better about how things are and ought to be than their subjects, be they spouses or employees. It's also a position commonly held by Protectors, whose sense of vulnerability leads them to regard the "forces out there" as dangerous and in need of definitional control, and by Fixers, who tend to believe they alone know what is right for the couple.

To overcome the tendency to hold to a One Truth perspective, remember these critical points:

- Your view may not be the only legitimate one. It may have gaps and embedded problems in it.
- Your partner's view may have some validity even if, at first, it seems improbable.
- When One Truth takes control of the ruling descriptions of self, other, and reality, the logic of "relationship" itself will be threatened.
- View your errors as interesting puzzles to be looked at, rather than as shameful and in need of covering up.
- Pay attention to your private thoughts and feelings, ideally before they build to an unresolvable emotional state.
- Seek help from your partner and others in identifying counterproductive patterns in your thinking and actions.
- Remember that the ways in which both of you have been used to thinking and acting are relatively comfortable, safe, and have "worked." Trying new behavior will probably not "work" at first, and requires reflection and practice to be internalized.
- To be named correctly by another is love. To repudiate false descriptions is also love.
- The rewriting of the feelings of another, the attributions of another's intent based on one's own untested assumptions, the remaking of another's meanings from one's own "partial perspectives," and descriptions of one's partner that extinguish her or his sense of autonomous identity are all equivalent to death in relationship.
- Because the life and death of the relationship itself is in question, every couple should place the highest value on *difference itself*.

Beginning lovers would do well to put into place some inviolable rules to guide them in the creative management of difference.

Before putting the rules to work, you may need to come to a mutual understanding of the four ways that differences can be resolved:

- Agreeing to agree
- Agreeing not to disagree
- Agreeing to disagree
- Finding a third way

People have very strong preferences as to which way or ways give them the most comfort and the most difficulty. Still, most of us, whatever our preferences, would concede in times of dispassionate reason that some situations call for one way over the others. Most of us would also acknowledge that in some situations we tend to send reason down the drain, all the while imposing our own preferred way on our mates.

Every couple, seasoned or ripe off the vine, would do well to come to a mutual understanding of their preferred ways of resolving differences in various circumstances.

Agreeing to Agree
In all matters, but especially in matters of importance, we take no action or stance and express no opinion in public except as we agree.

This resolution implicitly allows for some negotiation and discussion, but its express message is harmony.

Agreeing Not to Disagree
In matters of importance it is urgent that neither party deviate from strict action guidelines that are firmly in place, known, and observed.

This resolution allows for no ambiguity or negotiation.

Conformity is often unapologetically expected of all parties to any action, stance, or decision.

Agreeing to Disagree

In matters large and small, strict adherents of this style agree that both parties are free to disagree with impunity. Flexibility and autonomy are valued.

This type of resolution allows for imprecision, looseness, and delaying or deferring action.

Finding a Third Way

Proponents of this style of resolution argue that letting go and looking outside the box is the best approach to difference.

It seeks to bypass disagreement. It is a win-win model in which, ideally, the "third way" either creatively incorporates elements of the stances of both parties or proposes an entirely new stance that satisfies both parties.

EXERCISE

Once you understand these four styles of resolution, respond to the following:

1. Which type of resolution style are you likely to prefer in the majority of situations? Which do you perceive your partner would prefer in most situations?
2. Order the rest of the styles from most to least preferred.
3. Identify specific situations in which you are likely to choose different options. Try to identify situations that might influence your partner's choices.

Enter all of the above in your journal in a section called "Notes for Collaborative Negotiation." Use the exercise when you and your partner have or have not done well in managing difference. Don't forget to date your entries. You will probably want to refer to them when one or the other of you "calls a meeting"—when you've been having problems, or to review your good fortune if negotiations have been going particularly well.

The object of this exercise is to help you become aware of what is involved in your successful and unsuccessful negotiations. It alerts you to your biases, asks you to take responsibility for them, and makes vivid the notion that your way is not the only way. It promotes balance in each partner's right to influence the manner in which difference is managed and encourages creativity, flexibility, and fairness in matters which tend to divide most couples.

2. Protect sex from the politics of difference.

Couples who haven't done enough prophylactic work in time to forestall the withdrawal of desire which follows in the wake of broken contracts will often politicize lovemaking as a means of offsetting their helplessness or venting their anger. How do we politicize sex? We withhold in order to punish. Beginners, beware! Do everything you can to find more constructive sources of power. Put this admonition in your journal. Write it on your bathroom mirror in soap and do not wash it off until you have internalized it and burnt it into your memory. The withholding of sex is the Shadow's most complicit ally.

I have been thrown more times than I care to admit by couples who keep coming to therapy certain that their love is deep and abiding. Maintenance work, they say, is all they need. Sex is not mentioned. Other problems are brought in, worked through, mitigated. I push harder to get them launched, and the truth breaks out: "We haven't made love in years."

The last couple to speak this line were indeed deeply committed to one another. What makes them interesting is that their Personal and Gender Myth contracts were still intact, but the woman's Fixer-Protector heroes and the man's Survivor hero were having a hard time talking to each other. The would-be hero of the man's Personal Myth was torn between making his wife feel safe and making his way through the stressful times of starting a business. Politics were indeed responsible for this man's refusal to initiate lovemaking at the onset of their struggles. When the struggles ended, they still abstained and remained silent, months turning into years. When the truth came out, they said, "We got in the habit of not making love and simply forgot." They resumed lovemaking with unexpected ease, which liberated them from another dungeon of silence—their wish to have another child.

Initiates, take heed. Sex is without question the greatest balm to intimacy, but sexual identity and its fulfillment in the sexual dialogue between two Sexual Fantasy Myths rests on a fragile foundation until the couple has come through the inevitable mythic wars stronger than they began. Once any of the three Shadows launches an attack capable of threatening identity, sexual or otherwise, the couple's cumulative record of good sexual experience is put to the test. Make sure to build that record from the very beginning of your journey together, letting nothing short of incapacitation or absolute betrayal diminish it.

Many couples who "make it" set a period beyond which not making love is not tolerated. Observing their preset limit brings them closer if, for any reason, they have become distant. And, if their abstinence was simply due to forgetting, as many healthy couples commonly claim, after breaking the ice they often say something along the lines of "What the hell was the matter with us?"

Does this rule seem mechanical, does it encourage a kind of counting that kills off spontaneity? Hardly, since you need concern yourself with this rule only when spontaneity has failed.

3. Tell your stories in a safe environment.

If you are not already inclined to do so, become an inveterate storyteller. Within each of us are probably scores of stories which support the discipline of Deep Knowing, which focuses on the stories behind the three myths. Tell your stories in enough depth that your partner doesn't have to squint to see or dig to uncover who you really are as you know yourself through your stories. Tell of your childhood innocence, and the false bravado or painful shyness of adolescence. Tell each other what it was like when you had to face the world as an uncertain young adult. Speak of your lies and deceits and of your noblest deeds as well. In encouraging you to become storytellers, I am not recommending that you become self-obsessed bores. There is much more to it. We are all psychologically constructed to hide what is most painful. What we want most to hide from ourselves are the Shadows that announced our unworthiness after the initial childhood disappointment. Our reactions to the betrayal and disappointment (from guilt to shame, sadness to grief, anger to rage, or fear to anxiety) are the last things we wish to reveal, because of the pain associated with them. Eventually, we have to disclose the hurt self and unmask the false self we wear for protection. Or, at least we do if our intimate relationship is to survive the inevitable crisis of the second disappointment and the ensuing Myth Work needed to work through it. Storytelling, therefore, is a means to an end which you ignore at your own peril. Thorough, effective Myth and Shadow Work depend upon your ability to negotiate a safe passage to the parts of your past which matter.

As adults we are mired in sobered realism. It is only through one another's stories that we really come to know each other deeply. Storytelling is no less than a sharing of Self, something all companions do. But it's more than that, for what, after all, is a life of love but an anthology of stories, those that each partner brings and those they create together? Know, savor, and memorialize the new stories that celebrate the life you are creating together. Tell your lover good stories about himself. Tell family and friends good stories about her. Hold them in a library of stories to be brought out whenever you need to offset the bad memories of failed communication in the struggles to bridge your myths. Start with the archetypal encounter. Remember the rush of surprise and delight in discovering the "perfect other." Recall the sexual urge this particular individual ignited in you.

Now I feel compelled to urge a bit of paranoia. The forces that work against good memories are powerful and insidious. You must take these saboteurs on with a strong and conscious will. They spring from the subversive wreckage of mismanaged difference. When couples come to me in despair, they are likely to say, "We are unable to communicate," or, "Our differences are irreconcilable." Most trouble in the realm begins with the failure to manage difference.

4. Face your shadows with courage.

Medieval religion says that a man and a woman can become one soul. The ancient term "to know" suggests that the contact enables each to know the other from the inside—sexually and spiritually. But this deep knowing of the other is waylaid by the tendency of men and women to shape and tame their partners in the image of their ideal other. We get nowhere with this tendency until we discover that the shaping and taming must be of our own demons. The process of knowing the other fails unless and until we face the question of self-knowledge and come to know the true self. What keeps us from telling and rewriting our stories is the shadows they left in us. The demons of rage, grief, fear, and shame can be tamed. They are the voices telling you that you are unlovable and unworthy of love. You created them, paradoxically out of love and moral purity in childhood, as a way of explaining to yourself why you were betrayed by your parents or other important adults. Now these Shadows only harm you. Only you can get them to stop.

5. Keep a journal of personal responsibility.

Don't take the mirror (your partner's feedback) until it is given in the right spirit. Compassion, not blame, drives us when we are in the right spirit. There is no place for blame. If there is any hint of blame, do not take the mirror. If you cannot receive the mirror in a spirit free of blame, it is pointless to take it. Before asking your partner to look at something you know will be hard to face, ask whether you would do it yourself. If not, do not let your partner get there first in pointing this out to you.

In the back of your journal, title one section "Bin." Here you'll keep a list of differences you have not been able to resolve. There have probably been times when you have said or thought, "We're so different." But what on earth did you expect? If you want a re-lationship without difference, try cloning. If you want intimacy and to "grow up" through learning, anticipate difference and value it. Coming away from such an encounter with an agreement to name the difference and put it in the Bin is a way of getting enough distance to develop the skill of collaborating rather than fighting over differences.

6. Know your behavioral profile.

Getting to know your behavioral profile brings you closer to the secret of communication—*structure*. What makes communica-tion easy? What makes so much communication difficult? Is it really just about men and women? Why does it work between two people in some situations and fall apart in other circumstances?

Structure is invisible, ensconced in the words and themes we use in conversation. There are times, however, when structure takes over, when we are no longer responding to "what" our part-ner is saying but to the unseen structure—the choreography of the communication—which conveys as much about its content as the words themselves.

In all face-to-face communication, people use four kinds of be-haviors or actions. They can move, follow, oppose, or bystand. Each of us tends to have one or two "favorites," the actions in which we most frequently engage. The one we are best at and do most skilfully is called our *strong action*. Each of us also tends to shy away from certain actions and perform them less skillfully. This is our *weak action*. And we all do things from time to time which get us into trouble. This is our *stuck action*, the one we overuse or use at inappropriate times.

Each of these actions makes a unique contribution to com-munication:

- The *Mover provides direction, discipline, commitment, and clar-ity*. However, Movers can also have some of the same unin-tended effects upon communication as Fixers. They can act omnipotent, impatient, indecisive, scattered, and dicta-torial.

- The *Follower provides completion, compassion, loyalty, service, and continuity*. Like Protectors, Followers can also be pla-cating, indecisive, pliant, and over accommodating.

- The *Opposer provides correction, courage, protection, and in-tegrity*. On the downside, Opposers can also resemble Fixers by being critical, competitive, blaming, attacking, and con-trary.

- The *Bystander provides perspective, patience, preservation, and moderation*. Like Survivors, Bystanders can be disengaged, judgmental, deserting, withdrawn, and silent. Bystanders can also bridge other players, because from their position of "neutrality" outside the action, they are valued and trusted.

There cannot be effective communication unless all four ac-tions are present and permitted in the system of relationships.

And, as you know from personal experience, this is not always the case. We've all been in situations where we try to talk and want to be heard or listened to and it doesn't work. The secret lies in the choreography of the conversation. Observe the following couples:

Face-to-Face Communication #1

A:
I'd really like to go to the movies, okay?

B:
Sure, I'm up for a movie too.

A:
I've been dying to see *Titanic*.

B:
Not with me, you won't.

A:
You know how you've been saying that you've dropped too far out of the culture? Maybe *Titanic* is a good way to catch up.

B:
Okay. I may have to wear a disguise, but I get your point. I'm with you.

This is a successful communication. Take note of A's Bystander action and the perspective it affords B—who had first followed and then opposed A's suggestion—to follow once more, this time bringing the conversation to successful closure resulting in the joint action of going to the movies together.

Face-to-Face Communication #2

A:
That was a great movie.

B:
Yes, I loved it.

A:

How could you have? You fell asleep halfway through!

B:

(Says nothing, hangs head, looks diminished)

A:

There I go again—criticizing you when you're trying to be nice. I think I know why I keep doing that.

B:

Thanks—I really appreciate your honesty about yourself. I'm listening.

This too is a successful communication. A makes a move. B follows that move. A opposes B's following behavior, which crushes A, a weak action or a stuck one, but then A, resorting skilfully to the Bystander function, rescues the communication. It allows B to follow, giving closure to the sequence and inviting A to initiate a new sequence.

Face-to-Face Communication #3

A:

That was a great movie.

B:

Yes, I loved it.

A:

How could you? You fell asleep halfway through it!

B:

That's nonsense!

A:

You're calling *me* stupid?

B:

I hate it when you monitor me.

A:

I hate people who don't own up.

B:

Let's just drop it and go to bed.

A:

Go to bed yourself. I've got better things to do.

This is an unsuccessful communication, not because of its content, but because the structure is faulty. It is dominated by Opposer behaviors, not enough Follower actions, and a totally disabled Bystander.

How Did I Develop My Preferred Moves?

Your preferred choreography arises from your mythology as much as your heroic mode does. Was your mother always an Opposer? Did this make you a Bystander? If your father didn't let you speak at the table, did you become someone who prefers always to be a Follower or always a Mover? Your preferred conversational moves represent internalized structures which invisibly guide your communications, while your heroic mode determines their content. These conversational structures form an invisible dimension which shapes your heroic behavior. They dictate how you express yourself rather than why. We've all heard the expression, "It's not what you say, it's how you say it."

Your propensity for particular moves comes from your childhood stories. How you communicate your myths is linked to this choreography. In order to fully understand how you communicate, you must learn to observe your stance and the types of moves you make.

Rules of Successful Conversation

If people were to observe the following rules of successful conversation, they would rarely get into trouble and would be able to reach successful resolutions.

- Have the ability to engage in all four actions in observable, balanced sequences.
- Have the flexibility to engage in more than one of the actions.
- Do not get caught frequently in repetitive, almost ritualized, patterns of action.
- Have an active, enabled Bystander function which helps prevent becoming stuck.
- Have the ability to make clear, rather than mixed and ambiguous, moves.

Alas, when the conversation heats up (when the stakes are raised), we all tend to break these rules. The most frequently broken rule, the one which does the most damage, is the silencing or otherwise disabling of the Bystander. When the Bystander is disabled, effective communication is doomed.

Both of you will do well to learn and practice these rules. We're all familiar with conversations in which one or more of them is being broken. Caught up in the content, we find ourselves entrapped in a faulty structure which inhibits productive conversation. Stepping back from the content and becoming a Bystander to your own and your partner's actions will allow you to correct faulty conversational choreography which leads you into your particular vicious cycle.

Unsuccessful Communication

- Individuals tend to get locked into their favorite role
- Opposers are punished by the group or else they dominate
- There are no strong Movers or no one ever follows a move
- Individuals attach double messages to their communications
- Ritualistic and unproductive patterns prevail
- The Bystander is disabled
- The individuals are unable to reach closure

7. Outwit the tyranny of time.

In the culture around us, time has become a commodity like any other. We are seduced into trading our *Now* for money to be spent in a future which may or may never come to pass. And if that future does become our present someday, what will we have left that will be of value? So many of the young couples I see in my practice feel driven to make a bargain with the devil—like the twenty-nine-year-old who has agreed virtually not to see the light of day for the next five years so that the two hundred thousand dollars a year he presently earns will jump to half a million with stock options. Or, the thirty-two-year-old mother of two who schedules sex with her husband so that she can return to her evening conference call between nine and ten every night. It's as though we are seduced into forgetting the reality that our own time on earth is limited. All any of us really has is today, the present moment. Do we really want to bargain it away for an extra hundred thousand a year in a future which may never come—or a future without a partner or a family?

Particularly in the early years of relationships, time spent together is a valuable deposit in your bank of shared memories, an account upon which you may have to draw heavily in later years when the Shadows are veiling your marriage and you are trying to work through a crisis. In fact, time spent together at the outset of your relationship may even lessen the extent of the crisis.

Young people trying to "have it all" are no doubt familiar with the concept of "quality time." It's a concept which was initially dreamt up to make working parents feel less guilty about missing the important days and hours of their growing children's lives. The falsely comforting belief is that quality is more important than quantity, that anyone can babysit and change diapers all day long, so long as the high point of the child's day is the "quality time" spent with Mom and Dad. But, as with young couples who try to manage to apportion their time together in this same way, "quality time" misses the point. Young couples and parents and children all need just to be able to savor the small moments of a life passing in one another's company—not just its high points.

Couples who want to avoid falling into the deep wells of their Shadows have to develop a different orientation to time. The first step toward doing so involves really believing in your own mortality so that you don't put anything off. Each day, ask yourself, "If not now, when?" In the bestselling book *Tuesdays with Morrie*, written about the last days of a beloved professor by one of his former students, the professor, who is staring a slow but certain death in the eyes, says: "What if today were my last day on earth? . . . The culture doesn't encourage you to think about such things until you're about to die. We're so wrapped up with egotistical things, career, family, having enough money, meeting the mortgage, getting a new car, fixing the radiator when it breaks—we're involved in trillions of little acts just to keep going. So we don't get into the habit of standing back and looking at our lives and saying, Is this all? Is this all I want? Is something missing?"

One of my patients, a woman in her late thirties, told me that she had always visualized her deathbed in her mind's eye. In it she was always an old lady dying peacefully at home. Then she spent time as a volunteer on a rural ambulance route; there, as she put it, "I became intimately acquainted with death, and what so often surprised me was how young some of the car accident victims and even heart attack patients were. And each time I saw one of these deaths, I would say to myself, 'and just this morning, this person got up, put on his underwear and left the house not realizing at all that it was to be the last time he ever crossed his threshold.' "

My message to young partners trying to get ahead in the work world is to take a stand. Do not internalize the powers of enslavement. There are more options than you think. Be a fearless subversive in the corporate culture that demands the days of your life now for a future which may not be as certain as promised. I have spent a great deal of time as a consultant for many large corporations, and in all those years, I have not seen a single person be fired for holding out for a quality life. In most cases, you will be respected for it, because secretly everyone else wants to have the courage to ask for the same things.

Even if you're not a corporate slave, consider the other ways in which you may be robbing your relationship of the shared time it needs to bloom. As one of my patients said, "We never have sex anymore. He's always fucking the Web." Television, the Internet, drinking, and pursuing our own goals too single-mindedly are all common ways in which we steal time from our relationships and set ourselves up for later problems.

8. Pursue well-being as a serious investment.

Abraham Lincoln said, "A man is as happy as his mind allows him to be." Perhaps that is why happiness is so elusive. It certainly was for Lincoln. But it need not be for us. Except in obviously extreme circumstances, the mind can alter the experience of reality—even terrible reality, as some survivors of brutal torture, extreme isolation, and the incredible torments of the Holocaust can attest. Vastly simplified, the key is: how we view an event or experience depends on what we are comparing it with at the moment. Shifting our basis for judging events and experiences can allow us to experience greater happiness and well-being, in part by changing our frame of reference.

Objects that are "out there" have no inherent power to bring us happiness. I believe, and research supports my belief, that the joys of possession, and even of fulfilled desires, are not sustainable without an understanding of the nature of well-being and the mind's power both to give us happiness and to take it away. The scientific understanding of the links between frame of mind, emotion, pleasure, well-being, values, relationships and health is increasing. There is even dramatic research which links changes in emotions to the health of the immune system. It is now clear that

278

immune function can be radically altered by our mood and our perceptions. Happiness, then, is a state of mind that is largely, if not completely, under our control. Dr. Dean Ornish's book *Love and Survival: The Scientific Basis for the Healing Power of Intimacy* takes this a step further by linking intimacy and love to health.

The business culture, like the culture at large, does not make people feel good about themselves. Their unhappiness leads them to seek happiness in the wrong ways: more possessions, greater wealth, more power, material success. Many successful people I have known and worked with have admitted to me that they do not know real joy, perhaps have not known it since childhood or since launching their careers. The experience of joy is fleeting or escapes them altogether.

Happiness and well-being are not found in memorable events, or in great successes, power, or money. They are found in mind states that are completely under our control, states which we can learn to call forth at will. I believe that the capacity for happiness can be learned.

- Learning how to live and be well is not a luxury. It is a necessity and a responsibility. Learn to live well before you die.
- People who experience joy and pleasure know how to live in the present moment and to take pleasure in the moment. Even if you are in the midst of a distressing day, there's no reason not to savor for a moment the feel of a breeze on your face, the flowers in the park below you, or a comic moment in the office.
- The key ingredient to well-being is, above all, in your thoughts—rather than just in your genes, your diet, or your exercise program.
- Remember how to feel real joy, the kind of joy which came so easily to you as a child.

9. Keep your body and all of its senses alive.

Your body and your senses are the portals through which you experience love and desire as well as well-being and happiness. There is an abundance of information available on diet and exercise programs designed to maintain the strength, suppleness, and general health of your body. Therefore I will concentrate here on exercises for enhancing and maintaining your senses.

EXERCISE

Recall the scents of your childhood: your mother's fragrance, the aroma of your father's pipe or his clothes closet, the cooking smells wafting through your household, your grandparents' attic, books in the library. Constantly trying to recall the scents of childhood helps to recapture your story of perfect love. Many people who perform this simple exercise report a rush of emotion and memory. Consciously use your aromatic memory to connect the pleasures of the past with those of the present.

Each of my children has his or her own "personal smellprint." They are all grown now. When we've been apart for a while, some of them, as part of their greeting, will bend their heads to my waiting nostrils—"Here, Daddy, say hello to your baby [boy or girl]." They and I are not the least embarrassed by this primitive, somewhat animalistic re-bonding ceremony.

Smell is the most ignored and underappreciated of human senses. Its influence on our moods, memories, and sense of joy is often subconscious. Once registered, smells are not forgotten. Even many years later, the scent of a particular perfume or the first days of autumn or lilacs in summer can put us right back into a scene. Marcel Proust, the French novelist, believed that the hours of our lives are stored in tastes and scents which, when recalled, can trigger detailed memories. His *Remembrance of Things Past* begins with the recollection of the scent of lime blossoms. The German poet Friedrich von Schiller kept rotting apples in his desk because their scent helped him write.

EXERCISE

Command your mind to memorize and remember your partner's best fragrance, the situation in which you first encountered it and your reaction to it. Fill your lives with these sensory memories, scents which call forth good feelings. Expand your olfactory memory of your partner's aromas—public and private.

It is possible to develop a more acute and sensitive olfactory capacity. Nearly everyone can, although some people have natural, intense sensitivity to scents.

- Sex is strongly linked with the sense of smell.
- Aromatic chemicals known as pheromones are released by our skin. In a sense, our respective pheromones engage in dialogue with one another.

10. Maintain a positive balance in your emotional ledger.

Be sure to save more than you spend. Begin your bank account with your first shared memory. Victor happened to look up from his computer in time to catch sight of Gail's legs and hear the clickety-clack of her heels as she passed his cubicle at work. It is clear that this recollection gives him pleasure each time he retells it. "I usually have total concentration at work, but in that moment, some hidden force turned my head, lifted me by the shoulders and directed me to where I could glimpse this beautiful butt sitting right on top of the legs I was tracking. 'I will get to know her,' I told this force." In sad contrast to this happy memory was Victor's story of his archetypal encounter with Rosa, his first wife.

In it, Rosa invaded his sexual boundaries before he was ready. Victor and Rosa's emotional ledger never knew a positive balance. Rosa was never able to offset the negative value of her first deposit. Spending without regard for the other side of the ledger can end in bankruptcy. Bankrupt relationships are far too common. Many of these tragedies are unnecessary. Deficit spending can be offset by timely deposits of good memories and in continuing to add good stories from the present.

- Know your and your partner's myths and shadows
- Enhance desire by preserving the Mystery of sex
- Allow your heart to experience Gratitude for every act of love you receive

EXERCISE

You are standing next to your lover's coffin. Imagine that death came unexpectedly, prematurely. What do you want to say to your lover? Then why wait? Say it today. Express in life your gratitude for the blessings that this person has shared with you and contributed.

Succeeding at Efforts to Change

Expect failure despite all your good intentions to change. So many couples say to me, "We try and try but get nowhere." Probably you have bitten off more than you can chew at one sitting. It's a common mistake to try to change everything at once. Remember that the shared feeling of success is more important than success itself. Couples sometimes appear to change. Perhaps they drive their relationship close to disaster and then back off in terror without having learned anything.

- Experience the buoyant feelings of success and of having achieved it together in a shared effort. Do a lot of "high-fiving" to reinforce this vital sense of confidence.

- Reduce your expectations. Don't try to achieve your highest goals immediately.
- Design "experiments" together.
- Set yourselves up for success by agreeing to change those things you know you can change. Then up the ante just a little.
- Let the feeling of success take over and let it drive failure off the field.
- Sustain and build confidence that you will, as a two-person team, defeat the shadowy forces which destroy so many relationships.

EXERCISE

Interrupt your everyday life and/or the work you are doing to find ways to reinforce or increase the confidence or health of the relationship. Encourage each other to articulate positive assessments of the relationship—"This works, that doesn't." Find a balance.

EXERCISE

Selectively remember positive events at the expense of negative ones. Show yourselves how the past can influence the future with the spirit of what can be done, rather than what cannot.

Acts of kindness raise the level of desire.

Appendix B

Two Couples

What follows are two stories of relationships between people who were willing to do the work of discovering the content of their myths in order to heal old wounds and grow. In the second story, the couple Ashley and Gio, whom we met earlier in the book, were able to strengthen their love and desire for each other and move on with very little work. In the other case, Rebecca and Carlton were also able to strengthen their relationship, but they worked hard in therapy to do so. There were times when I wasn't sure they would make it, but after Carlton finally discovered the contents of his personal myths and was able to reconnect with his feelings, he and Rebecca began to make love for the first time in years.

The Blue Handkerchief

Carlton's face was flaming and his head throbbed as he made his way down the hall to his mother's office. He had held out as long as he could, because he wasn't supposed to bother her when she was working. If Shirley caught him she'd send him back to his room and minister to him herself. But he wanted his real mother, not a woman in a starched uniform. Forbidding and preoccupied as she was, she was still his mother. He liked the way she smelled and the feel of her hands on the occasions when she was being motherly. She alone could soothe him tonight.

He didn't hear any sounds from behind her office door—no frantic tapping of the typewriter, no voice on the telephone. That was a good sign. Maybe she would smile when she saw him. He rapped tentatively at the door. No answer. He knocked louder and then opened the door. His head twinged again. He felt very sick. He wanted her to get up and take him to his room and put him to bed. As he peered around the door into the office he could see his mother sitting at her desk. She was massaging her temples. Carlton's heart sank. How could he ask her for anything? He knew how busy she was. These things called *dead lines* that she was always talking about. She always seemed to have them and they always seemed to worry her more than whatever he needed. Even his father tiptoed around and gave her wide berth when she had a dead line.

"Is that you, Carlton?" she asked without releasing her temples or turning around.

"Yes, Mother."

"Carlton, I have *the* worst headache and I'm in the middle of a deadline. Please wet this under the cold water tap and wring it out and bring it back to me." She handed him a blue silk handkerchief twisted and rumpled from being pressed to her head. His own head and sore throat forgotten, he did as she asked. She pressed the dampened handkerchief to her temples. "Thank you. Was there something you needed?"

"No, Mother."

"I'm so glad. I don't think I could have borne one more problem. I'll just finish what I'm working on and then I'll be down for dinner. Tell Shirley we'll eat at seven."

At that moment Shirley herself arrived. "Oh, Mrs. Smythe, I'm so sorry he came in and bothered you. I told him to leave you alone. Come on, Carlton, you naughty little boy. Let's get you cleaned up for dinner." The kindly maid collared Carlton and marched him out of his mother's presence.

Carlton wanted to run back into his mother's room and throw himself on her lap and sob until she had to take care of him, but he knew he wouldn't. Instead, he wrenched his hand away from Shirley's and drew back and hit her as hard as he could. Then he burst into tears. "Oh, you must be a very sick little boy," she said indulgently, scuttling him down the hall and away from his mother.

In many ways Carlton was proud of his mother. Very few of his friends' mothers worked, and none had her own business. Carlton's mother ran a public relations firm which represented well-known writers and artists all over the country. But, proud as he sometimes was, usually he just wished he had a normal cozy mother who would love him and take care of him, instead of the high-strung one he had.

"Your mother is so fascinating," his friends' parents would say to him in a tone of voice which made it clear that they regarded her as an oddity. She seemed somehow larger than his friends' mothers. She was considered a great beauty, something she flaunted and used both in her work and to control the men around her. Her clothes were bolder, her laughter louder, and her tears and rages more frequent. She knew how to get her way. Was life really so up-and-down in his friends' houses, he wondered.

Each week, Carlton, now in his mid-fifties, and Rebecca, his wife, would seat themselves on the couch facing me. Almost as soon as she sat down Rebecca would squint once and tears would start to stream down her face. She never sobbed or tried to stop them from falling. She just let them slide down her face and puddle in her lap.

The effect of Rebecca's tears was remarkable and unvarying. As soon as she began, Carlton would pivot his hip ten degrees to the left, turning his right shoulder and back to his distressed wife. Then he would produce from his pocket a large blue silk handkerchief which he would push in her direction.

Carlton talked a lot about his mother in response to my questioning, and always with clear distaste. He had told me the story about the blue handkerchief several times before over the two years I had been seeing him and Rebecca, but it was always reportage, dredged up from his past to humor me and always related in a dull monotone.

As I sat facing them week after week I often couldn't help but feel that they seemed the most likely of candidates for a divorce. They had begun therapy after Rebecca admitted to Carlton that she had carried on for seven years what she preferred not to call an affair, but rather her "other life." In this life she was in love with a lawyer who worked in the same building she did. He was older, a widower, and from Rebecca's account, a Fixer with no deep shadows. Dan's highly evolved capacity for the language of the Personal Myth left Carlton at the starting gate of love. In bed, Dan had the patience of a Tao master, meandering through the pathways and interstices of sensuality, lingering in Rebecca's favorite places; a man who wanted above all to please his partner. Outside of bed, he listened to Rebecca. "He saw me," she once explained to Carlton. "He was interested in my life, my thoughts and reactions. That was seductive. You always seemed to be looking right through me."

Dan outdid Carlton in every department, in a competition where, admittedly, every illicit lover has an instant advantage and every mate a handicap. Carlton never noticed, never even suspected, so perfectly was Rebecca the Survivor able to split off that part of her life. She regarded her hours with Dan as parallel to the rest of her life, never touching it in any way. So oblivious was Carlton that she could have continued with Dan for as long as she could sustain the deception in her own heart. It was her love of her daughters that made her give up what was the happiest relationship of her life so far. The failure of intimacy between Rebecca and Carlton made their parenting incomplete. It lacked the warmth and juice that parents who "make love" provide. As they entered adolescence, the two girls began to sense their mother's frozen desire and began to question her as a model. When at last she did re- veal it to him, Carlton professed not to be offended by Rebecca's relationship with Dan or even curious. "I'm mostly just interested in how you managed to pull it off, what there is in your character which made a double life possible. Actually I'm kind of surprised you didn't fuck it up."

During those seven years Carlton hadn't been unhappy. He didn't really give their marriage much thought. He enjoyed his intellect and his job and his children. As for Rebecca, he liked her best when they were working side-by-side in the garden. Much of the rest of the time she got on his nerves because she seemed such a raw bundle of needs that he had no idea how to fulfill and no real interest in fulfilling. "How could I? How could anyone? All that emoting she did just to control me made me very angry. Every time I walked in the door there she'd be. I had no feelings like that for her." He was busy as a rising star in the biotech industry and didn't really notice the withdrawal of passion and intimacy. "In the early years I was full of myself and saw myself as the original Renaissance Man; science, art, literature, politics—nothing was outside the grasp of my hungry intellect. As a hero, Ulysses is my man. He went off for ten years to fight the Trojans and took ten more adventure-filled years getting home. Modern men spend twenty years on a career journey. Of course they neglect their family. That's part of the deal."

"I hated those Biomax years," Rebecca interjected. "I hated every moment. That doesn't mean I wasn't proud of Carlton's accomplishments. I just wanted him home more. When we married, women didn't ask, 'Who is this man I'm marrying?' like they do today. Carlton was a good catch. I never questioned that until my heart began to break off piece by piece."

"My ideal wife would be one of two kinds which might on the surface appear different but which are two parts of the same woman. The first is a woman who goes on a career journey with her man, like Marie Curie. She was a real partner. My second ideal is Penelope, who faithfully tended the hearth and educated the children, all the while ingeniously outwitting suitors and awaiting Ulysses' return."

"Whereas if I'd known then what I know now, I would have married someone like Hector," Rebecca cut in. "Hector wept when he said goodbye to his wife, Andromache, and their children as he went off to fight Achilles and face death. Andromache was sure of her husband's love. She knew he had to fight knowing he would probably die, but he preferred being with his wife and family. He was able to cry. I wanted a man like that, yet chose one who was very different."

Rebecca's father was a philanderer. Robust and sexy, a Fixer like Ulysses, he was on the road for his work much of the time, leaving behind a faithful and self-effacing wife. Rebecca was both fascinated and terrified by the edge of sexuality which pervaded his aura. "I remember lying in bed at night and hearing him start up the stairs. Would he come in and kiss me? I both hoped and feared that he would. But often something would tell me to turn off my light quickly so that he wouldn't see that I was awake. When I heard his footsteps receding I'd be relieved, though I wasn't sure why. He was too much man for my mother and certainly too much for me."

Rebecca grew up confused about Fixers. From her descriptions of her father's take-over and charge-forth energies, his explosive sexual drive, he sounded like a Fixer with an abusive shadow. Part of Rebecca wanted Carlton to come through as a heroic Fixer without a shadow, a man who could take charge and make love to her skillfully, yet she also wanted a Protector.

"When we married in the sixties," she said, "there were two worlds: the straight academic one we lived in and then that 'other world.' There was a couple we knew and still visit to this day. The wife, Mary, was my best friend in those early days in Cambridge when Carlton was doing his post-doctoral work and trying to become head of his lab. Peter, her husband, was a successful architect who taught at Harvard. First Mary and then Peter realized that their high-stress life was killing them. At Mary's encouragement they sold their house and moved to Maine, where Peter restored several old houses and, with the help of other stressed-out academics, built an alternative school, which flourishes to this day. I was envious of Mary, still am. She had everything she wanted: a man who had already proven he could make it in the straight world, as Carlton was so bent on doing, and who was willing to leave that world to be with his family and live his ideals—something Carlton would never have considered. Peter was a man who could cry. Carlton has never come within a mile of a good cry."

Carlton cut in abruptly. "Frankly, I don't think delving into the mists of time to discover some terrible buried pain—if such ever actually existed—is ever going to help us. Our problem is that we don't fuck enough. And when we do, all I hear is 'This is wrong for me . . .' and then she cries."

Carlton was confused because whenever he tried, at Rebecca's unstated urging, to act like a Fixer, particularly in bed, she was dissatisfied with his efforts.

"Sex is the most natural thing in the world," Carlton continued. "Two bodies releasing powerful energy and enjoying the act for its own sake. Instead, this psychodrama culture takes hold of this simple, physically gratifying act and mutilates it beyond recognition with self-indulgent scrutiny."

"He can make love two or three times a day, even now at age fifty-three," Rebecca said, "but I get the feeling I'm invisible or interchangeable, an object. Tenderness in sex is a foreign concept to Carlton. The very idea of intimate talk and slowly building physical sensation, which I need before I even want to make love, is like a foreign language to him. Two out of three times he comes before I even get my imagination going. To say that I don't look forward to sex with Carlton is a gross understatement that makes me sad for both of us."

"I just don't understand her need for all this *emotion* during sex," Carlton said. "As far as I'm concerned, emotions are manipulative and for that reason alone have absolutely no place in bed. It's bad enough all these tears and emoting in the rest of our lives, including in this office. Sometimes I feel like you two are trying to manipulate me into some great confession or some breakthrough, when there really isn't one. Sure, I didn't much like my mother, but she no longer has any effect on me. I don't go in for this garbage about my relationship with my mother affecting my relationship with Rebecca, although I've got to say that the emotional blackmail that goes on around here reminds me of my mother to some degree."

Rebecca continued to weep. She sat at the other end of the couch, her tears sliding silently down her face like a slow but perpetual waterfall. She didn't bother wiping her face or even mopping up the tears which runnelled at her jawline. It was as if here in my office she was able, for an hour at a time, to experience the undamming of her long-suppressed feelings, to express the Protector part of her psyche which had been forced underground in order to survive in the emotional desert of their marriage.

Carlton had already performed his cold ritual of handing Rebecca the blue handkerchief. This time, in a gesture so woefully tentative and unconvincing as to be embarrassing, he laid a cold hand onto the couch in the space that separated them as if he were handing her a rat. Carlton rejected emotions so thoroughly that he became almost visibly nauseated. Such emotions flow from the Personal Myth, but, as is painfully clear, Carlton had completely rejected this part of his past, which rendered him unable to communicate with Rebecca sexually, or in any other way for that matter. Carlton was well aware that his wife was sexually unfulfilled and this—not her unhappiness at his coldness, at the wall around him and between them—is what troubled him.

Carlton was as entrenched a Survivor as I had ever met, with an interesting twist to his anger. Many people openly admit their anger at their parents and others. But, as a rule, Survivors whose martyr shadow dominates find it a very difficult step. Carlton could *feel* anger at his colleagues who acted stupidly. He could *feel* angry at Rebecca when she "fucked up as usual in the kitchen." But the anger he "felt" toward his mother was never more than an idea that existed in his mind. He did not *feel* it. Carlton couldn't even acknowledge feeling physical pain. One winter day he tripped on the ice on his back stairs, breaking his wrist. "Go see a doctor right away," Rebecca fretted. "If you don't you could wind up with arthritis."

"Why do you always have to turn to the 'experts'?" Carlton fumed. "I doubt I broke it, but even if I did it'll heal on its own," his martyr declared firmly, cutting off both advice and sympathy. Rebecca felt abandoned by Carlton. But Carlton was also abandoning himself, as had been done to him in childhood by the mother whose needs always came first. Taking a lover who was able to express his own Personal Myth, and draw out Rebecca's also, was her way of balancing her painful and distorted life with her shut-down husband. As for Carlton, he sought release in masturbation or in quick ejaculatory sex with his unhappy wife.

Carlton was so disgusted by Rebecca's tears, and his feeling that she was using them to manipulate him, because the shades of his mother were in the room. It wasn't until much later, however, in a session without Rebecca, that he could accept this idea.

"All emotions are manipulative, by definition," he repeated for perhaps the fiftieth time since starting therapy. "They make me angry."

"Where did you learn that?" I asked.

"My mother was a manipulative bitch," he said in a flat voice. "She used me in every way she could."

"And that made you an angry boy?" I asked. Staring off into his past, he nodded with his eyes only. "It seems to me, Carlton, that in all you have told me you didn't have anything but the ordinary needs of a child. Your mother was too self-centered to pay attention."

Upon hearing these words, Carlton sat a long time silent and brooding. It was the first time he hadn't dismissed me when I attempted to get him to talk about his past.

"He is revisiting his story but won't say so," I thought. I knew enough not to push him too fast. I also knew that at that moment the door to the repressed Protector part of his psyche was starting to open. For the first time, he was revisiting his story without the wall he had built around himself. At this point, some people like Carlton, particularly if caught earlier before their fortifications are as impenetrable, cry for the first time in many years. But Carlton did not cry. I knew that he knew that I was inside the wall. He was silently pleading with me not to expose him or his shadow. There was no need to expose what we had learned together. It was enough for Carlton to accept it. The next step was for him to accept—intellectually at first, and then later down the line, emotionally—that he had to meet his shadow, a shadow that misled him in the ways of obtaining love; that corrupted his ways of showing love and greatly limited his ways of making love.

I was elated as I closed the door on Carlton that night. This was the moment I had been hoping for for several years. Carlton had been so difficult to unpack. There were many times when I wasn't sure he'd ever be able to get past his defenses and feel the anger and pain that were obviously in there.

A few months later, a curious thing happened. Carlton slipped into a depression which, for the first time in his life, he admitted feeling. He didn't even try to cover up the unpleasant moods and the sadness which overcame him. He was even willing to discuss them with me in our solo sessions and, to some extent, with Rebecca, although he was still wary of letting her in too close. With his depression came a brief loss of his priapic sexuality. For the first time in his life he couldn't be aroused at all, much less twice or three times each day. This loss of physiological readiness had the salutary effect of deepening his understanding of intimacy and feelings and their roles in sex.

As the priapic beast retreated and a more tender Carlton began to emerge, Rebecca began to have sexual dreams which starred her husband. She was vibrant and sexual in a way she had never seemed before. The cascade of tears had stopped. The two were playful.

Rebecca and Carlton have been living abroad for the last six months while Carlton is on sabbatical. Much of this time has been spent living in and observing a therapeutic community in Sweden. Living surrounded by so much unguarded feeling and emotion has been remarkably healing for Carlton. It has opened him to deep feelings which have been chafing to be admitted back into the light of day. The vulnerability he sees around him reminds him of that which is vulnerable and raw within himself. Finally, Carlton has accessed his Personal Myth, and the walls which have entombed him have more than crumbled. Rebecca, who told me early in our work together that eleven years into their marriage she had awoken "to find a stranger in my bed," wrote not long ago. "David," her note read. "It's not perfect between us, but it's better than all right."

Ashley and Gio:
It Began with a Secret

Ashley sighed contentedly as she shifted into a higher gear to make the light before it turned red. She was almost home, and she was looking forward to a blissful evening. She had finally managed to find a rare CD of the magnificent recording of Richard Strauss's Four Last Songs sung by Elisabeth Schwarzkopf. She had been searching for the CD to replace a thirty-year-old record which had once belonged to her father. Ashley remembered the first time she had heard these songs, sitting in her father's paneled study in their Beacon Hill house as he sat home alone one Saturday evening, unaccountably sad-looking, sadder even than the tragic beauty of the music seemed to warrant.

Tonight her childhood seemed far away and all the strange pain she felt for her father was erased by the prospect of sitting by the fire with Gio, her adored and adoring husband, sipping Bénédictine, their favorite liqueur, their special aphrodisiac. As she pulled her car into the mews behind their house she could see the light on in Gio's study. She couldn't wait to see him and surprise him with her find. She let herself in quietly and made her way up to the door of his study. She had meant to open the door silently and to come up behind him, making just enough noise not to startle him with the kiss she longed to plant on one of her favorite spots on his body, the smooth, tanned skin at the nape of his neck. She opened the door and stood around the corner where he couldn't yet see her. He was on the telephone. Probably a client, she thought. But something about the somberness of his voice contrasted with the authoritative, optimistic voice he normally used with the clients whose fortunes he managed.

"I don't know what to say, Georgie," he said, with a deep sigh. "This is a shock. Do you need me to come over? I can tell Ashley I need to go out for dinner. . . . All right, remember—we're both in this together. I'll call you tomorrow." Gio sighed deeply and hung up the telephone, still unaware of Ashley's presence around the corner.

A nauseating heat spread from Ashley's neck to her forehead and for a moment she thought she was going to be sick. Gio must have heard something, for he rose from his desk chair and came around the corner to where she stood with the bag containing the CD.

"Hi, darling," Gio said, coming over and planting what felt like a rather discouraged kiss on the top of her head. "How was your day?"

"It was fine," she said, but there was more on her mind. Her antennae were up. "Who was that you were just talking to?" she asked, trying to sound merely curious but somehow aware that it wasn't a client.

"It's no one you need to know about," Gio replied looking her straight in the eye but kindly.

"What do you mean 'no one I need to know about'? I like to know about your clients."

"Ashley, I really have to ask you to leave this one alone," Gio answered with uncharacteristic somberness.

"But who is Georgie?" she persisted, all the happy anticipation of twenty minutes ago destroyed. Somehow she knew the evening was spoiled, at least for her. Something strange was going on. She wanted to keep herself under control, but she felt shock waves of panic rising inside her one after another, barely giving her a chance to catch her breath. She had to find out what was going on, what it was that he was guarding.

"Look, Georgie isn't another woman, nor are Georgie and I involved in any nefarious dealings. It's just a private matter." Gio knew how Ashley hated secrets, how threatened they made her feel, how left-out. He knew how she had been damaged by the secrecy in her household surrounding her mother's lover and the air of sadness she felt in her father. He wished it could be otherwise, because he didn't want to frighten this woman he had come to love more than life itself. He knew that Georgie was no threat to them, but at the same time he refused to divulge the nature of the relationship. He held his ground. "Ashley, your trust in me is not misplaced. If you believe I am an honorable man, trust me and I will never hurt you. That I promise."

But this wasn't a good answer for Ashley. Something was going on that she didn't understand. She felt like she could barely breathe or eat until she knew.

When they had married four years before, Ashley and Gio had made a pact never to let any argument prevent them from making love for more than three weeks. This conversation about the mysterious Georgie had begun a painful impasse which had now extended to nearly two months. The sense of betrayal was physically painful to them both as they awoke, morning after morning, backs turned to one another, shoulders curled inward. The air between them was cold and charged with unspoken hurt and rage. Was this going to be another long silent day, the anger and fear palpable yet nothing they could even talk about? How odd, Gio thought, that this Ashley was so different from the strong yet gentle woman he thought he had married. She had never been anything but wise and understanding, a solver of problems. How could she have erected such an unbreachable wall between them over such a trivial issue?

How terrifying and yet how enraging, Ashley thought, that this man, a second husband she had chosen for his power, his wit, and the goodness of his heart could act like a hurt child and over something so silly. Why were his damned secrets more important than she, than even their relationship? She simply did not understand when people couldn't talk things out. Why was he suddenly incapable of loving her as she longed to be loved? They were so polarized now that neither was capable of making the first step to reach out, even though both knew instinctively that making love was the only way to find one another again. They had tried to talk it out, each trying to state his or her views, but each attempt had ended in an argument, the gates between them clanging shut, leaving each wondering where their love had gone.

This was the second marriage for each of them and they had chosen cautiously. They were so unlike each other in so many ways, their abilities and approaches to life so different, that they had even gone to a couples therapist briefly before their marriage so as to leave no stone unturned, to prevent ever again the personal Hiroshimas that each had gone through in the breakups of their previous worlds. They realized that although each was strong and very complicated, they respected each other's views. Communication, both verbal and physical, was essential to their harmony. They had always been able to talk to each other—and hear each other—from the deepest parts of their souls, and they had always been able to get through the hard times by making love. Or so they had believed.

Only once before had they exceeded their three-week limit—in an argument over a detail in the dream house they were designing together. But that time it had only gone on for a week and had been punctuated by a rip-roaring fight in which Ashley had thrown a crystal tumbler hard against the banister they had been arguing over, thus permanently registering her opinion in an object they touched every day. That fight had ended deliciously in bed and, until now, they had been able to laugh over that incident, certain that nothing like that would ever befall them again.

"Was this Cold War never going to end?" Ashley asked herself as she lay in bed trying to will herself to get up. Gio, who had gotten up some time before, was only a warm spot in the bed. Her stomach churned and she wondered whether she could even face another day. She wanted to go up to the roof and scream, she wanted to hurt herself, do anything to make Gio even look at her. He was punishing her, but why? All she wanted to do was to force the issue, to make things right between them, and his only response was to go deeper into his unfathomable interior. She kept hearing that conversation with the mysterious Georgie, and as she replayed it she strained desperately to find the meaning. She even found herself going over phone bills. If only she had sneaked back into his study that night and pushed the redial button, perhaps she'd know. She *had* to know. Now there was no going back. She knew their relationship would never get back on track until this was all cleared up, explained, and fixed. She could smell the coffee that Gio had made downstairs, but whereas on other mornings it was an invitation to come down and begin the day with him, she knew he was already in his study, busy on the telephone with people in Japan or Singapore as those markets were closing down.

Well, she would make the best of another day. One thing her mother had always told her and her sister was to keep their standards up, and so even though she felt so little pleasure in the small things which usually added delight to her mornings, she selected a perfume from the large collection in the bedroom. This morning, she chose a small splash from her remaining supply of Le De Givenchy, a perfume from her youth which had recently been discontinued. She had scoured the world looking for remaining bottles of this scent, which could bring her right back to her bathroom in the Beacon Hill house. The Givenchy was the first bottle of perfume she had ever been given and nothing could lift her spirits as it did.

She remembered conversations from childhood where friends would ask, "If you had to lose one of your senses, which one would it be?" And Ashley had always replied, much to the others' consternation, that her sense of smell was at least as precious to her as sight. Gio was the same way, and in fact, it was in a perfume store, Sephora, in Paris, that they had first met.

Ashley had been in Paris to finalize details for the French publication of her first novel. Although she had grown up in a wealthy old Boston Brahmin family, she had little money of her own, but on that day she felt successful enough to venture into this famous emporium dedicated exclusively to perfumes and indulge herself in a small bottle of something special that was unavailable at home.

She noticed Gio right away. He was just slightly taller than she, with gorgeous dark Italian-American looks and a thick black moustache. She had always favored men with moustaches. There was a Spanish saying: "A kiss without a moustache is like an egg without salt."

"Obedience!" he said, naming the very scent she was trying. He spoke the name with confidence and pleasure as if he and she and the clerk were old friends engaged in a game of "name the perfume."

"You're right!" she had found herself replying, hoping that he couldn't see the pulse pounding at her temples. "So many men don't seem to have much sense of smell. They only know what they like." She shot him a bemused glance.

"I have always been interested in scents. Obedience is special, because the quality of the flower essences is still so high. So many *parfumiers* are sneaking in synthetics whose first notes are wonderful—until they dry, when you can tell immediately that they don't involve real flowers."

"Monsieur is an American *parfumier*, perhaps?" the clerk interjected.

"No, Madame, merely an admirer of womanly scents."

Gio's double entendre escaped neither woman and, as one, they offered Ashley's fragrant wrist to Gio's waiting nostrils. He inhaled deeply. Ashley had chosen well, for the notes of the perfume seemed to meld with her own warm, honeyed scent, announcing it without overpowering it. "Wonderful! Truly," he said. Ashley met his eyes for a moment.

She purposely held herself back over the next few days in Paris, allowing him only the occasional brief lunch or drink, when so much of her was dying to give in to a Parisian romance with this man who seemed to share so many of her interests, a man so easy to talk to she felt like she had come home, yet whose background was as different as she needed it to be. But she was tired and more than a little discouraged. The success of her novel gave her pleasure, but she was still pained from the loss of a marriage she had thought was on track, weathering some turbulence perhaps, but basically safe from the kinds of precipitous divorces she had been witnessing among her friends. And then one day she had realized she was auditioning before her own husband, and soon thereafter he had discarded her for what he hoped would be a simpler life in the country with an uncomplicated and adoring woman. This trip to Paris and the success it symbolized was slowly repairing her soul. She had no desire to leap into complications and what might easily be another sorrowful romance just when she was beginning to feel her own wings.

As Gio sat in his study, his cup of coffee cooling before him, he thought back to that first encounter in Paris and the slow, careful romance which had followed. They had taken so much time to get to know each other. The very fact that they seemed so well-matched roused suspicions in him that he wasn't seeing the real picture, yet also made him feel that they had time to explore each other. Neither was going to be swept away by any others. But now another side of Ashley seemed to be emerging—an impatient side, a side that was battering at fortifications he could not allow her to enter. She was turning into a terrorist. It wasn't that he wanted to remain hidden from her just for the sake of remaining hidden. Why couldn't she understand that he needed this interior quiet, this sense of invisibility, in order to get through life safely, to accomplish all the things he needed to do? Just the night before she had started in again. The only conversations she seemed to be willing to have these days were attempts to pry him open like some help-less oyster only to chuck him back into the sea when she found no pearls within. He simply couldn't permit it.

"But why?" she had suddenly asked in the middle of a self-consciously silent dinner alone. Since the fight they had tried to surround themselves with friends and clients so that they wouldn't have to engage; so that she couldn't ask him any more questions about himself or torture him any further about Georgie.

"Why what?" he had asked, although he knew all too well where the conversation was inevitably headed.

"Why the hell do you have to shut yourself off? What could be so important for you to guard that you're willing to let our whole marriage go to hell in a hat? Can't you see you're shutting me out? Can't you see how unhealthy this all is? I can't believe this is us—Ashley and Gio. Listen, Gio, I know you're in pain. I don't know what the pain is and you won't tell me, but it's there. I can feel it, and I know if you won't let me in we're not going to make it."

"Can't you ever be patient?" Gio asked, glad that the waiter had come to pour some more wine for them so that she would have to desist for a moment from her interrogation.

"Patient!" she had exploded so that the waiter blushed, poured the wine and backed off. "Patient? What's the point in being pa-tient any more? You still won't dare come out. Look at you. I can see you're ten miles inside yourself. You look at me with these sad eyes full of secrets and pain and you tell me everything's just fine, just hunky-dory. Gio, don't you think I know what pain's about? Don't you think I've had pain in my life? Well, I can tell you right now it doesn't work to hold it in!"

"Jesus, you're relentless. Slow down, back off. Can't you see you're driving me away? I don't know what you mean about all this pain. If I were in that much pain do you think I'd be able to do the work I do? Do you think I'd be making almost a million dollars a year in the big-boy world? No! I'd be simpering in a bed down at Austen Riggs Center in Stockbridge like all the other wounded people you admire so much." That hadn't helped, although he had liked the sound of it.

"Fuck you," she'd muttered under her breath. "You don't know anything."

Gio had paid the bill and they'd driven home in silence. Another night on opposite sides of the bed, Gio crying inside because he wanted to hold Ashley, because he just wanted her to stop abusing him and let him be. He wanted his sweet and sweetly scented girl back in his arms, not this harridan of pop-psych who was acting like some idiot group-encounter leader. He had drifted asleep, touched by the sweetness of the Bulgarian roses in the Joy she wore when she was feeling upset and needed to settle herself, but furious at her reign of terror. Furious and unwilling to engage!

Ashley lay still, thinking about secrets and why even the merest hint that something was hidden frightened her and tortured her until she understood what was going on. Her first encounter with secrets and their power to hurt had come early. One day when Ashley was about seven, her older sister, Jill, had gone exploring in the bottom of her mother's bureau drawer and she discovered and read her mother's diary. Ashley was playing in her room one afternoon when the silence of the house exploded. "You're a damned little spy, Jill! I don't know why I trust either of you children. I never will again, but I swear to God that if you ever so much as cross the threshold into my dressing room ever again you're going straight to boarding school in Australia and you'll never surface again. Never!"

"But Mommy, I didn't read it!" Jill sobbed. "I didn't, I promise I didn't. I just wanted to try on your girdle and stockings and I moved it. I didn't read it." But her words were like drops of water thrown into a tempest. Later that night Ashley had sneaked into her sister's bedroom and asked, "What did it say?"

But Jill seemed shell-shocked. She shook her head and stared into the distance. "I didn't read it, I didn't even see it," was all she said. Later that night as Ashley lay in bed, she could hear her sister weeping on the other side of the wall. From that moment on, Ashley started to dream about someone who would come to the house and open up all the secrets—not to upset anyone, but just to restore safety to them all. He would be someone who was strong and kind and wise, like a doctor who could take away the pain.

By the time Ashley was ten, she realized she had a power. It frightened her at first, but frightening as it was, she realized it made her feel safer: she could see what was hidden, feel the presence of the unspoken or the hidden, and often she was correct in her intuitions. It wasn't until later that she realized that she, like many bright and sensitive children in a household full of secrets, had learned to survive by seeing below the surface.

After the incident with Jill and the diary, Jill was sent away to a boarding school in Connecticut, and their mother devoted herself more to Ashley. Unlike Jill, Ashley wasn't particularly afraid of their mother. Perhaps having an older sister shielded her from the worst of their mother's scorn and hatred. Perhaps having banished Jill, their mother felt safer with her secret life, and she decided to train Ashley to be the sort of woman who would understand why secrets needed to exist.

"Never forget, darling," she used to say, over tea in the library, before Ashley's father came home from the office, "that men are not as strong as we are. We have to allow them to think they are, but there's something slightly pathetic about men. They never really grow up. A smart woman is always one step ahead of her husband, just as a mother must always be one step ahead of her children."

Ashley just listened and watched, already aware that the uncovering of secrets was best done by pretending to be harmless and gullible, a receptive audience to her mother's wisdom. But she decided to make up her own mind, particularly about her father. Her intuition informed her that her mother did not love her father as a man, but why didn't he fight her, take charge, throw her out, she kept asking herself.

Occasionally she would dare to champion him in front of her mother. "Aren't we lucky to have Daddy?" she would exclaim. "When I spent the night at Martha's house last week, her father got drunk and yelled at Mrs. Niles all during dinner until I thought she was going to cry. And then he kept on yelling at her. I'm so glad Daddy isn't mean."

"Mean he is not," was about all she could get out of her mother. "That's certainly one of his better qualities." But later, as she entered her teens and "knew" that something was wrong, her mother no longer deigned to agree with her. "Please don't try to sell him to me, darling. Just don't," she would say, her voice as icy as the wicked queen in a Walt Disney movie.

Ashley's father was a humble man. Although he was descended from one of the oldest families in Boston—one which had held on to quite a lot of money as well—he was gentle and unassuming. He seemed happiest when he was at the helm of his sailboat up in Maine or playing with the dogs on the lawn. Ashley's mother had once told her that he wasn't particularly successful and that they were lucky everyone else in his family had been. Despite her rather haughty treatment of him, he gave his wife a great deal of room. On Wednesday nights he almost always stayed at the Saint Botolph's Club, where he played cards and enjoyed the cigars that were banned from the Beacon Hill house because of his wife's asthma. In Ashley's eyes he seemed to worship her mother unreasonably. Didn't he understand the disdain she had for him? His trustingness, his gentleness broke Ashley's heart. Something was very wrong, but even Ashley's internal radar couldn't precisely identify it yet.

And then, one day, it all became clear. All the inchoate suspicions, the sorrow in her father, the cruel triumph in her mother crystallized in one moment. Ashley was walking home from a friend's house in Back Bay. A block ahead of her she saw a figure which looked familiar, but because she was so out-of-context, she didn't recognize that the figure was her mother and with her mother was a man in a gray suit and a straw boater. They were holding hands and laughing in the spring sunshine. What broke Ashley's heart was the youthful joy her mother exuded. No longer the ice queen of the household, she was another woman, a woman in love, free from her husband and her children—free from the life they shared. She had betrayed them all.

Ashley ran home. She felt like she was breaking up into thousands of shards. She had to know the truth now. She went straight to the drawer with the brass keyhole where she knew the answers lay, but it was locked as she knew it would be. Her hands were shaking so hard she thought she might pull the whole dresser over on herself as she tugged hopelessly at the drawer of secrets. Horrible, horrible secrets. Only now the secret was out. She began to tremble with the pain of the deception. She couldn't shake the image of her mother with "him." The happiness on their faces was the worst pain she had ever felt.

Suddenly the air changed and Ashley looked to her right. Her mother was standing in the doorway staring at her as she sat in front of the locked drawer, the repository of all the cruel secrets that had hurt her for so many years. All the gaiety and beauty of an hour earlier on Marlborough Street were gone. The evil witch was descending.

"You little bitch!" she screamed. "Get out of my room! Get out of my house!"

Ashley stood up and looked at her. She was taller than her mother now, and she wasn't afraid. She stared directly into the wild anger and screamed "Now I know! Now I know all about you and your lies. You're evil and venal and you've destroyed this family with your secrets and your deceptions for too long. Well, you're not going to get away with it!" Then she pushed past her mother and ran upstairs to her bedroom. Ashley knew in her heart that her mother had lost her power, because her only power was deception.

The next morning, a Saturday, Ashley and her parents were gathered at the breakfast table. Ashley's mother regarded her coolly, almost as if daring her to speak up.

"I have something to say about what happened in this house

yesterday," Ashley announced, only a slight tremor in her voice belying the fear she felt.

But before she could go any further, her mother slammed both palms hard on the table, spilling her coffee. She uttered one word: "Edward!"

Ashley's father leapt up. "No!" he shouted, looking more angry than Ashley had ever seen him. "We are *not* going to speak about what happened last night. Come with me to the library, young lady. Right now."

Ashley's mother smoothed her hair and looked off in the distance as the maid cleaned up the spilled coffee and poured her some more. She smiled sweetly at Ashley as she followed her father to the library. Ashley was afraid, but more confused now than afraid. She realized all at once that her mother had made a preemptive strike. She had gotten to her husband before Ashley could.

"I want to tell you the truth, Daddy," Ashley said as soon as he had closed the door behind them. "There's something going on that you should know about."

"No, you are going to tell me nothing that you think you know about. Do you understand me?"

"But why? There's something going on and it's ruining our family and hurting you and you don't even know what it is."

"No. Nothing that you think you know about is hurting me. What you don't understand is that what you think you know could hurt your mother, me, and the whole family. You're too young to understand the whole picture. You are doing more harm than good. Do you understand?"

"But Daddy, it doesn't have to be this way. We can get it back on track, but everyone has to tell the truth. The secrets have to be exposed."

"My sweet child, I am asking you in the name of love to trust me that you do not understand. There's just so much that you can't yet understand."

These early experiences with secrets and their power to

destroy worlds shaped Ashley's life. They made her into a woman with a clear vision of how things should be and how to go about making them that way. Although Ashley was talented enough as a cellist that her teachers encouraged her to pursue a career in music, Ashley realized she wanted to be in the thick of the action, although she wasn't exactly certain what type of action she was looking for. She found it in journalism. While her friends were away on their "year abroad" before starting college, Ashley decided to volunteer as an assistant at the small local newspaper near her parents' summer house in Maine.

For old-time journalists, reporting is a kind of religion, and the editor under whom Ashley worked was a high priest in the church. His philosophy was simple, he told Ashley: People in power tended naturally toward corruption. It's the nature of their world, and of the human penchant for greed. Newspapers were one of the only ways in which people could be held accountable. In his own little way, Ashley thought, the old man held the world in balance. He loved his work, and he had found a reason for being honest, alert, and alive. One day, just after their weekly deadline, when he was relaxing and thinking back over a long day, he turned to Ashley and said, "We're in the business of exposing secrets. Never forget that. We hate secrets. That's what this business is all about. Every time newspaper people find a secret they shine the light on it. That's our job."

As Ashley finished scrolling these memories through her mind, she realized she had to make a move because Gio clearly couldn't. When she felt him stirring the next morning, she got up with him and followed him down into the kitchen as he made his coffee.

"Listen, Gio, this has gone on too long. I know you're mad at me, and I feel like my world is breaking apart without my having enough information to save myself, so the only thing I can think of to try to get us back on track is to just put all that to one side and make love tonight."

Gio said nothing. He didn't know what to say, but inside he

felt immensely grateful for Ashley's wisdom. He had missed her so much.

"I know we have problems," Ashley repeated, "and we can't ignore them forever, but tonight let's just agree to put them aside."

Gio nodded. "I think you're right."

She came over and kissed him on the cheek. This had to be taken slowly, she knew that. When she could think clearly about her contribution to their problem, part of her knew that her impatience to find a solution and get on with things somehow felt to Gio like a violation. "I'll be at the library all day. Why don't we meet in The Room at the end of the day?" The Room was their special sensorium designed expressly for making love. They had both participated in its design and furnishing. It had a fireplace and heavy velvet curtains for cold winter nights, and casement windows which let in warm, caressing breezes in temperate weather. The bed was large and outfitted with Italian linen sheets as soft as gauze on their naked bodies. Ashley took care to stock the room with their favorite foods and liquors and she made certain that fresh flowers or flowering plants were always there, scenting the air.

That afternoon, Ashley took a long bath in a tub scented with Gio's favorite tuberose bath oil, dressed in a thin silk caftan which whispered about her naked body, and started down the stairs to join him. Remembering the CD she had bought for just this sort of occasion over a month ago, she stopped off in her study and got it from her desk drawer. For the first time in so many weeks she was filled with joy, because she realized that their senseless withdrawal from one another was about to end, that they could finally begin to work on the problem. And that, for Ashley, felt life-saving. She felt that as long as she could bring to bear her prodigious powers to see solutions and apply them, nothing could harm her—unless her solution was rejected.

As she passed the spot where she had thrown the glass against the banister, the deep dent triggered a memory of the terrible fight which had occasioned it. Gio, who had grown up poor, and had made his first million before he was thirty, found nourishment in the beauty of old things which had endured, of objects which had been passed down and used by generations of the same family. As soon as he could afford to, he surrounded himself with furniture which had this patina, a patina that was so much more than just a finish. It supplied him with a sense of continuity and safety which had never been granted him in childhood, although he might not have identified his attraction for these objects in exactly that way. He had found the fine mahogany balustrade in a Federal house in Providence which was about to be destroyed to make way for a high-rise. Excited by this great find, he had had it shipped to the house they were building in Boston, ready to be installed that week. But Ashley had other plans. She wanted a new banister, something less traditional, something which did not remind her in any way of the house she had grown up in, also a Federal house full of dark polished wood—and secrets.

When Ashley arrived at the house one morning and found that Gio had bought the banister without her, she was enraged. "Why do you have to be so attached to every symbol of old money?" she asked, even though she knew that Gio, the son of poor Italian immigrants, still longed for aristocratic roots.

"For the same reason that you want to chuck any reminder of your own past and pretend you can create the present and future exactly as you want them!" he had retorted. "Just because you have the luxury of three hundred years of ancestors that you can reject doesn't mean you can deprive me of the beauty and comfort of all that is old and enduring."

"Oh, so all I am to you is a symbol of a past you wish you'd had? Am I just a living trophy for a poor little immigrant?" That was when Ashley had hurled the glass against the banister, cutting a deep gash into the old wood. Gio had "won" that round, but Ashley's abusive shadow, a side of her which appeared only when she wanted desperately to fix something and felt blocked, had left a visible stigmata.

As always, Gio had forgiven her words and even her destructive action quickly, but Ashley had never forgiven herself for the cruelty of her words and especially for the destruction of something she knew to be beautiful and important to her husband.

Tonight she put these painful recollections out of her mind as she made her way down to their special room. Tonight they could reopen their dialogue. That was the most important thing. It meant that there would be a future in which they could make up to one another gradually for the unintended cruelties each had inflicted upon the other while in the sway of the demon voices of their shadows.

Gio was already waiting for her with a fire roaring. He had dressed comfortably but not carelessly in a pair of soft flannel trousers and one of Ashley's favorite shirts of Sea Island cotton. He thought about Ashley, her beauty, her body, her scent, and as he did, he became aware of her presence in the room. His nostrils flared to take in her special scent, a sweet burnt smell, commingled with the tuberose, a flower both sweet and unctuous. As the first notes of the music swelled in the air, a wave of emotion something like melancholy swept over him and settled in his heart. He was overcome with a profound sense of gratitude to this beautiful woman he loved so much.

Sometimes, when they felt disconnected and came together in this room to reconnect, they would dance, but this was not dancing music. This was music that fused their two souls and brought tears to their eyes. Suddenly they were in each other's arms, devouring each other, sobbing together at the terrible aloneness they had felt all those nights they had turned their backs and tried to sleep in separate universes.

They awoke the next day in each other's arms and made love again in a shaft of dappled sunshine which sparkled around their bodies like champagne.

As they sat together drinking their coffee, Ashley, ever the repairer of the relationship, spoke up: "Listen, Gio, I know we still have some things to work out, and even though making love is one of our best ways of fixing things, there's something else we used to do."

Gio felt his equilibrium draining. Why couldn't she just let things be? Was she going to start in again about Georgie? "What's that?" he asked warily.

"Remember how we used to make lists of all the things which made us fall in love with each other? I want to do that again. I don't know exactly why, but I just think it might be a good idea. What do you think?"

"Do you really think it's necessary at this point? I mean we've been married for years. Aren't we pretty clear on each other's merits?"

"I just have a feeling it would help."

Gio knew that Ashley was usually ahead of him in matters of healing and the heart. She seemed to know things about her friends and lovers that opened them up to themselves in ways that were startling and illuminating. Ashley saw problems and obstacles as challenges, and pursued solutions like a dog with a bone. That was really the only flaw of any consequence that Gio perceived in her. She had to have answers and solutions. Everything had to be brought out into the light of day and examined from all angles lest any lurking secrets not be taken into account, explained, and stripped of their power to hurt or confuse.

"Is there a deadline?" Gio asked with a smile.

"Yesterday," she replied, laughing at a joke they shared about the impatience of some of her clients.

True to her word, Ashley began her list that very day. She had fallen in love with Gio's self-reliance. Her first husband had been a victim who had been unable to act with any conviction, leaving Ashley constantly searching for solutions to his and their life circumstances only to have them rejected, a situation she came to find intolerable. The more Jim had gone belly-up, the more Ashley had become embittered and, to his way of thinking, abusive.

She loved Gio's strength and his success in the venture capital world—or at least his way of achieving success. For in a world aswim with sharks—with men and women of no integrity or soul—Gio stood out. He never took his losses personally, nor did he complain about anyone who had bested him. Somehow he seemed certain that his determination and skill would, soon enough, earn him another victory. She loved his kindness. Although he refused to divulge the details, she knew that he had started a small private foundation which gave out scholarships anonymously to students who needed help.

Ashley and Gio complemented one another very well, and they had done some work on their relationship before their marriage. But what neither was clear on at the time they married—as couples almost never are—is that behind these positive qualities, beneath the strong, adapted adults each fell in love with, were shadows and unaddressed, unanswered needs spawned in the disappointments of their childhoods. These needs had never disappeared, and had to be brought out into the light of day, for they gave rise to the very different expectations each had for the other—which again is true for every couple. For Gio, the keeping of secrets was a matter of loyalty and a matter of love. Ashley was certain that her job was to force Gio to feel the pain she could see was poisoning his kind soul and endangering their intimacy. From the beginning, Ashley had viewed this secretive and wounded side of Gio as an exciting challenge.

That evening after dinner, they sat by the wood stove in the kitchen. Relieved that they were talking and making love again, the list she had made still fresh in her mind, Ashley couldn't help but return to her theme: "Gio," she began gently, but not gently enough to prevent Gio from stiffening inwardly. "You know sometime you're going to have to let me in. I don't just mean about Georgie although I want to hear about that too. But everything. I look at your face and I can see the pain under all that strength. I am your wife. You must let me know you completely, even if no one else ever does."

Gio sighed deeply, evidence again, to Ashley, of the wounds

he carried within. "Look, Ashley, you're like a battering ram. I am who I am. You knew who I was when you married me. I'm not a complainer. Your way of being strong is to talk endlessly about pain, to exorcise it from yourself and others. I don't need or want to talk about pain. My pain is in the past. I survived it. Are you now going to try to kill me with it?"

"Gio, you just don't get it, do you? The pain is there. It affects everything you do and everything that happens between us. Learning about yourself will never weaken you. I'm not asking you to be open to anyone but me, but if you can't do that then I'm scared for us. Those walls aren't just around you. They're between us."

"Ashley, can we just drop it for a night? I'm tired of this conversation. I'm tired in general. I've got to get an early start in the morning."

Following him up the stairs, Ashley was filled with old fears. Was Gio, like her father, going to refuse to reveal secrets which, if not aired, could expand like a radioactive cloud over their lives?

Gio, walking in front of her, felt anger boring into the pit of his stomach. Were her demands going to keep escalating until she had remade him in her image? He *wasn't* her father. His privacy was not weakening him. It empowered him. He was disappointed at how quickly her demands were escalating. He felt abused. She was certainly not going to reshape him. Her childhood had nothing to teach him.

But years of interviewing recalcitrant subjects had taught Ashley to be clever, and she decided to take a more circuitous route, one which she knew intuitively would help their situation. She waited until they were at their beach house in Gloucester. As they strolled along the shore, picking up rocks and shells, she suddenly asked, "Gio, do you remember the first money you ever made?"

"What? You mean after business school?"

"No, I mean the first money you ever made in your life."

"What a funny question," he replied. "Actually I was about

thirteen, and I decided to get a job as a delivery boy for a grocery store a bit out of the neighborhood so my parents wouldn't catch me."

"But why? I should think they'd be glad you were gainfully employed at that age."

"Well, you see, I had really begun to hate my father by then, and so when he got my mother to approach me and offer to go ask the Great Man himself for spending money for me, I refused. There was no way I was going to let him buy me off. I wasn't going to accept handouts from someone who had given me not much more than abuse. But I was in a bad situation because if I didn't accept his shit-faced gift I knew he'd make things even harder for my mother."

"So what did you do?"

"Finally I decided to accept the allowance and then just throw it away."

"Literally?"

"Literally. I started by pitching it and then I figured out that I could give it to beggars on the street."

"Did you ever get found out?"

"Almost. One day, I was riding my bike to my job, and I got sideswiped by a delivery truck. My bike was totaled, and I was bleeding and pretty badly cut, but I didn't dare go home. Mom had enough problems and I didn't want them to find out about my job. So I slipped into an alleyway, took off my underpants and made a bandage and tourniquet out of them. It hurt like hell for the next several days, and it was really hard not to limp in front of my parents. Then I began to realize that I had a very bad infection and so I went to the emergency room. The doctor who treated me was appalled. He said I'd just gotten there in time or I'd probably have gotten gangrene. Of course I, dumbshit that I was, just considered it a badge of courage."

"No wonder you're such a stoic today," Ashley said.

"And I guess that's why I need my privacy. I am a stoic, but never in a way that will hurt you. Only in ways to protect us both."

Ashley sighed deeply and dropped his hand. "God, Gio, if only you realized how wrong you are."

"Ashley, please don't start in on that again."

But Ashley couldn't help herself. A few days later they were back in Boston and again, Ashley heard Gio speaking in what she had come to call his "Georgie" voice. She tiptoed to the door and sure enough, she heard him say goodbye to Georgie in that same somber tone of voice which sent terror reeling through her stomach.

At dinner, she couldn't look him in the eye. Gio could see that something was wrong, but he certainly wasn't going to ask what.

"Gio, I can't stand this anymore," Ashley suddenly burst out. "I heard you talking to Georgie again today. You have to tell me now. You have to. It can't be more important for you to protect this Georgie person than for you to level with me."

Gio threw down his napkin. "Ashley, damn it, I told you that you have to trust me. All you can think about is how my privacy affects you. How do you think your prying affects me? This isn't working. You're not the woman I married. I can't deal with all of the problems from your past. I really can't!"

And then he was gone, out the door which opened onto the mews. Ashley heard the sound of his car. She put her head down on the kitchen table and sobbed. The silent treatment re-ensued, the sheets between them like a glacier.

It was at this point that Ashley came to me for a brief consultation. Gio had flat-out refused to attend the session, but I sensed that this couple wasn't yet in a great deal of trouble. There was plenty of love between them still. It was clear to me that the situation involved two people in their shadows, crying out for love and trying to remake the other according to his or her needs. So I spent several sessions with Ashley alone, telling her what I perceived. I told her about the heroic modes and their shadows and how she and Gio could begin the Myth and Shadow Work.

They embarked on their journey hand in hand. Neither was

so defensive as to be completely unable to look deeply into the mirror that the other held up.

Occasionally, Ashley became too aggressive with her mirror, a sure sign that her shadow was present. When she went over the line into her deepest shadows she would become wild and intolerant, verging on violent. Her ready anger merely made Gio recede even deeper into invisibility and invulnerability. And it wasn't just over Georgie or even secrets. Even going to the movies where the hero was a "strong, silent type" could occasion an offhand comment from Ashley couched as a critique of the movie but clearly a barb intended straight for Gio's heart.

"Thanks for the looking glass," he would say, "but I may need a plastic surgeon to pick the shards of glass out of my face." They were learning that if one person's shadow is present, he or she can't help the other person.

Ashley had her own journal work to do and she knew it. She came to realize that her willful pursuit of the truth—a source of pride, praise, and achievement in her professional life—gained her no accolades in her marriage. She came to understand that in pursuing the truth so fervently, as she did in the case of Georgie, she was imposing the will of the Fixer on her husband, and that in the darkest corners of that shadow zone she was an abuser. When Ashley made this connection, she told me in a session that she was "humbled." Strangely, she liked the feeling. It put her more lovingly in touch with all the characters in her Personal Myth, particularly her father. What if he knew what he was doing? Perhaps his playing the cuckold was a form of love she couldn't understand. Once she came to understand that perhaps her father didn't want to be "saved" by her, she was able to experience clearly her own frustration at not being able to help him and restore him to his place of power in the family.

One night, in sharing these insights with Gio, she found herself no longer angry, but crying with a curious nostalgia. He came over and put his arms around her. "I loved him so much, that's all," she sobbed. "I just wanted to make it all right for him, but he wouldn't let me. Did I hurt him even more by not letting him be who he was?"

Gio kissed the top of her head. He realized now just how important it was to confront the pain of the past. He saw the contradictions in Ashley so clearly now—her desire to help people, some of the sources of that desire, and the agonizing frustration she felt when people wouldn't accept her help, thereby leading her into her abusive shadow. Gio also realized that Ashley's courage in refusing to allow secrets had brought them closer together. Only now did he realize how right she was.

He thought back to some of the most painful scenes from his childhood, when he had learned to shut down. He too realized that there had been secrets in his household. His father was a drinker, explosive, ready to be ignited at any moment, but his mother kept very quiet and very still around him. He remembered the terrible ritual which recurred in slightly different forms throughout his childhood. He would be summoned by his father, who would demand, "So what are you doing in school?"

"Arithmetic, reading," Gio would answer.

"Numbers," his father would growl. "You've got to know numbers to get anywhere in this world. They measure your soul in numbers. Numbers are what they use to ruin you."

He would draw close to Gio, his eyes rheumy and terrifying, the smell of liquor sweet and rotting on his breath. "Why are you afraid of me? I'm your father!"

"I don't know why, sir."

"Everything scares you, doesn't it?"

"No. Not everything."

"What are you, some kind of coward?"

Gio wouldn't answer. He didn't know what to answer.

"I think you're a little coward, do you know that? You can't stand up to me or anyone else, can you? What are you afraid of?"

"I don't want you to hit me, sir."

"Who said anything about hitting you, you little pissant? Who

said anything about hitting you at all? You want me to hit you?"
Then he would hit Gio as hard as he could with the back of his
hand. As often as not, the strength of his blows would send Gio
into a heap on the floor. Stunned and dizzy, he would try to crawl
away, but his father would be at him again. Sometimes his father
would trip and fall. His mother would run out from where she was
hiding and try to help him up, but Gio's father would bellow and
throw her to the ground. And then he would be gone.

Lying in bed after these scenes, Gio would ask himself over and
over, "Where is my mother in all of this? Why won't she make him
stop?" He couldn't answer this question, but every day he had to
prove to himself that he wasn't a coward. He took on every bully
in his tough neighborhood, every dare, every challenge in school.
That was the only way he could think of to survive. But through
it all was the nagging question: Why wasn't his mother there for
him?

Gio's greatest breakthrough came when one night he and
Ashley were talking and he recalled a dream in which his mother
had come to him and said, "Gio, I want to tell you a secret. Your
father is under an evil spell. The man who hurts you isn't the real
man. When he is called he must go away by himself where he faces
unspeakable hardships. When he returns, if I have been loyal to
him, he will become the man he really is." And then she offered
him a pure white crystal. "Take this stone, my child," she said. "It
is my source and now it is yours. Keep it with you always and
squeeze it when you need its strength to endure." And that stone,
Gio realized that night, was the strength which he guarded still.

Later that evening Gio turned to Ashley and said, " You know,
I think I understand how your father felt."

"Oh?"

"I think I understand that he and I both felt that we had to
hide our own pain, our own perceptions, to honor or love someone else, and I guess that's why people like us don't want other people taking our strength away. Your father knew what was going on,
but his strength, and his way of loving your mother, was to hide his

pain and not let her have to feel the consequences of what she was doing. I think he really did love her."

A few weeks later, Ashley tried again about Georgie. "Why don't you tell me about Georgie—your truth, not mine," Ashley said.

At that point Gio decided he could make a full disclosure.

George Black had been Gio's roommate at Harvard. Although he was gay, his sexuality was never an issue between them. "We straightened it out early on," Gio explained to her. "After his first attempts at exploring my sexual orientation, he left that alone completely. Georgie has enormous dignity and self-respect, and of course I confessed my love for several goddesses, which I guess further clarified things for him."

Georgie became a mentor for Gio. He was an art major at Harvard and he had grown up in an aristocratic and artistic family. Georgie dabbled in everything—but dabbling, for Georgie, was like most people's spending five or ten years getting into something.

"He has a great gift," Gio continued, feeling more confident now because he could speak the truth to his wife. "He could have been at a museum, or the head of about five departments at Sotheby's. Instead he's with me."

"What do you mean?" she asked, pouring them each some more wine.

"Georgie's job is to discover new artists and funnel some of my foundation's money to them through anonymous grants. He's very good at it."

"Gio, why don't you want to be known for what you do?"

"I really don't like the burden of being responsible for fixing anything," Gio replied. "Once you do some good, there's often an odd reaction. You'd think it would be enough, but often it's not. Those you've helped want even more. It ends up creating dependencies and relationships I'd sooner not deal with. I'm not like you. You love to fix people and make their lives right, but I hate it."

"I can do it without creating leeches."

"I know. I've seen you do it, and I marvel at it, but I really hate being a fixer."

Ashley had trouble containing her annoyance at these words, honestly spoken as they were. Nothing in what Gio had revealed about Georgie warranted such secrecy as she had suffered through—the clandestine phone calls, the muffled conversations. They hearkened back to when she had overheard laughter and discussions about sex behind her mother's bedroom door. She made discoveries by overhearing things, by having things appear before her in the dark, so to speak. Then she was forced to bring them to light. "I hate this pattern," she thought to herself.

She felt the frustration of her Fixer descending into the shadow, but in some new place she found a shelf where she could stop and rest before she made the full descent into that Hades. "Maybe there is something to learn here, a deeper truth," a voice whispered to her.

"Were you afraid of having to take care of your mother when you were little?" she asked Gio.

"Maybe. I was very confused and ambivalent. On one hand, she catered to my father even as he was beating me, but on the other hand I loved her and I wanted to protect her even though she wouldn't let me. She didn't want to create any burdens for me. Maybe that's why she never spoke up for me when my father beat me. I always sensed she wanted me to be strong. Maybe that was her way of setting me free. Even the way she died—suddenly— managed to avoid putting any burden on me."

"How does that relate to Georgie?"

Gio said nothing. Ashley waited. "Georgie's got AIDS," Gio said finally. "Once he found out, he asked me to keep the secret. He is an intensely private man and so am I, so I understood why he needed to guard his privacy. I want to do everything I can to help him stay alive. Georgie is my family, and I remind him of that when his spirits are down. But you are my family now too, and I was wrong to keep these things from you."

"It was painful because of who I am."

"I know it hurt you and perhaps on some level I always knew it. I think I do a lot to maintain my identity as an independent man, without realizing that I am married and responsible for my actions upon you. I need to work on this."

Ashley took his hand.

"In any case, Georgie has been very weak lately and he needs support. I've done all I can for him, but he and I both need help now. I'm worried that the secrecy is going to compromise his medical care and he'll end up dying prematurely. I've been going crazy with worry. I actually needed to tell you this a long time ago. I need your help and support."

This confession broke open the door to Gio's heart. He had finally let Ashley in. More importantly, he understood that this opening was just the beginning.

When Georgie and Ashley met, they were like old friends. Chastened now by the understanding that in her shadow zone she could become too insistent on following the path she thought correct, Ashley was brilliant in her assistance. As she laid out her plan of action, Gio's heart opened. She was up on everything in AIDS therapy. "We will keep you alive with the best available treatment until they find a cure. Please believe that, Georgie," she said, reaching out to touch his frail wrist. "I will leave no stone unturned."

Ashley and Gio experienced a new high in their relationship that opened up many doors to their myths. Gio was finally ready to enter his own Personal Myth, albeit at his own speed. There was so much to discover, so much he wanted to discuss with his wife.

Ashley felt the same. Her recognition of her shadow and its links to her Personal Myth, especially to her frustrated desire to save her father, opened up the possibility of becoming a freer and more open human being. She realized that she could let people be themselves and still love them. She didn't have to change everyone to make her world as safe as she needed it. She had awakened to a higher love, she realized, in which both she and the person she cared about were free to be themselves without tampering or "fixing." Even though she realized that such a recognition would take years to fully adopt, she felt freed because it revealed a new path.

Yet the work is never finished even after both partners commit to the path.

One morning at breakfast a couple of weeks later, Gio told Ashley about a bad dream he had just had.

"A little boy was sitting in a chair in an otherwise empty room that was bathed in an eerie light," he said. "His hands were bound behind his back, and he was gagged."

"That seems like more than a bad dream," Ashley said.

"I don't know what you mean."

"Well, was that all of it? Was there more?"

"No, not that I can remember," Gio said.

"What do you think?" Ashley asked.

"I don't know."

Ashley said nothing. Instead she got up from the table and began to do the dishes. "What are you doing today?" she asked.

"I'm working," Gio replied, rising abruptly from the table and leaving the room.

That night, out of nowhere, they had an explosive argument over whether or not they would go out to the movies after dinner. "I think your anger at me is more than a little exaggerated," Ashley said. "What's really eating you?"

The next morning Gio appeared at the table with his journal. "After our fight last night, I went up to my office and wrote in my journal. I realized I was angry with your reaction to my dream. When you asked me if there was more to it and I said no, you just went over and started the dishes. I wanted your attention. I needed you to pull the rest of the dream out of me."

"I'm sorry," Ashley said. "I kind of thought you didn't want to talk about it anymore. Actually, I was still thinking about it, and I was wondering whether I should bring it up later."

"There was actually more to the dream than what I said. When I woke up, I suddenly thought, 'Why isn't he crying?' That was an odd thought, but I let it go, because it didn't make sense to me then. And when you asked if there was more to it, I didn't really want to tell you the thought I'd had. The moment I said to you, 'No, there wasn't any more to the dream,' I knew I was sort of lying. I kept hearing this one sentence in my mind: 'Why isn't he crying?' I tried, but I couldn't stop thinking about it, and then I realized that the first time I cried as an adult was when I heard about Georgie's diagnosis. I remembered not wanting to cry when my father hit me, but recently I know I've been needing to let out a lot of feelings. I feel vulnerable and threatened, and I need your attention and support. I need help. I need to release all these weird feelings that have been colliding inside of me ever since we started talking about this stuff."

Ashley embraced Gio, who was crying, in her arms.